THE BLUE PLAQUE GUIDE TO LONDON

THE BLUE PLAQUE GUIDE TO LONDON

Caroline Dakers

M

First published 1981 by
Macmillan Reference Books
a division of
MACMILLAN PUBLISHERS LTD

London and Basingstoke
Associated Companies throughout the world

ISBN 0 333 28462 3 8206 D R

Typeset by Leaper & Gard Ltd, Bristol
Printed in Great Britain

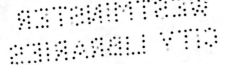

PREFACE

One of the greatest rewards for sitting on the Historic Buildings Advisory Committee of the GLC is the end of the meeting where plaques are discussed and who should have them. Everyone slacks off and tries to become a distinterested Spectator of the particular London village where the house is situated. Obviously there are more famous names in Carlton House Terrace than Clapham Road. Then does Donald McGill, who designed so many naughty seaside postcards qualify as an artist worthy of a plaque? This sort of discussion keeps us happily walking down Ralph Knott's broad corridors in County Hall.

In this book the results of those discussions are summarized. In this street there lived at one time Lloyd Osborne who collaborated with R.L.S. in writing 'The Wrong Box'. Does he qualify? With this question I leave you.

Sir John Betjeman

Introduction

William Ewart MP, an ardent reformer and founder of the free public library system was, in 1863, the first to suggest publicly that a scheme might be adopted for commemorating the houses of the famous in London: 'the places which have been the residences of the ornaments of their history cannot but be precious to all so thinking Englishmen'. The government did not respond to Ewart's appeal but the Royal Society of Arts decided to establish such a scheme, and in 1864 a committee was formed to 'promote the erection of statues or other memorials of persons eminent in the Arts, Manufactures and Commerce'. The plaques were designed both to give pleasure to 'travellers up and down in omnibuses etc. [for whom] they might sometimes prove an agreeable and instructive mode of beguiling a somewhat dull and not very rapid progress through the streets' and to ensure that 'the old haunts of London, teeming with historic interest, may be preserved from the ruthless hands of modern destroyers and improvers'. The first plaque erected by the RSA was to Byron at 24 Holles Street (since demolished) and a further 35 plaques were erected between 1867 and 1900. William Ewart received his own plaque in 1963, exactly 100 years after his original suggestion.

In 1901 the London County Council took over the scheme from the RSA and their first plaque was erected in 1903 to Lord Macaulay. It was unveiled by Lord Rosebery, first chairman of the LCC, who was himself commemorated by a plaque in 1962. Lord Rosebery felt, like the RSA committee, that London streets needed brightening up: 'I ask anybody, who is in the habit of taking long walks in London . . . whether it is not an immense relief to the eye and to the thoughts to come on some tablet which suggests a new train of thought, which may call to your mind the career of some distinguished person, and which takes off the intolerable pressure of the monotony of endless streets'.

By 31 December 1980 there were 438 plaques in London erected by the RSA and the LCC/GLC. These have come to be known as 'blue' plaques although the familiar blue glaze was not used until 1937. They are the 'official' plaques as opposed to the many 'rogue' plaques put up throughout London by individuals, societies and local councils.

Introduction

Most of the blue plaques and many of the 'rogue' ones are to be found in the borough of Westminster. The borough not only includes some of the oldest residential areas of London, such as Soho and St James's, but also those which were rapidly developed in the 19th century, like Mayfair, Belgravia, Pimlico, Paddington and Bayswater. By the end of 1981 there will be over 180 blue plaques in Westminster alone. Several are to the architects involved in the borough's expansion, including Thomas Cubitt, who built extensively in Belgravia and Pimlico. Since the establishment of the GLC in 1965 plaques are beginning to appear in more suburban boroughs but there are still very few in comparison with those in the centre. Sutton, Redbridge, Merton, Hounslow, Ealing, Bromley, Brent and Bexley have one plaque each; Barking, Enfield, Havering, Hillingdon, Kingston, Newham and Waltham Forest have none.

To qualify for a blue plaque a person has to fulfil one of several requirements laid down by the GLC. He or she should be regarded 'as eminent in his sphere by a majority of members of the person's own profession or calling'; he should have 'made some important positive contribution to human welfare or happiness'; and his name should be known to the 'well-informed passer-by' and his work should 'deserve recognition'. The individual must also have been dead for 20 years or have passed his 100th birthday, whichever is sooner. There have been occasional exceptions to the rule: Joseph Chamberlain was considered so important that he received a plaque on his home in Highbury the year after his death (in 1914 when he was 78); five years later he received another plaque on his home in Camberwell.

In spite of the GLC's own rules, anyone can put up a plaque; all that is required is the permission of the owner of the property concerned. The boroughs of Islington and Barnet have their own schemes and several plaques now maintained by the GLC were first erected by individual boroughs including St Pancras and Hampstead. The Dukes of Westminster and Bedford placed plaques on houses on their estates between about 1900 and 1914 though many have been demolished, particularly in the Grosvenor Square area and in Bloomsbury as a result of the development of London University.

Societies and individuals often erect plaques when the GLC reject their suggestions. Marie Corelli, who has a plaque on her home in Earl's Court (now the Embassy of the Arab State of Egypt), was rejected by the LCC in 1958 and again in 1963 for not having sufficient merit as a writer. Her popular novels did, however, contribute to the happiness of thousands of readers, as did the fiction of 'Ouida', R.M. Ballantyne and G.A. Henty, who have received blue plaques. The Vauxhall Society placed a plaque on an early home of Charles Chaplin in 1980 (he died too recently to qualify for a GLC one). The Heath and Old Hampstead Society erected a plaque on Maggie's Corner in Hampstead High Street to Maggie Richardson (1901–74) 'who sold flowers here for 60 years'. Only an enthusiastic friend or relative would have erected the plaque at 115 Maze Hill, Greenwich, to the minor poet Helena Pare Lydia Mott: 'the Summers Breath is spent upon the Hills / Behold, remember and rejoice'.

With an annual plaque budget of £7300 of ratepayers' money the GLC obviously has to answer for whoever it decides to commemorate. In spite of the many qualifications it has imposed, there has been a surprising amount of controversy over the official selection of candidates for a plaque. The GLC member for Brent North objected to the erection of one to Arthur Lucan, 'Old Mother Riley', the music-hall comedian. He was Conservative finance spokesman at the GLC and claimed the Labour-controlled council wanted the plaque 'as a misguided effort to curry popular favour'. There has indeed been a recent flurry of plaques commemorating the doyens of the music hall: Dan Leno (1962), Albert Chevalier (1965), Harry Lauder (1969), Harry Relph (1969), George Leybourne (1970), Marie Lloyd (1977), Arthur Lucan (1978) and Gus Elen (1980).

The GLC also seems to have a special affection for minor British artists. Plaques have been almost indiscriminately awarded to Sir Frank Short (1951), Sir Richard Westmacott (1955), Sir Hamo Thornycroft (1957), Benjamin Haydon (1959), Charles Rossi (1959), George Richmond (1961), William Strang (1962), John F. Sartorius (1963), Sir John Lavery (1966), Philip Wilson Steer (1967), W.P. Frith (1973), Sir Laurence Alma-Tadema (1975), George Frampton (1977), Sir William Orpen (1978) and Augustus John (1981).

The first plaques erected by the RSA were made by Minton of chocolate brown terracotta. The oldest still in position were put up in 1875 to Napoleon III and John Dryden. Doulton took over from 1921 to 1955 and in 1937 introduced blue glaze, which shows up considerably better on the invariably grimy brickwork of London. The GLC plaques are now made by Carter of Poole; they cost about £455 each, including erection.

As well as ceramic ones, there are plaques of lead, stone, bronze and steel. The condition of the house to be commemorated may dictate the style and composition of the plaque. A niche 2" deep and 20" in diameter has to be gouged out of the wall to fix the conventional ceramic blue plaque whereas steel can be screwed to the face of the building. Old Wyldes, the Hampstead home of John Linnell, is covered in commemorated. A house may be 'listed' when it receives a plaque, but the schemes of builders (private and public) inevitably find a way over such hurdles as 'preservation' and 'conservation'.

Only 13 of the early RSA plaques have survived. Of these, Edmund Burke's house in Soho has lost its upper storeys and is apparently to be rebuilt for office accommodation with a façade that is a facsimile of the original. Sir Harry Vane's house in Hampstead has been completely demolished; the plaque clings to a surviving gatepost.

Of the houses with LCC plaques 76 have been destroyed through demolition or (only a handful) bombing, though subsequently 21 plaques have been erected marking sites — scant consolation for the loss of the buildings. Not surprisingly most demolition occurs at the time of building expansion. For example, 30 houses were demolished in the period 1959–68. In 1936 the Adelphi Terrace was knocked down to be replaced by a ponderous apartment block. Sacheverell Sitwell commented 'willing hands did more damage to London than a German land-mine'. The magnificent four-storey terrace, raised above the river on an arched and vaulted brick substructure, was designed by Robert Adam as part of his ambitious Adelphi project. Since its completion in 1774 the terrace was continuously occupied, often by celebrities in the world of arts: David Garrick, Richard D'Oyly Carte, Thomas Hardy and George Bernard Shaw. J.M. Barrie watched its destruction from his rooms in Robert Street: 'you can't think what a stage of squalid demolition the Adelphi has reached. Roofs in tatters, windows gone, great holes in walls . . . Sad to have to say goodbye to it'.

I have attempted to give a comprehensive list of the plaques in London commemorating the residences of the famous, including both official blue plaques and the rogue plaques erected by individuals, societies and local boroughs. Because anyone, with the permission of the owner of the property concerned, may erect a plaque, there are inevitably several that I have missed.

I would like to thank all the members of the Greater London Council historic buildings division who have given me invaluable information about the GLC and LCC plaques; and also Miss Cobb of the GLC History Library. I would also like to thank the Royal Society of Arts, the local history librarians of all the London boroughs, the city engineer of the Corporation of London, Ralph Wade of the Hampstead Plaque Fund and the Dickens Fellowship. Many friends have helped in my research, especially Neil Burton, Hazel Dakers, John Falding, Nicandra Walker and Nigel Cross.

C.D. 1981

weather-boarding so could only have a steel plaque. The block of flats in which Norman Douglas lived had no area of plain brickwork sufficiently large for the round plaque so a rectangular one was designed.

With some 600 official and rogue plaques in London marking houses of historic interest it is surprising more mistakes have not been made. One error was only discovered at the official unveiling: Lily Langtry was born in 1853 and not, as the GLC plaque on the Cadogan Hotel states, in 1852. Changes of street names and numberings, the rebuilding of houses or parts of houses and inadequate biographical information may create problems of identification. The plaques to John Dryden in Gerrard Street (RSA), Joshua Reynolds in Great Newport Street (private) and the Beauclerks in Great Russell Street (Duke of Bedford) are all on the wrong houses. The plaque by the Hampstead Plaque Fund to Elgar marking the site of his house in Netherhall Gardens should be on the house next door.

The residents of houses earmarked for blue plaques are not always cooperative. Some owners are unwilling to expose their house to the curious gaze of passers-by. Not all passers-by gaze: the bronze plaque in the King's Road to Hans Sloane was stolen and had to be replaced by one of enamelled steel, of 'low scrap value'. The first plaque to Karl Marx was erected in 1935 and smashed the same year; its replacement was smashed the following year. Another location was eventually found in Dean Street, Soho, and a new plaque to Marx was erected, which seems to be surviving vandalism. The treatment Marx received deterred the owner of a house in which Lenin stayed from allowing a plaque to him to be put up (particularly as the house had become a vicarage). Lenin received his plaque only when the original house in Percy Circus had been demolished and the hotel on the site put up its own plaque in 1972.

Progress through the streets of London is still 'somewhat dull and not very rapid' and 'the old haunts of London' are still being threatened by the 'ruthless hands of modern destroyers and improvers' even though it is nearly 120 years since the Royal Society of Arts decided to erect plaques. The number of plaques has increased but the number of houses left standing of any considerable age has decreased. Now blue plaques can be spotted on the most unprepossessing 'semis' in suburbia while in central London plaques reading 'site of' proliferate. Even a blue plaque cannot prevent a house succumbing to the relentless force of the speculator's bulldozer. In Soho alone property developers and their architects have destroyed the birthplace of William Blake and the homes of Coleridge, John Hunter, Thomas De Quincey, Sir Joseph Banks and Arthur Onslow as well as countless residences so far un-

Adam, Robert.

1-3 Robert Street, Adelphi, WC2
Robert Adam, Thomas Hood, John Galsworthy, Sir James Barrie and other eminent artists and writers lived here (LCC 1950).

Robert Adam lived at 3 Robert Street from 1778 to 1785. He was involved in extensive building in London throughout his life: the ambitious Adelphi Terrace venture, the south and east sides of Fitzroy Square and Kenwood House. No.3 later became the Caledonian Hotel and in 1824 the King of the Sandwich Islands died of smallpox while staying there.

Thomas Hood, poet and author of *The Song of the Shirt*, lived at no.2 from 1828 to 1830 and the Victorian engraver Henry Ryall lived at no.1 from 1841 to 1850.

J.M. Barrie lived in a flat in Robert Street from 1909 until his death in 1937, a period of increasing sadness for him as he became estranged from the Llewellyn Davies boys who had inspired much of his work.

Adams, Henry Brook.

98 Portland Place, W1
United States Embassy (1863-1866) Henry Brook Adams (1838-1918) US historian lived here (GLC 1978).

Adams, John

Henry Brook Adams was the great-grandson of John Adams, the second president of the USA, and came from one of the most influential families in New England. He first went to London in 1861 when his father, Charles Francis Adams, was appointed ambassador to Great Britain by Abraham Lincoln at the outbreak of the Civil War. Henry worked as private secretary to his father until 1868, living at the embassy in Portland Place. Adam's most distinguished work and one of the finest American autobiographies, *The Education of Henry Adams*, was printed privately in 1907. His attempt to find continuity between the apparently secure and traditional past and the seeming chaos of the 20th century was futile: 'all he could prove was change'.

Adams, John.

9 Grosvenor Square, SW1

In this house lived John Adams First American Minister to Great Britain, May 1785 to March 1788 afterwards second President of the United States. From here his daughter Abigail was married to Colonel William Stephens Smith First Secretary of the Legation and an officer in the Revolutionary Army on Washington's staff. John Adams and Abigail his wife through character and personality did much to create understanding between the two English-speaking countries. In their memory this tablet is placed by the Colonia Dames of America 1933.

John Adams was made first United States ambassador to the Court of St James's in 1785; he and his family settled at 9 Grosvenor Square. Adams was a blunt New Englander, distrustful of European morals and ill at ease in London, particularly as he felt his allowance was not sufficient for him to maintain a suitably high standard of living. While he lived at Grosvenor Square he published *A Defence of the Constitutions of the Government of the USA* in time to influence the Philadelphia Convention of 1789. He was chosen to be vice-president under George Washington.

Adelphi Terrace.

WC2

This building stands on the site of Adelphi Terrace built by the brothers Adam in 1768–1774. Famous residents in the Terrace include Topham and Lady Diana Beauclerk, David Garrick, Richard D'Oyly Carte, Thomas Hardy and George Bernard Shaw. The London School of Economics and the Savage Club also had their premises here (LCC 1952).

The Adelphi Terrace was a magnificent four-storey terrace designed by Robert Adam as part of the Adam brothers' scheme to build houses and roads on a three-acre site between the Strand and the Thames. The project was enormously expensive and nearly brought the Adam family to ruin. Four years after the start, the debts amounted to £140,000 and the annual costs of labour and materials were £100,000. In 1774, however, £218,500 was raised by lottery. The press praised the efforts of the Adam brothers 'to raise palaces from an offensive heap of mud and circulate an immense sum to make a palpable nuisance a principal ornament to the metropolis'.

From completion until its unwarranted demolition in 1936 the terrace was constantly occupied, often by celebrities in the world of arts. Richard D'Oyly Carte employed Whistler to design the colour scheme for no.4: his library was painted primrose yellow 'as if the sun was shining, however dark the day'. Thomas Hardy worked as an architect in the offices of Arthur Bloomfield (no.8) from 1862 to 1867. The view of the river from the office windows was particularly fine, but the Thames stank in the summer. George Bernard Shaw lived in a flat in the terrace with Charlotte Payne-Townshend after their marriage in 1898.

Alexander, Sir George.

57 Pont Street, SW1
Sir George Alexander (1858–1918) actor-manager lived here (LCC 1951).

George Alexander (his original name was George Samson) began his career as an actor-manager in London in 1889 at the Adelphi Theatre, but his longest and most memorable association was with St James's Theatre which he managed from 1891 until his death. He made it one of the leading theatres in London and notable plays were previewed there, including Oscar Wilde's *Lady Windermere's Fan* and *The Importance of Being Earnest* and Pinero's *The Second Mrs Tanqueray*. Alexander moved to Pont Street in 1896 and remained in Chelsea for the rest of his life.

Allenby, Edmund Henry Hynman, Viscount.

24 Wetherby Gardens, SW5
Field Marshal Viscount Allenby (1881–1936) lived here 1928–1936 (LCC 1960).

Edmund Allenby was in retirement from the army when he lived at

3

Wetherby Gardens. During the Boer War he took part in the relief of Kimberley and in World War I he was given the command of the cavalry in the British Expeditionary Force to France. Transferred to Egypt in 1917, he led a victorious campaign against the Turks with Colonel T.E. Lawrence, one of his most outstanding officers. After the war he was appointed High Commissioner for Egypt but he resigned in 1925. One of his favourite retirement hobbies was bird watching and he established an aviary in the small garden of 24 Wetherby Gardens.

Alma-Tadema, Sir Laurence.

44 Grove End Road, NW8
   Sir Laurence Alma-Tadema OM (1836-1912) painter lived here 1886-1912 (GLC 1975).

Laurence Alma-Tadema was born in Dronrijp, Holland, and his passion for archaeology was acquired in Antwerp where he studied art. His paintings (over 400) are characterised by meticulous re-creation of classical times. He designed for the stage and his sets for Henry Irving's production of *Coriolanus* in 1901 were particularly successful. He moved into Grove End Road after rebuilding the original late 18th-century house to his own design, with the technical assistance of Alfred Calderon. The main staircase was carpeted with brass and the windows were of onyx, but these unusual features were lost when the house was converted into flats in the 1950s. Alma-Tadema's summer house is now no.44a, but his initials remain intertwined on the front gate-piers of the main house.

Anderson, Elizabeth Garrett. *See* GARRETT ANDERSON, ELIZABETH.

Annesley, Susanna.

7 Spitalyard, Bishopsgate, EC2
   In this house Susanna Annesley mother of John Wesley was born January 20th, 1669 (City of London).

Susanna Annesley was the youngest daughter of Samuel Annesley, one of the most eminent of the Puritan nonconformists. In 1690 she married Samuel Wesley; she gave birth to 17 children and outlived her husband (*see* Charles Wesley and John Wesley).

Arnold, Sir Edwin.

31 Bolton Gardens, SW5
Sir Edwin Arnold (1832–1904) poet and humanist lived and died here (LCC 1931).

Edwin Arnold first went to India as a schoolmaster and was principal of the Government Deccan College at Poona, 1856–61. He returned to London and began writing for the *Daily Telegraph*, becoming its chief editor in 1873. He studied Eastern language and religion and published *The Light of Asia* in 1879, a blank verse poem rich in oriental luxury, exploring the life and teachings of Buddha. For the last ten years of his life Arnold's sight was failing and he died in his house in Bolton Gardens.

Arnold, Matthew.

2 Chester Square, SW1
Matthew Arnold (1822–1888) poet and critic lived here (LCC 1954).

In February 1858 Matthew Arnold wrote 'we have taken a house in Chester Square. It is a very small one, but it will be something to unpack one's portmanteau for the first time since I was married, now nearly seven years ago'. The Arnolds remained for ten years, during which time Arnold was recognised as one of the leading poets of the day and was elected to the non-residential Chair of Poetry at Oxford (1857–67). In his last year at Chester Square he published *New Poems*.

Arnold's first volume of poetry received little attention and when he married in 1851 he decided to pursue a routine career. He became Inspector of Schools and did much to improve the education system (continuing the work of his father, Thomas, headmaster of Rugby). His poetic output was seriously affected.

Asquith, Herbert Henry [1st Earl of Oxford].

20 Cavendish Square, W1
Herbert Henry Asquith 1st Earl of Oxford and Asquith (1852–1928) statesman lived here (LCC 1951).

Herbert Henry Asquith lived at 20 Cavendish Square from 1895 to 1908 with his second wife Margot Tennant. In the 1920s the house was converted into the Cowdray Club and two more storeys were added, and in 1932 the whole of the façade was refronted with new stone and a new portico was erected, giving the house a more forbidding aspect.

Asquith was out of office for most of the time he lived in Cavendish Square. The Liberal Party did not return to government until 1906 after 11 years 'of trouble and schism' and Asquith was able to earn a large income as a barrister. He became Chancellor of the Exchequer and made the first provisions for old-age pensions. He was Prime Minister at the outbreak of World War I. A thoughtful and cautious politician, he was blamed for much of the early setbacks in the fighting and was soon outmanoeuvred by Lloyd George who replaced him as Prime Minister in 1916.

Astafieva, Princess Seraphine.

152 King's Road, SW3
Princess Seraphine Astafieva (1876–1934) ballet dancer lived and danced here (GLC 1968).

Princess Astafieva lived at The Pheasantry in the King's Road from about 1918 until her death. She came to England with Diaghilev in 1910 but retired from the stage three years later. She established her teaching studio and home at The Pheasantry and her famous pupils included Margot Fonteyn, Anton Dolin and Alicia Markova, who was only 14 when Diaghilev watched her dance there.

Astley, Dame Joanna.

North Wall, St Bartholomew's Hospital, EC1
The site of the house of Dame Joanna Astley, nurse of King Henry VI (private).

Joanna, wife of Thomas Astley, was appointed nurse to Henry VI in 1424. The king was nearly three years old and Dame Joanna received a salary of £40 a year — as high as that of a Privy Councillor — for looking after him.

Austen, Jane.

23 Hans Place, SW1
Jane Austen, novelist, stayed with her brother Henry in a house on this site 1814–1815 (private).

Henry Austen, captain in the Oxfordshire Militia, left the army and established a firm of army bankers in London. In summer 1814, Henry moved to 23 Hans Place and was visited by Jane in November. She described the house to her sister Cassandra: 'It is a delightful Place. . . and the Garden is quite a Love. I am in the front Attic, which is the Bedchamber to be preferred'. Henry became ill in October 1815 and Jane helped to nurse him, but the strain affected her own health.

Avebury, Baron. *See* LUBBOCK, JOHN.

Baden-Powell, Robert.

9 Hyde Park Gate, SW7
Robert Baden-Powell (1857–1941) Chief Scout of the World lived here (GLC 1972).

Robert Baden-Powell spent much of his youth at 9 Hyde Park Gate, living there from 1861/2 until 1876. His father, the Rev. H.G. Baden-Powell, a naturalist and scientist, died in 1860 leaving his widow (his third wife) to bring up ten children. She bought no.9 which was built between 1844 and 1847 by the developer J.F. Hansom. The Baden-Powell children were encouraged by their mother to study natural history and to go on camping holidays. The departure of the family from Hyde Park Gate coincided with Robert joining the 13th Hussars in India. He became a major-general when he was only 43 after the famous defence of Mafeking. His devotion to the Boy Scout movement began with the publication of *Scouting for Boys* in 1908.

Bagehot, Walter.

12 Upper Belgrave Street, SW1
Walter Bagehot (1826–1877) writer, banker and economist lived here (GLC 1967).

Michael Foot called Bagehot 'one of the most honest students of political man who ever applied first class talents to the inquiry'. *The*

7

Robert Baden-Powell, 9 Hyde Park Gate

English Constitution, which was published in book form in 1867, has become a classic elucidation. 12 Upper Belgrave Street was Bagehot's first permanent London residence. Its former owner was James Wilson, proprietor of *The Economist*. Bagehot wrote articles on banking for *The Economist*, married one of Wilson's daughters and edited the paper after Wilson's death. He lived in Upper Belgrave Street from about the end of 1861 until 1870. The house was built in the 1840s when Thomas Cubitt developed Belgravia.

Baillie, Joanna.

Bolton House, Windmill Hill, NW3
Joanna Baillie, poet and dramatist, born 1762, died 1851, lived in this house for nearly fifty years (RSA 1900).

Joanna Baillie and her sister moved to Hampstead after the death of their mother in 1806. Bolton House was visited by many eminent writers and scientists, including Sir Walter Scott who was a close friend for over 50 years. She had little success on stage, but her tragedies were highly regarded. Two of her dramas, *Martyr* and *Bride*, were translated into Singalese for Sir Alexander Johnston, Chief Justice of Ceylon, to use to improve the natives and 'eradicate their vices'.

Baird, John Logie.

22 Frith Street, W1
John Logie Baird (1888-1946) first demonstrated television in this house in 1926 (LCC 1951).

132-5 Long Acre, WC2
From this site John Logie Baird broadcast the first television programme in Great Britain on the 30th September 1929 (Royal Television Society 1980).

3 Crescent Wood Road, Sydenham, SE26
John Logie Baird (1888-1946) television pioneer lived here (GLC 1977).

John Logie Baird first experimented with television in an attic in Hastings. The projection lamp was placed in an empty biscuit tin and the motor in an old tea chest. The machine was held together with glue, sealing wax and string and with it Baird was able to transmit the flickering image of a Maltese cross. Baird moved to London in August 1924 and his 'original television apparatus' was first demonstrated to members of the Royal Institution at 22 Frith Street where he rented an attic

John Logie Baird, 22 Frith Street

laboratory. Two years later Baird transmitted pictures which were received on the other side of the Atlantic. He set up the Baird Television Development Company Ltd which provided programmes until 1932, when the BBC took over responsibility for transmissions.

Baird married Margaret Albo in 1931; they lived in Crescent Wood Road until Baird's death in 1946.

Bairnsfather, Bruce.

1 Sterling Street, Montpellier Square, SW7
Bruce Bairnsfather (1888-1959) cartoonist lived here (GLC c1981).

After Bruce Bairnsfather was severely wounded at Ypres he was moved to hospital in London from where he sent sketches of army life for publication in *The Bystander* magazine. He returned to France and was promoted to captain with the special title of officer-cartoonist. His reputation was established with the invention of characters such as Old Bill, Bert and Alf, whom he placed in wryly comic situations amid the devastation of the Front Line. Bairnsfather had his home and studio at 1 Sterling Street from 1919 to 1921.

Baldwin, Stanley.

93 Eaton Square, SW1
Stanley Baldwin 1st Earl Baldwin of Bewdley (1867-1947) Prime Minister lived here (GLC 1969).

Stanley Baldwin lived at 93 Eaton Square from 1913 to 1924, the period when his political fortunes were steadily rising. He entered Parliament in 1908 and by 1916 was Parliamentary Private Secretary to Bonar Law, Chancellor of the Exchequer. Baldwin was Financial Secretary (1917-21) and then President of the Board of Trade. In October 1922 he left Eaton Square for 11 Downing Street, as Chancellor, and settled the British World War I debt to the United States. He moved from 11 to 10 Downing Street after the retirement of Bonar Law in July 1923 and was to serve as Prime Minister three times before his resignation in 1937 after the abdication of Edward VIII.

Balfe, Michael William.

12 Seymour Street, W1
Michael William Balfe (1808-1870) musical composer lived here (LCC 1912).

Michael Balfe has been called the 'English Rossini' and is chiefly remembered for his opera *The Bohemian Girl* (1843). He lived at 12 Seymour Street from about 1861 to 1865, when he produced his operas *The Puritan's Daughter, Blanche de Nevers* and *The Armourer of Nantes*. In 1864 he purchased Rowney Abbey, a small landed property in Hertfordshire, where he became a gentleman farmer.

Ballantyne, Robert Michael.

Duneaves, Mount Park Road, Harrow
   R.M. Ballantyne (1825–1894) author of books for boys lived here (GLC 1979).

When two of his sons became day boys at Harrow School, R.M. Ballantyne bought a piece of land in Harrow in June 1879 and built Duneaves in the 'domestic revival' style. He wrote nearly all his adventure stories from personal experience and travelled widely. *The Coral Island*, one of the most popular Victorian children's books, was published in 1857. Ballantyne died from overwork and ill-health in Rome. He had written over 80 books in 40 years, furiously competing with Verne, Henty and others, in a desperate attempt to keep his family at a reasonable standard of living.

Banks, Sir Joseph.

32 Soho Square, W1
   Sir Joseph Banks (1743–1820) President of the Royal Society and Robert Brown (1773–1858) and David Don (1800–1841) botanists lived in a house on this site. The Linnean Society met here 1820–1857 (LCC 1938).

The first house at 32 Soho Square was built about 1680 and occupied by John Cleland, the supposed author of *Fanny Hill*. It was rebuilt in 1773–4 for the city banker Sir George Colebrooke, who sold it to Sir Joseph Banks. In August 1777 Banks moved in and assembled his extensive natural history collections and library. A year later he was elected president of the Royal Society. His 'philosophical breakfasts' attracted scientists, inventors and scholars from all over the world. Shortly before his death, when he was suffering severely from gout, his house was attacked by rioters demonstrating against the Corn Bill before Parliament.

   Robert Brown was librarian to Sir Joseph Banks and after Banks's death he inherited both the house and the natural history collection. Brown leased the front portion of the house to the Linnean Society, acting as its librarian until he was succeeded by David Don in 1822

The society, founded in 1788, had come into being with the stimulus of Dr James Edward Smith, who had bought the botanical collection of the Swedith botanist Linnaeus after his death in 1781. 32 Soho Square was demolished in 1936.

Barbon, Nicholas. *See* ESSEX STREET.

Barbosa, Ruy.

17 Holland Park Gardens, W14
Ruy Barbosa (1849-1923) eminent Brazilian statesman and jurist lived here 1895 (Anglo-Brazilian Society c1953).

Ruy Barbosa, politician, writer, journalist and lawyer, became Minister of the Treasury in 1889 in the newly established republic of Brazil. Five years later he fled to Argentina and then to Britain after a military dictatorship was set up in Brazil under Fioriano Peixoto. Barbosa spent a year in exile staying in Holland Park Gardens and started a law practice to serve British merchants and investors in Brazil.

Baring, Sir **Francis.**

The Manor House, Manor House Library, Old Road, Lee, SE13
Sir Francis Baring Bart MP (1740-1810) merchant and banker lived here 1797-1810 (private).

Sir Francis Baring founded the financial house of Baring Brothers & Co.; Lord Erskine called him 'the first merchant in Europe'. Deaf from childhood, he became director and chairman of the East India Company, and was made a baronet for his services.

Barnardo, Thomas John.

58 Solent House, Ocean Estate, Ben Jonson Road, E1
Thomas John Barnardo (1845-1905) began his work for children in a building on this site in 1866 (LCC 1953).

Thomas Barnardo became convinced of the evils of drink while working in a wine merchant's office in his home town of Dublin and he began preaching in the city slums. He went to London in 1866 intending to travel to China as a missionary but the plight of the homeless children in the East End deflected him. He took a dilapidated donkey-shed on the west side of Hope Place (now the site of Ocean Estate) and began teaching poor children. He preached in the open air, visited lodging houses and slums and volunteered for service in the district during the cholera epidemic of 1866/7. The boys' home which he opened at 18 Stepney Causeway in 1870 became the first Dr Barnardo's Home. His unbroken principle was 'no destitute child ever refused admission'. Before his death in 1905 Barnardo brought up 59,384 destitute children and assisted another 250,000 in want.

Barratt, Thomas J.

Bell Moor, Hampstead Heath, NW3
On this site stood the house Bell Moor where the historian of Hampstead Thomas J. Barratt lived from 1877–1914 (Hampstead Borough Council).

The height above sea level here is 435' 7'', 16' 7'' higher than the cross on the top of St Paul's Cathedral.

Barrie, Sir James M.

100 Bayswater Road, W2
Sir James Barrie (1860–1937) novelist and dramatist lived here (LCC 1961).

J.M. Barrie lived at 100 Bayswater Road from 1902 to 1909. The cottage is one of a pair built between 1825 and 1830 and set behind small gardens. They are virtually the last pre-Metropolitan survivals of the former Uxbridge Road. Barrie designed the interior: panelling in the sitting-room, an 'Adam' gas fire set among tiles from the Glasgow school, door-knobs and finger-plates with thistle emblems.

Barrie met the Llewelyn Davies boys on his walks in Kensington Gardens and they provided the inspiration for *Peter Pan*, which was written in a small summer house at the bottom of the garden (*see also* ROBERT ADAM).

Barrowe, Henry. *See* CLINK PRISON.

Barry, Sir Charles.

The Elms, Clapham Common North Side, SW4
Sir Charles Barry (1795–1860) architect lived and died here (LCC 1950).

Sir Charles Barry achieved fame as an architect when he won the competition in 1836 for his Tudor Gothic design for the new Houses of Parliament. The original building burnt down in 1834 because of the faulty firing of the heating apparatus under the House of Lords.

In 1841 Barry designed a building for rather different inmates: Pentonville Prison. £85,000 was spent on the structure which provided better comfort for many of the prisoners then they experienced when at liberty, including proper sanitation and a fair-sized window in every cell.

Basevi, George.

17 Savile Row, W1
George Basevi (1794–1845) architect, lived here (LCC 1949).

Savile Row and Old Burlington Street attracted a number of architects in the 1820s and 1830s, including S.P. and C.R. Cockerell. George Basevi lived at 17 Savile Row from 1829 to 1845. His most important work was the Fitzwilliam Museum at Cambridge. The first stone was laid in 1837 and by 1845 only the library and staircase hall were incomplete. But on 16 October that year Basevi fell to his death while inspecting the bell-tower of Ely Cathedral; C.R. Cockerell completed the Fitzwilliam Museum 'in the interests of Mrs Basevi'.

Baylis, Lilian.

27 Stockwell Park Road, SW9
Lilian Baylis (1874–1937) manager of the Old Vic and Sadler's Wells Theatres lived and died here (GLC 1974).

Lilian Baylis began assisting her aunt Emma Cons in the management of the Old Vic in 1898. By the beginning of World War I the Old Vic had become established as a theatre for the classics and between 1914 and 1925 Lilian Baylis presented all Shakespeare's plays from the First Folio. Her association with Sadler's Wells Theatre also lasted many years. She rescued the 'poor wounded old playhouse' and opened on Twelfth Night 1931 with a performance of Shakespeare's *Twelfth Night*. Lilian Baylis lived at 27 Stockwell Park Road from 1917 to 1937. The house was built in about 1850; it is no longer a family home.

Bazalgette, Sir Joseph William.

17 Hamilton Terrace, NW8
Sir Joseph William Bazalgette (1819–1891) civil engineer lived here (GLC 1974).

Joseph Bazalgette was knighted in 1874 for designing the main drainage system for London. The system, which consisted of 83 miles of intercepting sewers, was opened in 1865 though not completed until

15

1875. Bazalgette also constructed the Victoria, Albert and Chelsea Embankments, new bridges over the Thames at Putney and Battersea and the Woolwich steam ferry.

Beaconsfield, Earl of. *See* DISRAELI, BENJAMIN.

Beardsley, Aubrey.

114 Cambridge Street, SW1
   Aubrey Beardsley (1872-1898) artist, lived here (LCC 1948).

Aubrey Beardsley and his sister Mabel set up house at 114 Cambridge Street in summer 1893, to be 'always at home on Thursday afternoons' to friends who included Max Beerbohm, Oscar Wilde and William Rothenstein. Beardsley decorated his rooms in the style of Des Esseintes, the amoral and decadent hero of Huysmans's novel *A Rebours*, painting the walls violent orange and the doors and skirtings black. Other walls in the house were decorated with stripes from floor to ceiling. Rothenstein, who used Beardsley's workroom, was shocked by the erotic Japanese woodcuts his friend displayed in his bedroom.

Beardsley illustrated Malory's *Morte d'Arthur* and Wilde's *Salome* while living in Cambridge Street and, in 1894, conceived *The Yellow Book* with Henry Harland and Max Beerbohm. His designs only appeared in the first four volumes because he was sacked as art editor after Wilde was convicted in 1895. With increasing debts and worsening tuberculosis, Beardsley was forced to leave Cambridge Street; he lived in various lodgings in London and abroad until his death.

Beatty, David Earl. *See* COCHRANE, THOMAS.

Beauclerk, Lady **Diana; Beauclerk, Topham.**

99 Great Russell Street, WC1
   Here lived Topham Beauclerk born 1739 died 1780, Lady Diana Beauclerk born 1734 died 1808 (Duke of Bedford 1905).

Lady 'Di' was the eldest daughter of Charles Spencer, 2nd Duke of Marlborough; Topham was the grandson of the 1st Duke of St Albans. Lady Di was considered 'handsome and agreeable and ingenious, far beyond the ordinary rate' by her contemporaries and she achieved slight fame as a painter. Topham is remembered for his close friendship with Samuel Johnson which lasted for 27 years until Topham's death in Great Russell Street (in no.100, not no.99 as stated in contemporary rate books). The Beauclerks also lived for a time in the Adelphi Terrace.

Beaufort, Sir **Francis.**

51 Manchester Street, W1
   Sir Francis Beaufort (1774–1857) admiral and hydrographer lived here (LCC 1959).

Francis Beaufort had a distinguished naval career. In action against Spain in 1800 he received 19 wounds in the head, arms and body, three sword cuts and 16 musket shots and was promoted to commander. More peaceful activities included making an accurate survey of the entrance to the Rio de la Plata. Beaufort was appointed hydrographer to the navy in 1829 and his name was given to the scale of numbers still used to indicate the force of the wind and also to a system of notation for the weather.

Beerbohm, Sir **Henry Maximilian.**

57 Palace Gardens Terrace, W8
   Sir Max Beerbohm (1872–1956) artist and writer born here (GLC 1969).

Henry Maximilian Beerbohm first achieved fame and notoriety through writing for *The Yellow Book*, one of the journals of the Aesthetic movement. He contributed an essay on 'A Defence of Cosmetics' to the first number in 1894 at a time when make-up was associated with prostitution, and he was attacked violently in the pages of *Punch*. He was associated with the Aesthetes throughout the 1890s, writing essays, drawing caricatures and spending evenings at the Café Royal with Aubrey Beardsley and Oscar Wilde. He married the actress Florence Kahn in 1910 and they went to live in Rapallo, Italy.

Belloc, Hilaire.

104 Cheyne Walk, SW3
   Hilaire Belloc (1870–1953) poet, essayist and historian lived here 1900–1905 (GLC 1973).

Hilaire Belloc and G.K. Chesterton became the leading English Catholic writers of their age. Belloc moved to Cheyne Walk from Oxford in 1900 and spent the next few years engaged in politics, becoming MP for Salford South in 1906. One of the first books to bring him fame was *The Bad Child's Book of Beasts* (1896). While living in Cheyne Walk he published *The Path to Rome* (1902) (*see also* WALTER GREAVES).

Benedict, Sir **Julius.**

2 Manchester Square, W1
   Sir Julius Benedict (1804–1885) musical composer, lived and died here (LCC 1934).

   Sir Julius Benedict lived at 2 Manchester Square for over 40 years. He conducted his first opera, *The Gypsy's Warning*, at Drury Lane Theatre in 1838. In 1850 he accompanied Jenny Lind on a tour of the USA and then returned to conducting at Her Majesty's Theatre. His most popular opera is *The Lily of Killarney* (1862). He was knighted in 1871.

Benes, Edvard.

26 Gwendolen Avenue, SW15
   Dr Edvard Benes (1884–1948) President of Czechoslovakia lived here (GLC 1978).

   Dr Edvard Benes stayed in his nephew's house in Putney from 1938 to 1940, the first two years of his seven-year exile in London. He had become President of Czechoslovakia in 1935 but was unable to prevent the crisis in 1938 which led to the destruction of his country. Abandoned by his allies he was forced to capitulate to Germany. He was active during his exile and in October 1939 became President of the Czechoslovakian National Committee, which he organised from the red-brick Putney house. He was recognised as President of the Czechoslovakian Republic in 1940 and moved to the Czech Embassy at 9 Grosvenor Place. At the end of the war Benes returned to his country.

Bennett, Arnold.

75 Cadogan Square, SW1
   Arnold Bennett (1867–1931) novelist lived here (LCC 1958).

   Novels like *The Old Wives' Tale* and *Anna of the Five Towns*, set in the Potteries, brought Arnold Bennett wealth as well as acclaim, and in 1922 he moved into 75 Cadogan Square, 'a rather fine thing in houses'. The next year he was completing *Riceyman Steps* while having an affair with the actress Dorothy Cheston. When their daughter Virginia was born in April 1926 Dorothy moved into the flat in Cadogan Square (she could not marry Bennett because his wife refused to give him a divorce). When the lease of 75 Cadogan Square expired in 1930 Bennett and Dorothy moved to a new block of flats, Chiltern Court, off Baker Street, in which Bennett's friend H.G. Wells was already installed.

Bentham, George.

25 Wilton Place, SW1
George Bentham (1800–1884) botanist lived here (GLC 1978).

George Bentham lived at Wilton Place from 1864 until his death. His concentration on botanical studies began in the 1830s and he became one of the greatest English systematic botanists. He made almost daily visits to Kew where, with Sir Joseph Hooker, he produced the major part of *Genera plantarum* (1862–83). It is Bentham's most important work, giving a revised definition of every kind of flowering plant — a model of scientific accuracy. His *Handbook of British Flora* (1858) is perhaps his best-known book.

Bentley, John Francis.

43 Old Town, SW4
John Francis Bentley (1839–1902) architect lived here (LCC 1950).

John Francis Bentley's most remarkable work as an architect (he specialised in church architecture) was his design of Westminster Cathedral. Halsey Ricardo described the impact of the building, which was begun in 1894, in his obituary of Bentley: 'the romance and piety of those great masses of brickwork effloresce from the plain, common-sense, and direct treatment of the problem, and consecrate it apart from the usual commonplace of building'. Bentley lived at 43 Old Town, Clapham, from 1876 to 1894.

Berlioz, Hector.

58 Queen Anne Street, W1
Hector Berlioz (1803–1869) composer, stayed here in 1851 (GLC 1969).

Berlioz was perhaps the greatest musical figure in the French Romantic movement. In 1851 he was chosen to be a member of the jury judging the qualities of musical instruments submitted to the Great Exhibition from manufacturers throughout Europe; he stayed at Queen Anne Street from May to July. The fine Georgian house belonged to a professor of music and the Beethoven Quartet Society gave regular concerts in the drawing-room, as Berlioz described: 'My apartment being situated above the main staircase, I could easily hear the whole performance by simply opening my door. One evening I heard Beethoven's Trio in C minor being played. I opened my door wide. Come in, come in, welcome proud melody!'

19

Besant, Annie.

39 Colby Road, SE19
Annie Besant (1847–1933) social reformer, lived here in 1874 (LCC 1963).

Annie Besant lived at 39 Colby Road, an early Victorian semi-detached house, for most of 1874. She had left her husband, Frank Besant, vicar of Sibsey in Lincolnshire, the previous year after losing her religious faith. While at Colby Road she joined the National Secular Society and began her close friendship with Charles Bradlaugh which lasted until her conversion to theosophy and her first visit to India in 1893. She became a constant supporter of trade unions, organising the Matchmakers' Union and strike in 1888. In 1885 she joined the Fabian Society and Social Democratic Federation and she played a leading part in the movement for birth control.

Besant, Sir Walter.

Frognal End, Frognal Gardens, NW3
Sir Walter Besant (1836–1901) novelist and antiquary lived and died here (LCC 1925).

Walter Besant began his literary career in London in 1867. Although his novels (some written jointly with James Rice) have been forgotten, his work for the cause of authorship continues to be honoured. He formed the Society of Authors in 1884 and *The Author* was founded and edited by him in 1890. George Meredith described Besant's aim 'to establish a system of fair dealing between the sagacious publishers of books and the inexperienced, often heedless, producers'.

Besant built the house at Frognal End for himself in 1893 and a year later started his project to prepare a historical survey of London. It was completed after his death but he prepared studies of *Westminster* (1895), *South London* (1899), *East London* (1901) and *The Thames* (1902).

Birkenhead, Earl of. *See* SMITH, FREDERICK EDWIN.

Blake, William.

8 Marshall Street, W1
William Blake was born on 28 November 1757 in a house on this site (private).

23 Hercules Road, SE1
  William Blake poet and painter lived in a house on this site (City Corporation 1907; re-erected on new building 1922).

17 South Molton Street, W1
  William Blake poet and painter lived here born 1757 died 1827 (City Corporation 1925).

The young Blake saw his first vision (a tree filled with angels) when he was only about ten years old. He left his parents' home in Broad (now Broadwick) Street at the age of 14 and was apprenticed to the engraver Basire for seven years. He then returned to Broad Street and lived with his parents until 1782, when he married Catherine Butcher.

The couple moved to 13 Hercules Buildings, Lambeth, in autumn 1790 and stayed there ten years, the only period in which Blake achieved anything approaching worldly prosperity. The 'pretty, clean house of 8 or 10 rooms' had a vine growing in the garden over an arbour, the setting for one of the most famous legends about the family life of this extraordinary mystic, poet and artist: 'Mr Butts calling one day found Mr and Mrs Blake sitting in this summer-house, freed from those troublesome disguises which have prevailed since the Fall. "Come in!" cried Blake; "It's only Adam and Eve, you know!" Husband and wife had been reciting passages from Paradise Lost, in character, and the garden of Hercules Buildings had to represent the Garden of Eden'. In Lambeth Blake wrote many of his best works, *The Marriage of Heaven and Hell*, *America* and *The Songs of Experience*.

The period the Blakes spent in a second-floor flat at 17 South Molton Street (1803–21) was considerably harder. Friends reported on their condition 'still poor still dirty' and 'drinking tea, durtyer than ever'. Blake produced less of his own work but was helped by commissions from his new friend and benefactor John Linnell whom he met in 1818.

In 1821 the Blakes moved to 3 Fountain Court (now demolished), off the Strand, where Blake died. He was buried in the dissenters' burial ground at Bunhill Fields; his faith could not be contained within any orthodox religion.

Bland, Dorothea. *See* JORDAN, DOROTHY.

Bligh, William.

100 Lambeth Road, SE1
  William Bligh (1754–1817) Commander of the 'Bounty' lived here (LCC 1952).

The mutiny on the *Bounty* which made William Bligh so notorious took place five years before he moved to Lambeth Road in 1794. The house had just been built and remained in his possession until about 1813. Bligh was bound for the West Indies with a cargo of bread fruit gathered at Otaheite (Tahiti) but the six-month stay on the island had a disastrous effect on the crew who 'became demoralised by the luxurious climate and their apparently unrestricted intercourse with the natives'. Bligh's ruthless behaviour towards them and general bad temper caused some of the crew, led by Fletcher Christian, to mutiny. With 18 loyal members Bligh was set adrift in a 23' boat with provisions but no chart. A brilliantly navigated three-month voyage of 3618 miles brought them to Timor, off the east coast of Java. The mutineers settled in Pitcairn Island.

Bloomfield, Robert.

Kent House, Telegraph Street, EC2
In a house on this site lived Robert Bloomfield poet (1766–1823)
(City of London).

Robert Bloomfield spent most of his life in squalor. He went to London to learn the shoemaking trade but when he married in 1790 he could still only afford to live in a garret. He achieved fame with the publication of *The Farmer's Boy* (1800), a volume of verse which sold 26,000 copies in less than three years. But Charles Lamb was less than complimentary: 'I have just opened him but he makes me sick'. Bloomfield received £3000 for *The Farmer's Boy* but it soon disappeared. His attempts to enter the book trade ended in bankruptcy. He died in great poverty in Shefford, Bedfordshire.

Blumlein, Alan Dower.

37 The Ridings, W5
Alan Dower Blumlein (1903–1942) electronics engineer and inventor lived here (GLC 1977).

Alan Blumlein was living at 37 The Ridings, a red-brick house in Ealing built between the wars, at the time of his death in 1942. He and two colleagues were killed when their Halifax bomber caught fire and crashed as it returned from a flight to test Blumlein's invention, H2S, 'blind bombing radar'. H2S transformed Bomber Command's ability to attack German industrial targets by providing a radar map in the bomber which guided it to the point where the bombs should be dropped.

Bonar Law, Andrew.

24 Onslow Gardens, SW7
  Andrew Bonar Law (1858–1923) Prime Minister, lived here (LCC 1958).

On Balfour's resignation in 1911 Andrew Bonar Law became Leader of the House of Commons; he served as Leader of the Conservative Party (1916–21), Chancellor of the Exchequer (1916–18) and Lord Privy Seal (1918–21). He retired for a year because of ill-health and in that period moved to 24 Onslow Gardens, his home until his death. He returned to Parliament in 1921, however, and was leader of the movement that broke up the Lloyd George combination, becoming Prime Minister from October 1922 to May 1923. Tranquillity and stability were the essence of his policy.

Booth, Charles.

6 Grenville Place, SW7
  Charles Booth (1840–1916) pioneer in social research lived here (LCC 1951).

Charles Booth and his brother Alfred began their successful shipping service between Europe and Brazil in 1866. Charles was deeply concerned at the suffering of the poor of London, and he published a monumental 17-volume work, *Life and Labour of the People in London* (1891–3). He studied 4076 cases to determine the causes of individual poverty and discovered that 62% were the result of low or irregular wages, 23% illness or large families and 15% squandered earnings, excessive drinking or refusal to work. He lived at Grenville Place from 1875 to 1890, the period in which he began his research.

Borough, Stephen; Borough, William. *See* WILLOUGHBY, Sir HUGH.

Borrow, George.

22 Hereford Square, W8
  George Borrow (1803–1881) author lived here (LCC 1911).

George Borrow took his wife and step-daughter from East Anglia in 1860 to look for 'a pleasant healthy residence within 3 to 10 miles of London', and on 25 September he took 22 Hereford Square, their home for the next 12 years. Borrow was already a well-known novelist: *Lavengro* (1851) and *Romany Rye* (1857) explored his particular interest in gypsies and the English countryside. During his time in

London his literary output and reputation diminished. With the death of his wife in 1869 and his own ill-health he was reduced to a 'sad state'. He let the house in 1872 and returned to Oulton Broad.

Boswell, James.

122 Great Portland Street, W1
James Boswell (1740-1795) biographer lived and died in a house on this site (LCC 1936).

James Boswell's masterpiece *The Life of Johnson* was published in 1791 shortly after he moved to Great Portland Street. He first met Samuel Johnson in 1763 and their friendship developed during Boswell's annual visits to London from Edinburgh (where he reluctantly practised as an advocate), until Johnson's death in 1784. Boswell moved permanently to London in 1788 and devoted himself to writing Johnson's life but his last years were marred by depression and alcoholism. Macaulay wrote of Boswell: 'Many of the greatest men that ever lived have written biography. Boswell was one of the smallest men that ever lived, and he has beaten them all. . .servile and impertinent, shallow and pedantic, a bigot and a sot'.

Bow Street.

19-20 Bow Street, WC2
Bow Street was formed about 1637. It has been the residence of many notable men among whom were Henry Fielding (1707-1754) novelist; Sir John Fielding (d.1780) magistrate; Grinling Gibbons (1648-1721) wood carver; Charles Macklin (1697?-1797), actor; John Radcliffe (1650-1714) physician; Charles Sackville Earl of Dorset (1638-1706) poet; and William Wycherley (1640?-1716) dramatist (LCC 1929).

Bow Street was so called because it curves in the shape of a bent bow. It was described in the 1720s as 'open and large, with very good Houses, well-inhabited, and resorted unto by Gentry for Lodgings', but declined after a poor house was built in the street. One of the first celebrities to live in Bow Street was the woodcarver Grinling Gibbons whose work may be seen on both the exterior and interior of St Paul's Cathedral. Will's Coffee House, a favourite haunt of Dryden, was at 1 Bow Street, and many artists were attracted to the area. William Wycherley, who was called licentious and indecent by Macaulay for his bawdy plays (*The Country Wife* was published in 1675), lived in Bow Street in 1715. Henry Fielding, a magistrate as well as a novelist,

19–20 Bow Street

was appointed to the Bow Street magistrates' office in 1747. He originated the Thief-Takers, later known as the Bow Street Runners.

Bridgeman, Sir **Orlando.** *See* ESSEX STREET.

Bright, Richard.

11 Savile Row, W1
Richard Bright (1789–1858) physician lived here (GLC 1979).

11 Savile Row was built on the Burlington Estate (*c*1733–5). It was originally three storeys but a fourth was added in 1836 during Bright's occupancy (1830–58). The ground floor has since been given a Victorian shop front and the upper parts of the house have been embellished with stucco.

Bright was the most eminent physician of his time and became a full physician at Guy's Hospital in 1824. In 1827 he published the first volume of *Reports of Medical Cases* in which he gave the first account of his research into dropsy: he traced its cause to a disease of the kidneys, later to be called *Morbus Brightii* (Bright's Disease). Dr Wilks wrote of him that he 'could not theorise and fortunately gave us no doctrines and no "views"; but he could *see*, and we are struck with astonishment at his powers of observation'.

Brockway, Archibald Fenner, Lord.

60 Myddelton Square, N1
Fenner Brockway, Lord Brockway (1888–   )lived here 1908–1910 (London Borough of Islington).

Archibald Fenner Brockway was born in Calcutta where his father was a missionary. In 1907 he joined the staff of the *Examiner* and in 1909, after moving to Myddelton Square, became sub-editor of the *Christian Commonwealth*. When World War I broke out Brockway was a pacifist and was sentenced to four separate periods of imprisonment and hard labour. His book *The Devil's Business* (1915) was proscribed during the war. His efforts towards peace in the world continued throughout his life. Lord Brockway is unique in having a plaque put on one of his homes during his lifetime.

Brougham, Henry Peter, Lord.

4 Grafton Street, W1
Henry Peter Lord Brougham resided in this house for the last thirty years of his life. Born 1778–Died 1868 (City Lands Committee 1903).

Henry Peter Brougham first practised law in Scotland (he was born in Edinburgh) but became a member of Lincoln's Inn in 1803. Before moving permanently to London in 1805, he was involved in the establishment of the *Edinburgh Review* and was an ardent anti-slavery campaigner. Brougham was made Lord Chancellor in 1830 and was a zealous reformer. He drove around London on his official duties in a small carriage specially built for him — 'an old little sort of garden chair' — the ancestor of all broughams. He was closely involved in education and science and helped to found London University and the Society for the Diffusion of Useful Knowledge.

Brown, Ford Madox.

56 Fortess Road, NW5
Ford Madox Brown (1821-1893) painter lived here (GLC 1976).

56 Fortess Road is part of a terrace built in the late 1820s. Ford Madox Brown lived there from 1856 to 1862 while working on one of his best-known paintings, *Work*, which depicts a street scene in Hampstead. Brown studied art in Bruges, Ghent, Antwerp and Paris and became friendly with the pre-Raphaelite group of artists; Dante Gabriel Rossetti was his pupil for a time. Although Brown was never an official member he belonged to the crafts firm of Morris, Marshall, Faulkner & Co. (1861-74). Another close friend was F.D. Maurice, and from 1854 Brown gave free tuition at the Working Men's College which Maurice had founded.

Brown, Robert. *See* BANKS, Sir JOSEPH.

Browning, Elizabeth Barrett.

99 Gloucester Place, W1
Elizabeth Barrett Browning (1806-1861) poet lived here (LCC 1924).

50 Wimpole Street, W1
Elizabeth Barrett Browning (1806-1861) poet lived in a house on this site 1838-46 (LCC 1937).

Elizabeth Barrett Browning is now perhaps more famous for her romance with Robert Browning than for her own poetry, although when they married and fled to Italy she was the more famous. Her invalid life was the result of a riding accident which damaged her spine. It was exacerbated by the strict régime of her father who refused to consider marriage for any of his daughters. Before her elopement

27

she summed up her predicament: 'a bird in a cage would have as good a story; most of my events and nearly all my intense pleasure have passed in my thoughts'. Excitement and subterfuge came into her life with her secret marriage to her fiery poet lover in 1846. The Brownings, together with Elizabeth's faithful dog Flush, established their home in Florence and in 1850 Elizabeth published *Sonnets from the Portuguese*, 44 love-poems to Robert.

Browning, Robert.

179 Southampton Way, SE5
   In memory of Robert Browning (1812–1889) who lived here. 'I spoke as I saw' (South London Immortals Club c1947).

29 De Vere Gardens, W8
   Robert Browning lived in this house 1887–1889. From here his body was taken for interment in Poet's Corner Westminster Abbey (private).

Robert Browning was born to respectable middle-class parents in Camberwell. His father was a clerk in the Bank of England and able to provide a private tutor for Robert. His education was mostly literary and encouraged the early development of his imagination; he later confessed to Elizabeth Barrett Browning: 'I myself am born supremely passionate — so I was born with light yellow hair'. He did not become very well known as a poet until his return to London after his wife Elizabeth's death in 1861, but finally his reputation rivalled Tennyson's.
   Browning's courtship and elopement with Elizabeth Barrett resulted in a contented and artistically productive marriage and he was desolate after her death. He returned to England with their young son but when his home in Warwick Crescent was threatened in 1887 by the construction of a railway he moved to De Vere Gardens. The following winter found him increasingly ill but he was able to complete the arrangements for a uniform edition of his works before dying in Venice where his son had settled.

Bruckner, Anton.

City Gate House, 39–45 Finsbury Square, EC2
   On 29 July 1871 the Austrian composer Anton Bruckner (1824–1896) stayed in the house which used to occupy this site. Bruckner started work on his second symphony during his period in London (private).

Anton Bruckner learnt the organ and studied composition under Sechter in Vienna and in 1868 became professor at the Vienna Conservatory. He visited London as an organ virtuoso in 1869 and again in 1871, when he stayed in Finsbury Square.

Brunel, Sir Marc Isambard; Brunel, Isambard Kingdom.

98 Cheyne Walk, SW3
Sir Marc Isambard Brunel (1769-1849) and Isambard Kingdom Brunel (1806-1859) civil engineers lived here (LCC 1954).

Marc and Sophia Brunel moved to part of Lindsey House (now no. 98), Cheyne Walk, in 1808 when their son Isambard was two years old. Marc was working for the Admiralty at Chatham and had also invested capital in a sawmill at Battersea. He was imprisoned for debt in 1814 and not discharged until 1821 when the Duke of Wellington granted him £5000 to prevent his departure to Russia because he was threatening to work for Tsar Alexander. A year later Isambard began working for his father and in 1824 they began work on one of their most ambitious projects: building a tunnel under the Thames. They started in 1825, and that year the family moved to Blackfriars to be nearer the work.

Lindsey House was first built by Sir Theodore Mayerne, physician to James I, on the site of Sir Thomas More's farm. In 1674 it was incorporated into a house built by Robert Bertie, 3rd Earl of Lindsey and Lord Chamberlain to Charles II. In 1752 it was used by Count Zinzendorf as the London headquarters of the Moravian brethren. Subdivided in 1774, it became 1-7 Lindsey Row. The Brunels occupied the part that included the original staircase and main rooms with wide fireplaces of marble and porphyry.

Burgoyne, John.

10 Hertford Street, W1
General John Burgoyne (1722-1792) lived and died here (LCC 1954).

General Burgoyne moved to 10 Hertford Street in 1771. He was a man of many talents: a General, an MP, dramatist, and leader of London fashion. The rise in his fortunes was helped by his friendship with the Derby family, particularly after he eloped with Lord Derby's daughter. He is best remembered for his defeat at Saratoga in 1777 during the American War of Independence.

Burgoyne's plays include *Maid of the Oaks*, produced by David Garrick at Drury Lane in 1775, and *The Heiress*, produced in 1786.

Marc Isambard and Isambard Kingdom Brunel, 98 Cheyne Walk

In 1787 Burgoyne fulfilled his last important political engagement as a manager of the trial of Warren Hastings (*see also* RICHARD BRINSLEY SHERIDAN).

Burke, Edmund.

37 Gerrard Street, W1
Edmund Burke author and statesman lived here b.1729, d.1797 (RSA 1876).

Edmund Burke lived at 37 Gerrard Street from about 1787 to 1790. A neighbour described his habits: 'Many a time when I had no inclination to go to bed at the dawn of day, I have looked down from my window to see whether the author of the "Sublime and Beautiful" had left his drawing-room, where I had seen that great orator during many a night after he had left the House of Commons, seated at a table covered with papers, attended by an amanuensis who sat opposite to him'. In Parliament (MP 1765–94) he was a zealous reformer of independent cast of mind.

Other eminent residents followed him including John Money, one of the earliest of the English balloonists. From 1805 to 1818 the house was the home of the Literary Fund (now the Royal Literary Fund) which had been established by the Rev. David Williams who died in Gerrard Street in 1816.

Burne-Jones, Sir **Edward.** *See* ROSSETTI, DANTE GABRIEL.

Burnett, Frances Hodgson.

63 Portland Place, W1
Frances Hodgson Burnett (1849–1924) writer lived here (GLC 1979).

The impoverished Hodgson family emigrated to Tennessee in 1865 and eight years later Frances married S.M. Burnett whom she later divorced. Her first novel was her most popular, *Little Lord Fauntleroy* (1886). Her other bestsellers were *The Little Princess* (1905) and *The Secret Garden* (1909).

The Burnetts went to London, acquiring 63 Portland Place in 1893 and remaining there until 1898. The street was built by the Adam brothers and is unusually wide because of a special Act of Parliament obtained by Lord Foley who was determined to protect his view from Foley House at the south end of the street north to the hills of Hampstead. Visitors to the Burnetts' house included Henry James and Israel Zangwill.

Fanny Burney, 11 Bolton Street

Burney, Fanny.

11 Bolton Street, W1
  Fanny Burney: Madam D'Arblay authoress lived here. Born 1752, died 1840 (RSA 1885).

Fanny Burney moved to 11 Bolton Street in 1818. Her first novel, *Evelina, or The History of a Young Lady's Entry into the World,* was published anonymously in 1778. It was an immediate sensation and as a result of her literary success she became acquainted with Mrs Thrale and Samuel Johnson. She was appointed second keeper of the robes to Queen Charlotte in 1786, retiring in 1797 with an annual pension of £100; two years later she married a French emigré General D'Arblay. She was interned in France for the next ten years, only obtaining permission to return to England when Napoleon set out for Moscow.

Burns, John.

110 North Side, Clapham Common, SW4
  John Burns (1858–1943) statesman lived here (LCC 1950).

John Burns was at the end of his active political career when he moved to 110 North Side in 1914. He was the only working-class member of the first LCC in 1889 and sat in Parliament as MP for Battersea from 1892 to 1918. He was an organiser of the dockers' strike in 1889 and helped to obtain a minimum wage of 6d an hour for dockers. Although Burns was a socialist he served in Campbell-Bannerman's Liberal government of 1905 as President of the Local Government Board and in 1914 was transferred to the Board of Trade. He resigned shortly afterwards as he was opposed to the declaration of war against Germany.

Butt, Dame Clara.

7 Harley Road, NW3
  Dame Clara Butt (1873–1937) singer lived here 1901–1929 (GLC 1969).

Clara Butt first went to London in 1890 when she won a scholarship to the Royal College of Music. She made her début at the Albert Hall two years later. Her striking appearance and powerful voice were to make her one of the most popular singers of her day. The well-known setting of *Abide with Me* was composed for her and Elgar wrote *Sea Pictures* for her. In 1900 she married Robert Kennerley Rumford; they

33

moved to 7 Harley Road in 1901. The house may have been built specially for them as they were the first occupants.

Butterfield, William.

42 Bedford Square, WC1
William Butterfield (1814–1900) architect lived here (GLC 1978).

William Butterfield first set up his own practice as an architect in 1840 at 38 Lincoln's Inn Fields. In 1842 he moved to 4 Adam Street, Adelphi, where he kept his offices for the rest of his life; his study, with its Adam chimney piece and grate and old Turkey carpet remained unchanged. Butterfield lived in Adam Street until 1886 when he moved to 42 Bedford Square. Butterfield was a devout man of unfashionable appearance. His work was far from conservative, however, and never achieved popularity in his lifetime. 'I do not think this generation will ever much admire it', Gerard Manley Hopkins wrote to him; 'They do not know how to look at a Pointed building as a whole having a single form governing it throughout. . . . And very few people seem to care for pure beauty of line, at least till they are taught to.' All Saints', Margaret Street, and St Augustine, Queen's Gate, are two of Butterfield's London churches.

William Butterfield, 42 Bedford Square

Caldecott, Randolph.

46 Great Russell Street, WC1
Randolph Caldecott (1846–1886) artist and book illustrator lived here (GLC 1977).

Randolph Caldecott left his work as a Manchester bank clerk and in 1872 he took rooms in Great Russell Street, opposite the British Museum. He spent his summers abroad, sketching and painting in rural surroundings: 'London is of course the proper place for a young man for seeing the manners and customs of society and for getting a living in some of the less frequented grooves of human labour, but for a residence give me a rural or marine retreat'. Success as an artist came with his illustrations for Washington Irving's *Sketch Book* (1875) and *Bracebridge Hall* (1876). Caldecott also illustrated children's books and produced his own series with two volumes every year until just before his death.

Campbell, Colen.

76 Brook Street, W1
Colen Campbell (1676–1729) architect and author of 'Vitruvius Britannicus' lived and died here (GLC 1977).

Colen Campbell was granted a lease of ground in Brook Street in 1726 when he was working for Sir Richard Grosvenor on his Mayfair estate. The houses he built are now nos.76 and 78. Some of the rooms in no.76 have retained their original decoration and the water tank in the area is dated 1726 (no.78 was demolished).

Campbell's career began in 1712 with his design of Shawfield Mansion, Glasgow, and he amassed a huge fortune from his designs of country mansions and town houses. He adapted the ideas of Palladio to suit English taste, publishing his revision of Palladio's *First Book of Architecture* in 1728. Mereworth Castle, Kent (1723), and Stourhead, Wiltshire (*c*1721), are close to Palladio's Villa Rotonda and Villa Emo. When Campbell moved to Brook Street he was not only working on private commissions but was also surveyor to Greenwich Hospital.

Campbell, Mrs Patrick.

33 Kensington Square, W8
Mrs Patrick Campbell (1865–1940) actress lived here (private).

Beatrice Stella Tanner was born in Kensington in 1865 and eloped at the age of 19 with Patrick Campbell, who held a minor post in the City. She made her first professional stage appearance in 1888, in *Bachelors* at the Alexandra Theatre, Liverpool. After touring in Philip Ben Greet's company Mrs Campbell went to London and made her triumphant début as Paula Tanqueray in the first performance of Pinero's *The Second Mrs Tanqueray* (1893). No other female actress of the time could match her portrayal of passionate, complex heroines.

Campbell, Thomas.

8 Victoria Square, SW1
Thomas Campbell (1777–1844) poet lived here 1840–44 (Duke of Westminster 1908).

Thomas Campbell was born in Glasgow. His first volume of verse, *Pleasures of Hope*, was published in 1799 and became instantly popular. Campbell went to London in 1801 and through an introduction to Lord Holland he became acquainted with the notable writers of the day. His seven-volume *Specimens of the British Poets* was published in 1819. One of Campbell's last projects was assisting in the founding of London University; he described the part he played as the only important event in his 'life's little history'. He lived at Victoria Square from 1840 until his death there in 1844.

Campbell-Bannerman, Sir Henry.

6 Grosvenor Place, SW1
  Sir Henry Campbell-Bannerman (1836–1908) Prime Minister lived here (LCC 1959).

Henry Campbell-Bannerman lived in several houses in London, in Kensington, Eaton Square and Belgrave Square, but he spent the longest time at 6 Grosvenor Place, from 1877 to 1904. It was a period of speedy political advancement: he was Financial Secretary to the War Office, 1880–82; Parliamentary and Financial Secretary to the Admiralty and spokesman in the Commons, 1882–4; Chief Secretary for Ireland, 1884–5; Secretary of State for War, 1886; and Leader of the Liberal Party, 1899.

Canaletto.

41 Beak Street, W1
  Antonio Canal called Canaletto (1697–1768) Venetian Painter lived here (LCC 1925).

Canaletto visited England several times between 1746 and 1756: he made an agreement with Joseph Smith (later the British consul in Venice) that he should act as his agent. Beak Street did not exist in 1746 but the house that is now no.41 was owned by Richard Wiggan and situated in Silver Street. An old studio with a skylight stood on what was formerly the garden of the house until the 1920s. Canaletto's style became more academic during and after his English period, losing much of its former breadth and freedom.

Canning, George.

50 Berkeley Square, W1
  George Canning (1770–1827) statesman lived here (GLC 1979).

50 Berkeley Square is traditionally the haunted house of the square. It was built in the mid-18th century and Canning lived there only briefly in 1806/7. He entered politics with the encouragement of William Pitt, who was his close friend. Canning was treasurer of the navy in Pitt's last ministry and, after his death, became Foreign Secretary. He planned the brilliant seizure of the Danish fleet and witnessed the beginning of the Peninsular War against Napoleon. In 1827 he became Prime Minister.

Carlile, Wilson.

34 Sheffield Terrace, W8
Wilson Carlile, Prebendary (1847–1942) Founder of the Church Army lived here (GLC 1972).

Prebendary Carlile lived in Sheffield Terrace from about April 1881 to 1891. The three-storey house is part of a long terrace built by Jeremiah Little in 1850; the architect was probably Thomas Allason, surveyor to the Pitt Estate. Carlile first went to Kensington in 1880 as curate of St Mary Abbot's church, but he resigned two years later to found the Church Army, along similar lines to the Salvation Army. By the time he left Sheffield Terrace he had established colleges to train working men and women for evangelistic work and set up homes for ex-prisoners and tramps.

Carlyle, Thomas.

33 Ampton Street, Gray's Inn Road, WC1
Thomas Carlyle (1795–1881) lived here (LCC 1907).

24 Cheyne Row, SW3
Thomas Carlyle (1795–1881) lived here (Carlyle Society).

Thomas Carlyle made two brief visits to London before settling permanently at 24 (then no.5) Cheyne Row, his home from 1834 until his death in 1881. On the second visit (1831–2) Carlyle was seeking a publisher for *Sartor Resartus* and he found lodgings in Ampton Street: 'clean, quiet and modestly comfortable'. The Carlyles were not rich and Carlyle described their simple life: 'plenty of people come about us, we go out little to anything like parties — never to dinner; or anywhere willingly, except for profit. . . . Towards two o'clock I am laying down my pen, to walk till as near dinner (at four) as I like; then comes usually resting stretched on a sofa, with such small talk as may be going till tea; after which, unless some interloper drop in (as happens fully oftener than not), I again open my desk and work till bedtime, about eleven'. When Thomas and Jane Carlyle returned to London in 1834, *Sartor Resartus* had been serialised in *Fraser's Magazine* and Carlyle's reputation as philosopher, critic and historian was affirmed.

24 Cheyne Row was built in the early 18th century. Carlyle found it 'a right old strong, roomy brick house, likely to see three races of their modern fashionable fall before it comes down'. But Cheyne Row became increasingly busy and he found the noise unbearable when he was trying to write. Jane was knocked down by a cab in 1863 and died

Thomas Carlyle, 33 Ampton Street

three years later. Carlyle's niece Mary Aitken and her husband went to look after him for the last sad and silent 15 years of his life.

After Carlyle's death the house was neglected but in 1895 it was bought for the nation and restored. It now belongs to the National Trust and is open to the public.

Caslon, William.

21–3 Chiswell Street, N1
The foundry established by William Caslon typefounder (1692–1766) stood on this site 1737–1909 (LCC 1958).

The foundry William Caslon established in Chiswell Street in 1737 was destroyed during World War II. Caslon was the first great English typefounder; he established his reputation with types based on the early 18th-century Dutch style derived from the Aldine Roman. He lived and worked in Chiswell Street and being particularly fond of chamber music he installed an organ in the concert room of his house. He also had a house in Bethnal Green (a rural retreat in the 18th century) and died there in 1766.

Catherine of Aragon. *See* WREN, CHRISTOPHER.

Cato Street Conspiracy.

1*a* Cato Street, W1
Cato Street Conspiracy discovered here 23 February 1820 (GLC 1977).

The increasing government repression of social change in the years after the Napoleonic wars led to violent action by reformers and radicals. The Cato Street conspirators planned to murder the whole of the Cabinet when it was meeting at Lord Harrowby's house, 44 Grosvenor Square, on 23 February 1820. It was Arthur Thistlewood's plan, and he and his companions assembled in a stable loft in Cato Street, just off the Edgware Road, armed with pikes, guns and hand-grenades. Ings the butcher had two bags ready for the heads of Castlereagh and Sidmouth. However, a member of the group, named Edwards, was a spy, and just before they left for Grosvenor Square Bow Street officers arrived. Thistlewood killed one of them and escaped but he was captured the next day; nine others were arrested. Five of the conspirators were hanged outside Newgate Prison and the rest were transported to Australia.

Cavafy, Constantine P.

5 Queensborough Terrace, W2
   Constantine Cavafy (1863–1933) Greek poet lived here 1873–1876 (London Hellenic Society).

The plaque to C.P. Cavafy was unveiled by Lawrence Durrell. Cavafy spent most of his life in Alexandria working as a civil servant. He spent part of his childhood in England and returned to London for brief visits. The world of the Hellenistic East provided him with the mythology and characters of his poetry, which is ironic, critical and disillusioned, and dwells with nostalgia on unfulfilled homosexual desire and fleeting moments of passion.

Cavendish, Henry.

11 Bedford Square, WC1
   Hon. Henry Cavendish natural philosopher lived here. Born 1731 Died 1810 (Duke of Bedford 1904).

Henry Cavendish was the first scientist to convert oxygen and hydrogen into water by purely inductive experiments. He was a shy man with unusual habits. He collected a large library from which friends could borrow freely, but whenever he himself took out a book he always left a receipt. Lord Brougham, who met him at the Royal Society and at meetings of Sir Joseph Banks, recollected: 'the shrill cry he uttered as he shuffled quickly from room to room, seeming to be annoyed if looked at, but sometimes approaching to hear what was passing among others. . . . He probably uttered fewer words in the course of his life than any man who ever lived to four score years, not at all excepting the monks of La Trappe'.

Cayley, Sir George.

20 Hertford Street, W1
   Sir George Cayley (1773–1857) scientist and pioneer of aviation lived here (LCC 1962).

Although the front of 20 Hertford Street dates from about 1880 parts of the interior date from 1840–48, when George Cayley lived in the house. Most of Cayley's experiments were carried out at his country house in Yorkshire. In 1852 or 1853 he built the first successful man-carrying glider, which carried his coachman in the air for a short distance. Cayley was concerned to promote public interest in engineering and science and in 1839 he founded the original Polytechnic Institution in Regent Street. He stayed in London to carry out his duties as an MP.

Henry Cavendish, 11 Bedford Square

Cecil, Edgar Algernon Gascoyne, Viscount.

16 South Eaton Place, SW1
Viscount Cecil of Chelwood (1864–1958) creator of the League of Nations lived here (GLC 1976).

16 South Eaton Place was built in the early 19th century. Edgar Algernon Robert Gascoyne Cecil, third son of the 3rd Marquess of Salisbury, lived in the house from 1922 until his death. During World War I Cecil worked for the Red Cross before being made Assistant Secretary of State for Foreign Affairs. He was so appalled by the bloodshed and suffering that he produced a document which was to become the first draft of the covenant of the League of Nations. Cecil dominated the conference on the League in 1919, persuading the neutral nations to join. After the League's failure to bring about disarmament, he said 'the League is dead. Long live the UN'.

Cecil, Robert Gascoyne [3rd Marquess of Salisbury].

21 Fitzroy Square, W1
Robert Gascoyne Cecil 3rd Marquess of Salisbury (1830–1903) Prime Minister lived here (GLC 1965).

The lineal descendant of Queen Elizabeth I's Robert Cecil, Salisbury was the first statesman to hold the offices of Prime Minister and Foreign Secretary at the same time, and the last Prime Minister to sit in the House of Lords. It was inevitable that as a Cecil he should enter politics and when he was only 23 he became an MP. He moved to Fitzroy Square in 1858 and remained there until 1862. He was to spend three periods as both Foreign Secretary and Prime Minister. From 1886 to 1892 he played a major part in averting war in Europe, the Near East and Africa. The death of this deeply conservative aristocrat marked the end of the Victorian age in British politics.

Central School of Arts and Crafts. *See* LETHABY, WILLIAM RICHARD.

Chadwick, Sir **Edwin.**

9 Stanhope Terrace, W2
Sir Edwin Chadwick (1800–1890) lived here (Chadwick Society 1975).

Edwin Chadwick was called to the Bar in 1830 but became increasingly interested in his 'sanitary idea' for the eradication of disease, particularly after becoming a close friend of Jeremy Bentham. When

Bentham died in 1832 he left Chadwick a legacy and part of his library. The same year Chadwick became assistant commissioner working on the poor-law commission; he worked on the influential royal commission investigating the condition of factory children. The first sanitary commission was appointed at Chadwick's instigation in 1839 after an epidemical outbreak in Whitechapel. In 1847 he advocated a separate drainage system for London and during the Crimean War he saw the Indian Army sanitary commission established.

Challoner, Bishop **Richard.**

44 Old Gloucester Street, WC1
   Bishop Richard Challoner (1691–1781) Vicar Apostolic of the London District died here (Catholic Record Society).

Richard Challoner spent 26 years at the English College at Douay. In 1730 he left France for the London Mission and ten years later he was consecrated Bishop of Debra. He established several schools, founded the Charitable Society, and in 1758 became the Vicar Apostolic of the London District. During the persecution of Catholics Challoner was evicted from his Lamb's Conduit Street home. He moved to 44 Gloucester Street, Holborn, but during the Gordon riots he again sought refuge elsewhere, with a friend in Highgate. He died soon after in his Holborn house. Challoner inaugurated a new era in Catholic literature and many of his writings have become standard works of doctrine or devotion.

Chamberlain, Joseph.

188 Camberwell Grove, SE5
   Joseph Chamberlain (1836–1914) lived here (LCC 1920).

25 Highbury Place, N5
   Joseph Chamberlain (1836–1914) lived here (LCC 1915).

Joseph Chamberlain was born at 188 Camberwell Grove (then 3 Grove Hill Terrace), the end house of a row of 'dignified 3-storey houses, with 3 rows of severely respectable windows and long flights of steps. . . with gardens of generous size. . .somewhat dark and gloomy-looking'. His father, also Joseph, was a prosperous merchant in the City of London.
   The family moved to 25 Highbury Place in 1845 and remained there for 20 years but Joseph was sent to Birmingham in 1854 to represent his father's interests in the screw-manufacturing firm of Nettlefold's. When Highbury Place was built by John Spiller for City merchants in

Joseph Chamberlain, 25 Highbury Place

the 1770s, it was possible to see to 'Limehouse Church, Greenwich Hospital and park, and the vessels navigating the river Thames'. Only the view across Highbury Fields remains unspoilt.

Chamberlain entered Parliament in 1876 as MP for Birmingham but did not establish a home in London until 1879. He finally settled at 40 Prince's Gardens on the south side of Hyde Park in about 1883 and died there in 1914.

Chamberlain, Neville.

37 Eaton Square, SW1
Neville Chamberlain (1869-1940) Prime Minister lived here 1923-1935 (LCC 1962).

Neville Chamberlain entered national politics in 1918 as Conservative MP for the Ladywood division of Birmingham. In 1923 he became Chancellor of the Exchequer and moved to Eaton Square, but he was out of office when Baldwin was defeated in the autumn. The Conservatives were only out of power for a year and from October 1924 to 1929 Chamberlain was Minister of Health, a post he returned to in 1931. He had a second term (1931-7) as Chancellor of the Exchequer.

Chamberlain left Eaton Square two years before he became Prime Minister in 1937. His attempts to negotiate with Germany and Italy and avert World War II have made his name synonymous with the policy of appeasement.

Champagne Charlie. *See* LEYBOURNE, GEORGE.

Chaplin, Charlie.

287 Kennington Road, SE11
Charlie Chaplin (1889-1978) lived here (Vauxhall Society 1980).

Charlie Chaplin spent his childhood in and around the Kennington Road. His parents were music-hall performers but because they lived apart and were never permanently in work Chaplin had an unhappy childhood attending boarding schools, orphanages and even the workhouse. On one occasion when his mother was taken away to an asylum he went to live with his father, his father's mistress and their child at 287 Kennington Road. Chaplin recalled in his autobiography: 'the family lived in two rooms and, although the front room had large windows, the light filtered in as if from under water. . .the wallpaper looked sad, the horse-hair furniture looked sad, and the stuffed pike in the glass case that had swallowed another pike as large as itself — the head sticking out of its mouth — looked gruesomely sad'.

Chaplin first appeared on stage at the age of eight in a clog-dancing act. His father died a year later. He joined Fred Karno's company when he was 17 and toured America until he signed up with the Keystone Film Company in 1913 and began his successful career as a film comedian.

Charles, Elizabeth Rundle.

Combe Edge, Branch Hill, NW3
Elizabeth Rundle Charles lived here 1894–1896. Author of the Chronicles of the Schonberg-Cotta Family (Rundle Charles Memorial Fund 1897).

The Chronicles of the Schonberg-Cotta Family was published in 1862 after Elizabeth Charles was offered £400 for a story about Luther for the periodical *Family Treasury*. In 1851 she married Andrew Paton Charles, who owned a soap and candle factory at Wapping. He died in 1868 and Mrs Charles built a house for herself, Combe Edge, in Hampstead. She wrote some 50 books.

Chatham, Earl of. *See* PITT, WILLIAM.

Chatterton, Thomas.

39 Brooke Street, EC1
In a house on this site Thomas Chatterton died August 24th 1770 (City of London).

Thomas Chatterton was literally starving when he committed suicide by swallowing arsenic, in his Brooke Street lodgings, at the age of 18. As a boy he became interested in the ancient archives of St Mary Redcliffe, Bristol, and invented a 15th-century monk called Thomas Rowley, a secular priest and poet. 'Rowley's' poems began appearing in print in 1768.
Chatterton went to London in April 1770 and began contributing songs and topical verse to magazines. He first found lodgings in Shoreditch but moved to Brooke Street in June in search of greater seclusion. For the first time in his life he had a bedroom to himself and could write throughout the night. But his writings were bringing him little return and his brief tragic life and lonely, poverty-stricken death became the epitomy of the romantic artist's fate.

Chelsea China.

16 Lawrence Street, SW3
Chelsea China was manufactured in a house at the north end of Lawrence Street 1745-1784. Tobias Smollett (1721-1771) novelist, also lived in part of the house from 1750 to 1762 (LCC 1950).

The Chelsea China factory probably started at the north end of Lawrence Street, shifting, expanding and contracting in the course of its existence, but it was centred on Monmouth House, the home of Nicholas Sprimont who was manager of the factory from 1749 to 1769. The house was previously the residence of the Duchess of Monmouth and it was demolished around 1834.

The factory produced different styles of china, from the goat and bee cream jugs of the first period to the floridly decorated large groups of figures, vases and dinner services of the gold anchor period. When the lease expired in 1784 the moulds, ovens and plants went to Derby and the kilns were demolished.

Tobias Smollett, writer of picaresque and satirical fiction, is now acclaimed for his influence on the development of the English novel, but he never achieved financial success or literary fame in his lifetime. His violent political, literary and personal partisanship often caused him trouble and he even spent a brief period in prison for libel. *The Adventures of Peregrine Pickle* were published while he lived in Monmouth House.

Chesterfield, Philip Stanhope [2nd Earl] ; **Chesterfield, Philip** [3rd Earl] ; **Chesterfield, Philip Dormer** [4th Earl].

45 Bloomsbury Square, WC1
Here lived Philip Second Earl of Chesterfield born 1633 died 1713. Also Philip Third Earl and Philip Dormer Fourth Earl of Chesterfield KC born 1694 died 1773 (Duke of Bedford 1907).

Rangers House, Chesterfield Walk, SE3
Philip Fourth Earl of Chesterfield (1694-1773) statesman and author lived in this house (LCC 1937).

Philip Stanhope, 2nd Earl of Chesterfield, was mostly educated in Holland where he was taken by his mother at the age of seven. According to his memoirs, after the death of his first wife he was offered a command in Cromwell's army and the hand of one of the Protector's daughters. He declined and took to drink, gambling and 'exceeding wildness', and he was committed to the Tower for duelling and dabbling in Royalist plots against the government.

His son Philip, the 3rd Earl, was born to his third wife, Lady Elizabeth Dormer.

The 4th Earl, Philip Dormer Stanhope, was neglected by his father who died in 1726. Shortly after inheriting the title he was appointed ambassador to The Hague where, in 1731, he negotiated the Second Treaty of Vienna. He returned to The Hague in 1744 to try and get the Dutch to cooperate in the War of Austrian Succession. He was successful and on his return to England he was made Lord-Lieutenant of Ireland and from 1746 to 1748 Secretary of State for the northern department. Chesterfield gradually withdrew from politics and he took possession of Rangers House in December 1748.

Chesterfield made extensive alterations to Rangers House, which was built in the early 18th century, adding the whole of the south wing. The house was used as a summer residence where he could indulge his hobbies of growing fruit, reading and writing.

Chesterfield is remembered today for his published letters to his bastard son, many of which were written at Rangers House. But the young Philip failed to benefit from his father's advice: he was awkward and inarticulate, and he died young.

Chesterton, Gilbert Keith.

32 Sheffield Terrace, W8
   Gilbert Keith Chesterton was born here 29th May 1874 (private).

11 Warwick Gardens, W14
   Gilbert Keith Chesterton (1874–1936) poet novelist and critic lived here (LCC 1952).

G.K. Chesterton was born at 32 Sheffield Terrace. When he was seven his parents moved to Warwick Gardens, his home until his marriage in 1901. Though Chesterton spent three years studying at the Slade School of Art his talent for writing was soon apparent and his first book of poems, *The Wild Knight*, was published in 1900. Chesterton was received into the Roman Catholic Church in 1922 by his friend Father O'Connor, on whom 'Father Brown', hero of some of his best-known stories, was modelled.

Chevalier, Albert.

17 St Ann's Villas, W11
   Albert Chevalier (1861–1923) music hall comedian was born here (LCC 1965).

Chevalier was born at 17 (then no.21) St Ann's Villas, Holland Park, to a French father and Welsh mother; his full name was Albert Onesiure Britannicus Gwathveoyd Louis. At the beginning of his professional acting career he abbreviated it to 'Mr Knight'. His success as a music-hall entertainer came after he adopted the mask of the cockney character of the coster; his most famous song was *My Old Dutch*. Chevalier not only performed in music halls but gave recitals in fashionable drawing-rooms, bringing a respectability to the music hall.

Chippendale, Thomas.

61 St Martin's Lane, WC2
The workshop of Thomas Chippendale and his son cabinet makers stood near this site 1753–1815 (LCC 1952).

Thomas Chippendale and his partner James Rennie were granted a 60-year lease in August 1754 on two houses, 60 and 61 St Martin's Lane and the stable yard and premises in the rear. All that survives of their workshops is the yard. In 1754 Chippendale published *The Gentleman and Cabinet-Maker's Director* which included 161 engraved plates of designs ranging from chairs to bookcases. Nothing comparable had been available for provincial furniture makers who were at last able to make goods in styles like those of London. The success of Chippendale's business and designs is shown by a notice in the press of 5 April 1755: 'a fire broke out at the workshop of Mr Chippendale, a cabinet maker near St Martin's Lane, which consumed the same, wherein were the chests of 22 workmen'. To be employing 22 workmen, Chippendale was doing a flourishing trade.

Chopin, Fryderyk [Frédéric].

99 Eaton Place, SW1
Fryderyk Chopin (1810–1849) gave his first London concert in this house June 23 1848 (private 1949).

4 St James's Place, SW1
From this house Frederic Chopin (1810–1849) went to Guildhall to give his last public performance in 1848 (GLC c1981).

Chopin was already seriously ill with tuberculosis when he gave his last Paris concert in February 1848. He left a politically disturbed Paris, where Polish exiles were hoping the February Revolution would bring about Poland's liberty, and went to London, where he was to spend seven months. From the end of October until 23 November he stayed at 4 St James's Place. The front wall of this late 17th-century house has been rebuilt as a facsimile of the original but the interior is little changed. Chopin gave his last concert at the Guildhall, in aid of Polish refugees. Chopin was unimpressed by the celebrities he met in London, though they included Dickens and Wellington, and he failed to comprehend British taste in music.

Churchill, Lord **Randolph.**

2 Connaught Place, W2
  Lord Randolph Churchill (1849–1895) statesman lived here 1883–1892 (LCC 1962).

The years Randolph Churchill lived at Connaught Place were among the most important of his life. He gained a reputation as one of the most brilliant parliamentary orators, and after the defeat of the Conservatives in 1880 he came forward as the leader of the 'Fourth Party', a group pledged to uphold true Tory principles. The new Prime Minister Salisbury appointed him Secretary of State for India. In 1886 he became Chancellor of the Exchequer and Leader of the House of Commons but he resigned in December. Randolph Churchill married an American, Jennie Jerome, in 1874 and their eldest son, Winston Churchill, was born the same year.

Churchill, Sir **Winston.**

34 Eccleston Square, SW1
  Sir Winston Churchill lived here 1909–1913 (private).

Winston Churchill held several important offices while living at Eccleston Square: President of the Board of Trade (1908–10), Home Secretary (1910–11) and First Lord of the Admiralty (1911–15). No man except Gladstone has held high office over such a long span. Churchill resigned as Prime Minister in 1955.

Clarkson, **Willy.**

41–3 Wardour Street, W1
  Willy Clarkson (1861–1934) theatrical wig-maker lived and died here (GLC 1966).

Willy Clarkson joined his father's wig-making business and began to develop its theatrical side. At the height of his prosperity he hired out nearly 10,000 wigs each Christmas. He also became a theatrical costumier. Some of his clients had far from innocent reasons for disguising themselves and they included Crippen and Charles Peace.

Clarkson moved to Wardour Street in 1905. The building was designed for him by H.M. Wakley, blending Baroque and Art Nouveau forms. Sarah Bernhardt laid the foundation stone and Sir Henry Irving the coping stone. Clarkson lived in a flat over his shop until his death.

Clementi, Muzio.

128 Kensington Church Street, W8
Muzio Clementi (1752-1832) composer lived here (LCC 1963).

Clementi had given up public performances and devoted himself to composition when he lived at 128 Kensington Church Street (1820-23). He was born in Rome but spent most of his life in England, making his début as a pianist and composer in London in 1770. He made a considerable fortune conducting, performing and teaching (one of his most famous pupils was John Field).

Clementi sold the lease of his Kensington house to the organist and composer William Horsley (1774-1858). The Horsley family were friendly with Mendelssohn, who was a frequent visitor. Horsley's son John Callcott lived in the house from 1858 to 1903. He is remembered for designing the first Christmas card and for his nickname 'Clothes-Horsley' — earned through his campaign against the use of nude models.

Clink Prison.

Clink Street, SE1
Near this site stood the Clink Prison. Prisoners for their religion in the 16th century in this and other Southwark prisons included Henry Barrowe, John Greenwood, John Penry. They all three suffered martyrdom in 1593. John Penry was imprisoned in the King's Bench Prison in Southwark and hanged at St. Thomas a Watering Old Kent Road. They were founders of an independent church in Southwark and precursors of the movement which led to the emigration of the Pilgrim Fathers (private).

Clive, Robert, Lord.

45 Berkeley Square, W1
Clive of India (1725-1774) soldier and administrator lived here (LCC 1953).

Lord Clive bought 45 Berkeley Square in 1761 on returning to England after a triumphant period as Governor of Bengal. The house (together with no.46) was built *c*1750–60, probably by Isaac Ware, and its first occupier was William Kerr, Earl of Ancrum. Clive's descendants, the Earls of Powis, lived there until the 4th Earl sold it in 1937. Clive had to return to India in 1764 and wrote to his wife in London concerning their house in Berkeley Square: 'I would have the Grand Flight of Rooms furnished in the richest and most elegant manner, a man of taste and judgement should be consulted and if any additional rooms can be built without spoiling or darkening the others you have my consent for erecting them. I do empower you to make the house at Berkeley Square as fine and convenient as you please immediately'.

After his final return to England in 1766, Clive was accused of accepting bribes from Indian princes and an inquiry in 1773 censured him for abusing his powers. Clive was already a sick man, taking laudanum to kill the pain. He took his own life with it at the age of 48.

Cobden, Richard.

23 Suffolk Street, SW1
Richard Cobden (1804–1865) died here (LCC 1905).

Richard Cobden spent only a short time in lodgings in Suffolk Street. He had made his last speech in the House of Commons in July the previous year. In November the effort of addressing a large meeting in his constituency confined him to his country home with asthma and bronchitis and when he travelled to London to take part in the discussion of a scheme of Canadian fortification, his bronchitis returned and he died in Suffolk Street in April.

As a young man Cobden started a calico-printing business in Manchester which was soon a thriving concern. He read extensively, travelled abroad and wrote economic pamphlets. In 1838 he joined the anti-Cornlaw League, and in 1841 he became an MP.

Cobden-Sanderson, Thomas James.

15 Upper Mall, W6
Thomas James Cobden-Sanderson (1840–1922) founded the Doves Bindery and Doves Press in this house and later lived and died here (GLC 1974).

T.J. Cobden-Sanderson practised as a barrister for over ten years before taking up bookbinding in 1883 under the influence of William Morris and Edward Burne-Jones. In 1893 he moved to Hammersmith and established the Doves Bindery at 13–15 Upper Mall. By 1898 he was teaching bookbinding at the Royal College of Art and in 1900 with Emery Walker he founded the Doves Press which continued the tradition of Morris's Kelmscott Press in producing fine books until forced to close for financial reasons in 1916. Fifty titles were published, using a modified version of the 15th-century Jensen type.

Codeb-Sanderson did not live at 13-15 Upper Mall until after the financial failure of the Doves Press. His wife continued to live in the small two-storey brick house overlooking the river after his death there in 1922.

Cochrane, Thomas [Earl of Dundonald].

Hanover Lodge, Outer Circle, NW1
Thomas Cochrane Earl of Dundonald (1775–1860) and later David Earl Beatty OM (1871–1936) admirals lived here (GLC 1974).

Hanover Lodge, designed by John Nash in the 1820s, was first the home of Sir Robert Arbuthnot; Thomas Cochrane lived there in the 1830s and early 1840s and David Earl Beatty lived there from 1910 to about 1925. A contemporary of Cochrane described the interior: 'a stone stair-case of good proportions leads to the upper storey, which comprises of handsome bedchambers, a bathing room with every accommodation for that healthful luxury, dressing rooms and other requisites for a respectable family'. Additions were made to the house in 1909 by Lutyens and it is now used by Bedford College.

Cochrane lived at Hanover Lodge after his stormy career in the navy was at an end. He proved himself a daring, skilful leader, preying on Spanish and French shipping, but he made enemies at home through his outspoken criticism of those in command. He was accused of involvement in a Stock Exchange swindle in 1814 and spent a year in prison but he was later exonerated.

Beatty's career in the Royal Navy was of unbroken distinction. He was made captain when he was 29 after action in the Nile, in Kitchener's invasion of the Sudan. By the time he moved to Hanover Lodge he was a rear admiral, the youngest flag-officer since Nelson, and when war broke out in 1914 he was commander of the battle-cruiser squadron. At the end of the war be became Admiral of the Fleet and was made an earl.

Cole, Sir Henry.

3 Elm Row, NW3
Sir Henry Cole lived here 1879–1880 (Hampstead Plaque Fund).

55

Henry Cole was knighted in 1875 for his services as public servant, art patron and educationist. He was a co-founder of *The Journal of Design and Manufactures* (1849) to promote 'the germs of a style which England of the nineteenth century may call its own' and was on the committee of the Great Exhibition of 1851. He returned to London in 1879 after a period living in Birmingham and Manchester.

Coleridge, Samuel Taylor.

7 Addison Bridge Place, W14
   Samuel Taylor Coleridge (1772-1834) poet and philosopher lived here (LCC 1950).

71 Berners Street, W1
   Samuel Taylor Coleridge (1772-1834) poet and philosopher lived here (GLC 1966).

3 The Grove, N6
   Samuel Taylor Coleridge English poet and critic. Lived in Highgate Village for nineteen years and in this house from 1825 until his death in 1834 (St Pancras Borough Council).

By the time Coleridge moved into 7 Addison Bridge Place (formerly Portland Place) in 1810 his greatest poetry, including *Kubla Khan* and *The Ancient Mariner*, had been written. Coleridge was heavily addicted to opium, separated from his wife Sara Fricker and no longer on speaking terms with his great friend Wordsworth. He lived with John Morgan, a successful lawyer, and his family and followed them to Berners Street (no.71, demolished 1907) in 1812. While there (1812-13) Coleridge tried to give up opium.

He was finally taken in hand by Dr James Gillman and went to live in his house in Highgate in 1816, remaining with the Gillmans until his death in 1834. After the completion of *Biographia literaria* in 1816 Coleridge did little writing but spent his time advising and inspiring his young disciples 'like a sage escaped from the inanity of life's battle' (Carlyle); among the most famous of them was the young John Keats.

Coleridge-Taylor, Samuel.

30 Dagnall Park, South Norwood, Croydon
   Samuel Coleridge-Taylor (1875-1912) composer of the 'Song of Hiawatha' lived here (GLC 1975).

Samuel Coleridge-Taylor lived nearly all his life in Croydon. He spent the first two years of married life (1900-02) in the small late

Samuel Taylor Coleridge, 3 The Grove

19th-century, semi-detached yellow-brick house in Dagnall Park. Colonel Herbert Walters, a local resident, provided Coleridge-Taylor with a musical education, sending him to the Royal College of Music in 1891. His most famous composition, *Hiawatha's Wedding Feast*, was first performed there in 1898 and became a popular success at the Royal Albert Hall two years later. Coleridge-Taylor was in demand as a composer for the rest of his life. He died suddenly in 1912.

Collins, William Wilkie.

65 Gloucester Place, W1
William Wilkie Collins (1824–1889) novelist lived here (LCC 1951).

Wilkie Collins lived at 65 (formerly 90) Gloucester Place from 1868 to 1876 and from 1883 to 1888. He had achieved popularity in 1860 with his mystery story *The Woman in White* which was a bestseller. But from 1862 until his death Collins suffered from rheumatic gout and took increasing amounts of opium to dull the pain. By the time he started writing *The Moonstone* in Gloucester Place he was 'taking enough opium to put a dinner party of 12 under the table'.

After the success of his mysteries, Collins turned to social reform and didactic novels. He was himself a radical and ardent feminist and he braved Victorian morals by living with one mistress and keeping another in a separate establishment.

Collins's Music Hall.

10–11 Islington Green, N1
Collins Music Hall was here from 1862–1958 (GLC 1968).

Sam Vagg, a chimney-sweep who had made his name on the stage as Sam Collins, was responsible for turning the Lansdowne Arms into a music hall. It had only been open for three years when Sam died in 1865 at the age of 39. He was famous for his Irish songs, *Limerick Races* and *The Rocky Road to Dublin*.

His death did not affect business and Collins's was known as the 'little goldmine' in the 1870s. Famous performers who played there before it closed in 1958 included Marie Lloyd, Harry Lauder, Charlie Chaplin, Norman Wisdom, Gracie Fields and Tommy Trinder. Walter Sickert went night after night from his lodgings in Islington to study the performers. Unlike many music halls Collins's had a reputation for such clean jokes that it was called the 'chapel-on-the-green'.

Collinson, Peter.

The Ridgeway, Mill Hill, NW7
Site of Ridgeway House, residence of Peter Collinson (1694–1768) author, naturalist and botanist (Hendon Corporation).

Mary Bushell, wife of Peter Collinson, inherited Ridgeway House and Dollis Farm from her father and the couple moved to Mill Hill in 1749. Collinson had already begun collecting plants at his home in Peckham and the collection he assembled at Mill Hill was to improve considerably the English horticultural system. He brought some 170 new plants to Ridgeway House, many of them exotica from America. He exchanged seeds with a correspondent in Philadelphia and sent them all over England, including to Kew and Kenwood; many of the trees in the garden of Mill Hill School (built on the site of Ridgeway House) are believed to have been planted by him.

Conan Doyle, Sir Arthur.

12 Tennison Road, SE25
Sir Arthur Conan Doyle (1859–1930) creator of Sherlock Holmes lived here 1891–1894 (GLC 1973).

Conan Doyle qualified as a doctor but after failing to become established as an eye specialist he devoted himself to writing. He moved to South Norwood in June 1891 and in his study to the left of the front door of 12 Tennison Road he wrote the six short stories that became the first of *The Adventures of Sherlock Holmes*. They were published in *Strand Magazine*. He began a further series, *The Memoirs of Sherlock Holmes*, in 1893 but was growing to dislike the detached, superior character he had created. On holiday in Switzerland in the same year he found the ideal setting for Holmes's death, the Reichenbach Falls. Popular outrage at Holmes's death led to his resurrection, and the last Holmes story was not published until 1905.

Cons, Emma.

136 Seymour Place, W1
Emma Cons (1837–1912) philanthropist and founder of the Old Vic lived here (GLC 1978).

The establishment of the Old Vic, which opened in 1880, was initiated by Emma Cons's work among the poor of London. Through managing various residential properties she discovered the violent side of slum life. She regarded the theatre as an essential form of entertainment and an escape for working people. When the Old Vic opened it was run by Emma Cons and her niece Lillian Baylis. Emma Cons helped to establish a wide range of facilities for the poor and was one of three women members of the first LCC.

Constable, John.

40 Well Walk, NW3
   John Constable (1776–1837) painter lived here (LCC 1923).

Constable married Maria Bicknell in 1816. He had met her 16 years before in East Bergholt church, Suffolk, and they settled near Russell Square a year later. Neither liked the noise and dirt of London and from 1819 until Maria's death in 1828 Constable rented houses in Hampstead for his wife and children. The Constables had only one contented year at 40 (then 5) Well Walk (1827–8). After Maria's death Constable remained there for about five years looking after his children. He returned to the rooms he had kept from 1822 at 76 Charlotte Street, where he died in the attic bedroom.

Cook, James.

88 Mile End Road, E1
   Captain James Cook (1728–1779) circumnavigator and explorer lived in a house on this site (GLC 1970).

Walter Besant described Cook's house in the Mile End Road as being 'a small and rather mean house...one of a row of shops'. In the middle of the 20th century it was demolished and its site formed the entrance to a brewer's yard, but the GLC erected a memorial plaque in 1970 to commemorate the bicentenary of Cook's landing at Botany Bay. Cook returned to Mile End after the first of his great voyages (1768–71) in which he circumnavigated the world. His second voyage (1772–5) disproved the existence of a great southern continent in the Pacific by sailing across its supposed position; it incidentally led to the discovery of a successful treatment for scurvy. His final voyage began in July 1776. Cook left England in command of the *Resolution* and the *Discovery* but he did not complete a third circumnavigation, dying at Hawaii after being attacked by natives.

Corelli, Marie.

47 Longridge Road, SW5
   Famous Victorian novelist Marie Corelli lived here 1883–1899 (private).

Marie Corelli's real name was Mary Mackay. She first adopted her pseudonym when intending to pursue a musical career. Her precocious talent on the piano had been encouraged by George Meredith, her parents' neighbour in Box Hill, but she turned to writing. She lived with her widowed father at Longridge Road from 1883 to 1899. Real popularity came with the publication of *Barabbas: a Dream of the World's Tragedy* (1893). The fervent religiosity of the novel thrilled the reading public. Two years later the equally sensational and over-written novel, *The Sorrows of Satan*, was greeted with near-hysteria by her followers.

Cox, David.

34 Foxley Street, SW8
David Cox (1783-1859) artist lived here (LCC 1951).

David Cox began helping in his father's smithy in Birmingham but went to London in 1804 as a scene painter. After two of his water-colour landscapes were accepted at the Royal Academy in 1805 he took up painting professionally. He lived at 34 Foxley Street from 1827, shortly after the house was built, until 1841. Cox did not take up oil painting until 1840. He was an ardent lover of nature and travelled extensively in Britain, especially in the Lake District and Wales, painting the landscape. The rough paper he favoured is still called 'Cox paper'.

Crane, Walter.

13 Holland Street, W8
Walter Crane (1845-1915) artist lived here (LCC 1952).

Walter Crane moved to 13 Holland Street in 1892 when his home in Shepherd's Bush was threatened with demolition to make way for the Central London Railway. He was an established artist by that time and best known for his illustrated children's books. He was also an ardent supporter of William Morris's Socialist League.

No.13 Holland Street immediately caught his eye: 'returning one day after a long and fruitless search [for a house], my wife and I happened to pass along Holland Street, Kensington and noticed no. 13 was to let. The house had an eighteenth-century brick front, which was attractive, and on entering we found instead of the usual squeezy passage a square hall with a fireplace in it. There was a garden at the back towards St Mary Abbott's Church, and on a fine old leaden cistern there was the date 1674. The style of some of the mouldings

61

and woodwork suggested an earlier date'. Crane lived in Holland Street until 1915.

Creed, Frederick George.

20 Outram Road, Addiscombe, Croydon
Frederick George Creed (1871–1957) electrical engineer inventor of the teleprinter lived and died here (GLC 1973).

Frederick and Valerie Creed lived in Croydon for over 50 years, moving from Glasgow in 1909. The house at 20 Outram Road was only 100 yards from the premises of the old factory in Cherry Orchard Road which was once the hub of Creed's teleprinter empire. Creed first perfected the teleprinter in Glasgow; the *Daily Mail* was the first national newspaper to adopt the system, subsequently installed in newspaper offices all over the world.

Crookes, Sir William.

7 Kensington Park Gardens, W11
Sir William Crookes (1832–1919) scientist lived here from 1880 until his death (GLC 1967).

William Crookes bought 7 Kensington Park Gardens in 1880. His biographer claims that the mid-Victorian house was the first in England to be lit by electricity. Sir Oliver Lodge described the house: 'when one. . .saw his fine library with the well-ordered though small laboratory opening out of it, and admired the neatness of his records and his untiring industry, one felt that here was a workshop from which phenomena of stimulating novelty might at any time emerge'. Crookes was elected a Fellow of the Royal Society in 1863 for the experiments in spectroscopy which led to his discovery of a new element, thallium. He also studied radiation and invented a radiometer.

Crosby, Brass. *See* ESSEX STREET.

Cruden, Alexander.

45 Camden Passage, N1
Alexander Cruden (1699–1770) Humanist, scholar and intellectual. Born Aberdeen. Educated Marischal College. Came to London 1719 as tutor. Appointed bookseller to Queen Caroline. In 1737 compiled the Concordance to the Bible. Died here in Camden Passage November 1st (Camden Passage Association 1962).

Alexander Cruden started his bookshop in the Royal Exchange in 1732 and in 1737 he compiled his concordance to the Bible, which he had dedicated to Queen Caroline. He hoped for her patronage but she died a few days later, leaving Cruden with a book that failed to make a profit and a business quite beyond his resources. He became insane and had to be confined to an asylum. He managed to escape and found work as a proof-reader. Calling himself 'Alexander the Corrector' he toured the country rebuking Sabbath-breaking and the general profanity of his contemporaries. He died suddenly while praying in his lodgings in Camden Passage.

Cruikshank, George.

69/71 Amwell Street, N1
George Cruikshank (1792–1878) engraver and illustrator lived here 1824–1849 (London Borough of Islington).

263 Hampstead Road, NW1
George Cruikshank artist lived here from 1850 to 1878. B. September 27th 1792, d. February 1st 1878 (RSA 1885).

George Cruikshank achieved fame and notoriety in 1818 when his cartoon appeared attacking hanging as a penalty for forging bank notes. He was shocked by the harsh punishment: 'I passed Newgate jail and saw several persons suspended from the gibbet, two of these were women who had been executed for passing one pound forged notes'. The etching created a sensation. During his lifetime Cruikshank became the pre-eminent illustrator of Victorian fiction. His face was described by a contemporary: 'prominent aquiline nose, and a mouth cut in firm, sharp lines, and from whose corners grew an ambiguous pair of ornaments, which were neither moustaches, nor whiskers, nor beard, but partook vaguely of the characteristics of all three'.

Cubitt, Thomas.

3 Lyall Street, SW1
Thomas Cubitt (1788–1855) master builder lived here (LCC 1959).

By the time Thomas Cubitt moved to Lyall Street in 1847 his buildings had dramatically altered parts of Bloomsbury, Belgravia and Pimlico. By the age of 32 he was famous in the building world for his workshops in the Gray's Inn Road in which he employed craftsmen in all trades on a permanent wage basis, something never done before. Cubitt built Belgrave Square, Lowndes Square, Chesham Place and

Eaton Square in Belgravia. In Pimlico he built on soil excavated from St Katherine's Dock and used to replace the local clay. He lived in Lyall Street from 1847 to 1855 and guaranteed funds for the Great Exhibition of 1851. He also built Osborne for Queen Victoria. His son Lewis carried on in the family business and designed King's Cross Station.

Curtis, William.

51 Gracechurch Street, EC3
In a house on this site lived William Curtis Botanist. B.1746 – D.1799 (City of London).

William Curtis went to London in about 1766 to finish his medical education and soon began to establish a reputation as a botanist. He gave practical demonstrations of botany at the London medical schools and his students visited the gardens he planted at Bermondsey, Lambeth Marsh and Brompton. Curtis was one of the original fellows of the Linnean Society (*see* JOSEPH BANKS); he translated Linneaus's *Fundamenta entomologiae* in 1772 and in 1777 began his *Flora Londinensis*.

Curzon, George Nathaniel.

1 Carlton House Terrace, SW1
George Nathaniel Curzon Marquess Curzon of Kedleston (1859–1925) statesman Viceroy of India lived and died here (GLC 1976).

Curzon bought 1 Carlton House Terrace (designed by John Nash *c*1827-33) in late 1904 or early 1905, about the same time he resigned from his position as Viceroy of India. He was concerned for the welfare of the Indian people but his autocratic behaviour towards the civil service and army developed into a long and bitter struggle with Kitchener which only ended on his departure for England.

Curzon was out of office between 1905 and 1915 but pursued his interest in the arts, purchasing and restoring Tattershall and Bodiam Castles which he later bequeathed to the nation. He returned to politics in 1915 and was Foreign Secretary (1919-24). He was often regarded as the personification of imperialism but his aloof manner may partly be explained by the effects of a harsh upbringing and lifelong pain from his spine.

Dadd, Richard.

15 Suffolk Street, SW1
Richard Dadd (1817–1886) painter lived here (GLC 1977).

Robert Dadd, Richard's father, went to London in 1836 and took over the silver-gilding and ormolu business of Messrs Pincott at 15 Suffolk Street. Richard 'found himself at once in the midst of the advantages which polish and refine' and lived above the family shop when he began his career as a landscape and portrait painter, attending the Royal Academy Schools. In 1843 Dadd savagely murdered his father and fled to France. He was brought back to England and admitted to the Criminal Lunatic Department of Bethlem Hospital suffering (as we know now) from paranoid schizophrenia. In 1864 Dadd became one of the first male patients admitted to Broadmoor where he remained for the rest of his life. But he produced his finest paintings there 'with all the poetry of imagination and the frenzy of insanity'.

Dale, Sir Henry.

Mount Vernon House, Mount Vernon, NW3
Sir Henry Dale (1875–1968) physiologist lived here (GLC c1981).

The attractive house in which Henry Dale lived from 1919 to 1942 dates from c1800 and is set behind an 18th-century brick wall: both house and wall are listed. Dale held some of the most eminent positions

Henry Dale, Mount Vernon House, Mount Vernon

in the medical and scientific world during his distinguished career, which culminated in his election to the presidency of the Royal Society in 1940. It is his work on the pharmacology of nervous impulses which has been of fundamental importance for the understanding of numerous body functions and diseases; he shared the Nobel Prize for Medicine in 1936.

Dance [the Younger], George.

91 Gower Street, WC1
  George Dance the Younger (1741-1825) architect lived and died here (GLC 1970).

George Dance the Younger moved into 91 Gower Street in 1790 when the house was only a year old. It was part of a group of houses built on ground belonging to the Duke of Bedford. Dance's wife died shortly after the move there and he was left with three sons to support. He was already a successful architect, however: his practice thrived from its beginnings in 1765 to his retirement in 1815. He designed many streets and squares in London, including the area of Finsbury Square, Chiswell Street and City Road and John Wesley's chapel and house. His most celebrated work was Newgate Prison, demolished in 1902. Dickens described its massive portals 'as if they were made for the express purpose of letting people in, and never letting them out again'.

D'Arblay, Madam. *See* BURNEY, FANNY.

Darwin, Charles.

Biological Science Buildings, University College, [site of] 110 Gower Street, WC1
  Charles Darwin (1809-1882) naturalist lived in a house on this site 1838-1842 (LCC 1961).

Down House, Luxted Road, Downe
  Here Darwin thought and worked for 40 years and died in 1882 (London Borough of Bromley 1964).

After marrying Emma Wedgwood in 1839 Darwin moved into 110 Gower Street (then 12 Upper Gower Street). The house was demolished during World War II but Darwin's son described it as 'a small common-place London house with a drawing-room in front, a small room behind, in which they lived for the sake of quietness. In later years my father

Charles Darwin, Down House, Downe

used to laugh over the surpassing ugliness of the furniture, carpets, etc. The only redeeming feature was a better garden than most London houses have, a strip as wide as the house, and thirty yards long'. The house was rented and Darwin called it Macaw Cottage in honour of the drawing-room colour scheme. While there he worked on *Coral Reefs*.

Frequent ill-health forced Darwin to move to the country and he bought Down House and 18 acres of land for £2200 in 1842. The house he found to be 'moderate-sized. . .square, unpretentious and uninspired'. The landscape, however, was particularly varied with 'waterless uninhabited valleys, bleak uplands, with occasional yews in the hedges, and here and there a white chalkpit', and he was 'pleased with the diversified appearance of the vegetation, proper to a chalk district'.

The Darwins led quiet, secluded lives. One of the most influential books ever published was written at Down House: *On the Origin of Species* (1859). While fierce debates raged in London and Oxford over Darwin's theory of evolution he followed his daily routine, walking his fox terrier Polly along the 'sand walk' at midday (*see also* ROBERT FITZROY).

Davies, Emily.

17 Cunningham Place, St John's Wood, NW8
Emily Davies (1830–1921) founder of Girton College Cambridge lived here (GLC 1978).

Emily Davies lived in Cunningham Place from 1862 to 1886. She went to London in 1861 and immediately became involved with movements for furthering women's rights, particularly equal educational opportunities. She started a campaign to have women admitted to university local examinations and in 1865 Cambridge University yielded; Oxford followed in 1870. Emily Davies is best remembered for founding Girton College, Cambridge. It was first set up at Hitchin in 1869 and four years later transferred to new accommodation outside Cambridge. Emily Davies was secretary (1867–1904) and mistress (1872–5). Cambridge did not agree to grant titles of degrees to women until the year of her death in 1921.

Defoe, Daniel.

95 Stoke Newington Church Street, N16
Daniel Defoe (1661–1731) lived in a house on this site (LCC 1932).

Daniel Defoe lived in two houses in Stoke Newington between 1709 and 1729. Both have been demolished and only the site of the second, where Defoe lived from about 1714 to September 1729, has been conclusively established. The house was in Church Street and had extensive grounds but it was demolished in 1859; Defoe Road now cuts through the site of the greater part of the house.

Defoe led an adventurous life: merchant, economist, journalist, spy and novelist. He was arrested for writing a satire against High Church tyranny after a description had been circulated for his apprehension: 'a middle-sized, spare man about forty years old, of a brown complexion, a dark brown-coloured hair, but wears a wig; a hooked nose, a sharp chin, grey eyes, and a large mole near his mouth'. He acted as a spy for Robert Harley, whose intervention saved him from a severe prison sentence. Defoe wrote some 500 works; his most famous novels include *Robinson Crusoe* (1719) and *Moll Flanders* (1722).

De Gaulle, Charles.

4 Carlton Gardens, SW1

A tous les français
La France a perdu une bataille!
Mais la France n'a pas perdu la guerre!
Des gouvernants de rencontre ont capituler, cedant à la panique, oubliant l'honneur, livrant le pays à la servitude. Cependant, rien n'est perdu!
Rien n'est perdu, parce que cette guerre est une guerre mondiale, dans l'univers libre, des forces immenses n'ont pas encore donné. Un jour, ces forces écraseront l'ennemi. Il faut que la France, ce jour la soit présente à la Victoire. Alors, elle retouvera sa liberté et sa grandeur. Tel est mon but, mon seul but!
Voilà pourquoi je convie tous les français ou qu'ils se trouvent, a s'unir à moi dans l'action, dans le sacrifice et dans l'espérance. Notre patrie est en peril de mort. Luttons tous pour la sauver!
Vive la France!   *18 juin 1940*

Ici le Général de Gaulle établit son quartier général des Français libres, ses compagnons refusant que lui d'accepter la defaite, y ont poursuivi la lutte jusqu'à la victoire (private).

De Gaulle came to England in June 1940 after the French government under Marshal Pétain declared their intention to seek an armistice with Germany. From London he appealed to his compatriots to continue the war under his leadership, and posters appeared in England: 'France has lost a battle; she has not lost the war'. In August a French military court sentenced him in absentia to death but De Gaulle continued to broadcast and to organise the Free French Forces, until moving to Algiers in 1943. Winston Churchill described his impact on the British: 'he had to be rude to the British to prove to French eyes that he was not a British puppet. He certainly carried out this policy with perseverance'.

De Laszlo, Philip A.

3 Fitzjohns Avenue, NW3
From 1921 to 1937 here lived and in his adjoining studio worked Philip A. De Laszlo MVO Portrait Painter President of the RBA Born 1869 Died 1937 (private).

Philip De Laszlo was born in Hungary and studied art in Budapest, Munich and Paris. He became a naturalised British subject in 1914, seven years after moving to London, and became well known for his portraits; he painted many famous sitters including Edward VII. De Laszlo became president of the Royal Society of British Artists in 1930 and he died in his Hampstead home.

De Morgan, William; De Morgan, Evelyn.

127 Old Church Street, SW3
William De Morgan (1839–1917) ceramic artist and novelist and his wife Evelyn De Morgan (1855–1919) artist lived and died here (LCC 1937).

William and Evelyn De Morgan moved into 127 Old Church Street in autumn 1910 after their home for over 20 years in the Vale, a quiet backwater off the King's Road, had been demolished. William De Morgan had first moved to Chelsea in 1872. He built a kiln and established workrooms and a showroom at the Orange House, Cheyne Row (where the Church of the Holy Redeemer now stands), and made tiles, thickly glazed in blues and greens. His friendship with the Pre-Raphaelites (Evelyn followed their school of painting) and particularly William Morris led him to produce tiles at Morris's factory at Merton Abbey and in 1888 he established his own factory at Sands End, Fulham.
When the Fulham factory closed in 1907 because of financial difficulties William De Morgan began a new career as an author. His first novel *Joseph Vance* (1906) was an immediate success. The seven years in Old Church Street were devoted to writing novels, but at the outbreak of World War I he turned his attention to inventing, studying the problems of submarine and aircraft defence.

Denman, Thomas, Lord.

50-51 Russell Square, WC1
Lord Denman Lord Chief Justice of England lived in this house 1816-1834 and his son Rt. Hon. George Denman Judge of the High Court 1872-1892 was born here 1819 (private).
The adjoining plaque was removed from the house which stood upon this site from 1800 to 1862.

Thomas Denman was called to the Bar in 1806 and in about 1818 he moved to 50 Russell Square, then the most fashionable region for leading lawyers. Denman and his friend Brougham were involved in the trial of Queen Caroline; they became popular figures for defending the queen, but Denman lost the favour of the crown and his chances of becoming a King's Counsel. In Parliament Denman spoke in favour of reforms in the law, including abolition of the death penalty for forgery; he was an ardent supporter of negro emancipation and the abolition of slavery.

De Quincey, Thomas.

36 Tavistock Street, WC2
Thomas De Quincey (1785-1859) wrote 'Confessions of an English Opium Eater' in this house (GLC c1981).

The *Confessions of an English Opium Eater* describe De Quincey's early privations in London, as a consequence of which he had a painful gastric disease which drove him to take opium when he was at university. By 1816, when he was living in the Wordsworths' former cottage at Grasmere, he was heavily addicted, but with a wife and children to support he had to write articles for magazines; in 1821 he went to London, beginning the *Confessions* in late summer. Their publication aroused intense interest but brought De Quincey little reward. He spent the rest of his life alone and poverty-stricken. His wife and children died and he became a celebrated eccentric.

Derby, Earl of. *See* PITT, WILLIAM [Earl of Chatham].

Dickens, Charles.

141 Bayham Street, NW1
Charles Dickens lived in a house on this site when a boy in 1823 (Dickens Fellowship 1924).

92 North Road, N6
Charles Dickens (1812–1870) author stayed here in 1832 (Haringey Borough Council 1969).

Prudential Building, High Holborn, WC1
Charles Dickens novelist Born 1812 Died 1870 lived for a time in Furnivals Inn close to this spot and there wrote Pickwick in the year 1836. This bust was modelled and presented by Percy Fitzgerald

48 Doughty Street, WC1
Charles Dickens (1812–1870) novelist lived here (LCC 1903).

15–17 Marylebone Road, NW1
While living in a house on this site Charles Dickens wrote 6 of his principal works, characters from which appear in this sculptured panel (Dickens Fellowship).

BMA House, Tavistock Square, WC1
1851–1860 Charles Dickens novelist lived in Tavistock House near this site

14 Great Russell Street, WC1
Here lived Charles Kitterbell as related by Chas. Dickens in Sketches by Boz "The Bloomsbury Christening" (private).

The Dickens family moved to Bayham Street, Camden Town, in 1822 and lived there for about a year, until Dickens's father (the original of Mr Micawber) was imprisoned in the Marshalsea for debt and Charles was employed in a blacking factory on Hungerford Stairs. Dickens called the area Stagg's Gardens in *Dombey and Son*: 'it was a little row of houses, with little squalid patches of ground before them, fenced off with old doors, barrel-staves, scraps of tarpaulin, and dead bushes; with bottomless tin kettles and exhausted iron fenders thrust into the gaps. Here the Stagg's gardeners trained scarlet beans, kept fowls and rabbits, erected rotten summer houses (one was an old boat), dried clothes, and smoked pipes'.

After Dickens was appointed a reporter on the *Morning Chronicle* he lodged at Furnival's Inn in Holborn where *Sketches by Boz* was written. It was published in 1836, the year Dickens married. He spent a year sharing his cramped lodgings with his wife, her sister and his brother and a baby son and then moved to a larger home, 48 Doughty Street. In the 19th century there were gates at either end of the road, attended by porters in gold-laced hats and with the Doughty arms on the buttons of their mulberry-coloured livery. Many of Dickens's friends called at no.48 — W. Harrison Ainsworth, Leigh Hunt, George

Charles Dickens, 48 Doughty Street

Cruikshank, Daniel Maclise, John Forster — but the atmosphere was permanently affected by the sudden death of his wife's sister, aged only 17, in May 1837. Dickens had been infatuated with her and her death affected his depiction of women.

After the births of two daughters Dickens had to leave Doughty Street at the end of 1839 for a larger house. A new home was found at 1 Devonshire Terrace, Regent's Park, but the property has been demolished. It was a 'handsome house with a considerable garden' and stood at the corner of Marylebone Road and Marylebone High Street.

Their last and grandest home was Tavistock House in Tavistock Square, Bloomsbury. This has also been demolished and the British Medical Association headquarters occupies the site. Dickens began *Bleak House* shortly after moving in and was to complete *Little Dorrit* before separating from his wife in 1858. He had bought Gad's Hill Place, Rochester, in 1857 and although he owned Tavistock House until 1860 his family left London for the country. While they were at Gad's Hill, Dickens had various lodgings in London, paying for the houses of an actress, Ellen Ternan, in Slough and Peckham.

Dickinson, Goldsworthy Lowes.

11 Edwardes Square, W8
This was the London home of Goldsworthy Lowes Dickinson author and humanist. He was born 1862 and died 1932 (LCC 1956; privately erected).

Goldsworthy Lowes Dickinson lived for most of his life in King's College, Cambridge, but he shared a London home with his sisters. From 1912 to 1920 this was at 11 Edwardes Square. Dickinson was deeply shocked by the outbreak of World War I and worked with Lord Bryce on planning the League of Nations. His namesake Lord Dickinson recalled: 'he was modestly personified and when others took the work over he quietly dropped out of sight. But, nevertheless, the League of Nations owes its birth very largely to his idealism'.

Dilke, Sir Charles Wentworth.

76 Sloane Street, SW1
Sir Charles Wentworth Dilke (1843–1911) statesman and author lived here (LCC 1959).

Charles Wentworth Dilke lived at 76 Sloane Street as a boy and young man. His grandfather, whose name he inherited, had built

75

Wentworth Place in Hampstead with Charles Brown, the house in which both Keats and his adored Fanny Brawne lived. Dilke followed a political career, entering Parliament as a Liberal MP in 1868. He was a radical in sympathy and was largely responsible for the legalising of trade unions and limiting hours of work. (*See also* Sir HERBERT BEERBOHM TREE.)

Disraeli, Benjamin [Earl of Beaconsfield].

22 Theobalds Road, WC1
Benjamin Disraeli, Earl of Beaconsfield (1804–1881) Born here 1804 (LCC 1948).

6 Frederick's Place, Old Jewry, EC2
Benjamin Disraeli Prime Minister in 1868 and 1874–80 worked in this building 1821–1824 (City of London).

93 Park Lane, W1
Here lived Benjamin Disraeli Earl of Beaconsfield from 1839 to 1873

19 Curzon Street, W1
Benjamin Disraeli Earl of Beaconsfield (1804–1881) died here (LCC 1908).

Benjamin Disraeli's family was distinguished and relatively prosperous, and he had a comfortable childhood at 22 Theobalds Road. In July 1817, a few months after his father Isaac D'Israeli left the Jewish faith, Benjamin was baptised in St Andrew's, Holborn; he remained a staunch member of the Church of England for the rest of his life.

From 1821 to 1825 Disraeli was articled to a firm of solicitors in Frederick's Place. Disraeli later recalled his 'utter unfitness to become a solicitor' even though 'it gave [him] great facility with [his] pen and no inconsiderable knowledge of human nature'.

Disraeli became an MP in 1837 but had already published his first novel, *Vivien Grey*, in 1826. In 1839 he married Mary Anne Lewis, a widow ten years his senior. They settled down to a contented marriage and Mary Anne's house at 1 Grosvenor Gate (now 93 Park Lane) remained their London address until her death in 1872. The Disraelis' main home, however, was Hughenden Manor, Buckinghamshire, into which they moved in 1848.

Disraeli first served as Prime Minister in 1868, shortly after carrying the 1867 Reform Bill through Parliament (when he was Chancellor of the Exchequer and Leader of the House of Commons). As Prime Minister from 1874 to 1880 he purchased the Khedive's Suez Canal Shares (1875).

Benjamin Disraeli, 6 Frederick's Place

After his defeat in the 1880 election Disraeli bought the seven-year lease of 19 Curzon Street from Lord Tankerville. He paid for it with the proceeds of his last novel, *Endymion*.

D'Israeli, Isaac.

6 Bloomsbury Square, WC1
   Isaac D'Israeli, author, lived here. Born 1766. Died 1848 (Duke of Bedford 1904).

The D'Israeli family moved from Theobalds Road, where Benjamin Disraeli was born, to Bloomsbury Square where they lived from 1818 to 1829. Isaac D'Israeli was born in England of a family of Sephardic Jews who had fled from Spain to Venice and then to England. He was educated at Amsterdam and Leyden and his literary works are of particular value because he had access to traditions and documents now lost. The first volume of his anecdotes and essays *Curiosities of Literature* appeared in 1791 and went into 12 editions; as an anecdotalist and anthologist he had scarcely a rival in his own day or since.

Dobson, Henry Austin.

10 Redcliffe Street, SW10
   Austin Dobson (1840–1921) poet and essayist lived here (LCC 1959).

Austin Dobson combined a career in the civil service with writing. His first volume of poetry *Vignettes in Rhyme* was published in 1873, a year after he moved into the suburban villa at 10 Redcliffe Street (where he lived until 1879). Several other writers worked in the Board of Trade with Dobson, including Edmund Gosse, and an American referred to the Board as 'a nest of singing birds'. Dobson specialized in studies of 18th-century literature.

Don, David. *See* BANKS, Sir JOSEPH.

Dorset, Earl of. *See* BOW STREET.

Douglas, Norman.

63 Albany Mansions, Albert Bridge Road, SW11
   Norman Douglas (1868–1952) writer lived here (GLC 1980).

Norman Douglas spent most of his life abroad, living in Italy and on Capri, where his homosexuality was less subject to censure. Between

1910 and 1917, however, he stayed in London and from 1913 to 1917 he took a flat in Albany Mansions. *Old Calabria*, often regarded as his masterpiece, was published in 1915 and his best-known novel *South Wind* was completed on his return to Capri in 1917. D.H. Lawrence described him: 'D — was decidedly shabby and a gentleman, with his wicked red face and tufted eyebrows'.

Dowson, Ernest Christopher.

1 Dowson Court, Belmont Grove, SE13
Ernest Christopher Dowson poet (1867-1900) lived in a house which stood on this site (Lewisham Borough Council).

Ernest Dowson was one of the leading 'decadent' artists at the end of the 19th century, whom Yeats called 'the tragic generation'. Influenced by Verlaine and Swinburne, Dowson wrote of the renunciation of the world, of hopeless love and of death. He lived according to his aesthetic vision and died a young man, poverty-stricken, addicted to drink and suffering from tuberculosis.

D'Oyly Carte, Richard. *See* ADELPHI TERRACE.

Dryden, John.

43 Gerrard Street, W1
John Dryden poet lived here, b.1631, d.1700 (RSA 1875).

The plaque to Dryden erected by the Royal Society of Arts is one of the oldest surviving in London but it is unfortunately on the wrong house. Dryden moved to 44, not 43 Gerrard Street from Long Acre in 1687: 'my house is in Gerrard Street, the 5th door on the left hand, coming from Newport Street'. He 'used most commonly to write in the ground-room next the street' and in a letter of 1698/9 he describes the great gale which 'blew down three of my chimneys, and dismantled all one side of my House, by throwing down the tiles'. Dryden's poetry was redolent with classical allusion; Robert Graves described him as the poet who 'found English poetry brick and left it marble — native brick, imported marble'.

Du Maurier, George.

91 Great Russell Street, WC1
George Du Maurier (1834–1896) artist and writer lived here 1863–1868 (LCC 1960).

Du Maurier, Sir Gerald

New Grove House, 28 Hampstead Grove, NW3
George Du Maurier (1834–1896) artist and writer lived here 1874–1895 (privately erected 1900; LCC 1959).

George Du Maurier was at the height of his artistic powers when he lived at 91 Great Russell Street, above the offices of Pears Soap. He began working for the *Cornhill Magazine* as an illustrator while at Great Russell Street, and in 1864 produced some of his finest designs, for Mrs Gaskell's novel *Wives and Daughters*, the first serial he illustrated.

The change from his comparatively humble rooms in Bloomsbury to the magnificent house in Hampstead Grove reflects the change in his artistic interests. His work became more of a commentary on fashionable society as he turned from artist to journalist. His association with *Punch* (he became a permanent member of the staff in 1864) encouraged his satirical drawing. He began to write novels towards the end of his life and his most successful prose works were based on his childhood and student days in Paris. The novel *Trilby* (1894) was a bestseller and a success on stage for Herbert Beerbohm Tree.

Du Maurier, Sir **Gerald.**

Cannon Hall, 14 Cannon Place, NW3
Sir Gerald Du Maurier (1873–1934) actor manager lived here from 1916 until his death (GLC 1967).

Gerald Du Maurier, the youngest child of George Du Maurier, made his first professional appearance in 1894 at the Garrick Theatre. He achieved fame with his interpretation of J.M. Barrie's plays, particularly his role as Mr Darling and Captain Hook in *Peter Pan*. Cannon Hall was built in the 18th century and was a residence and courthouse for several Hampstead magistrates in the 19th and early 20th centuries. It was the home of eminent professional people in the 18th century, including a physician to George III. While living there Du Maurier was manager of Wyndham's Theatre and, from 1925, of St James's Theatre.

Duncan, Leland Lewis.

8 Lingards Road, SE13
Leland Lewis Duncan (1862–1923) local historian lived here 1873–1923 (Lewisham Borough Council).

Dundonald, Earl. *See* COCHRANE, THOMAS.

Earnshaw, Thomas.

119 High Holborn, WC1
Site of the business premises of Thomas Earnshaw (1749–1829) noted watch and chronometer maker (LCC 1948).

Thomas Earnshaw, the 'creator of the modern marine chronometer', carried on his business in Holborn from 1806 until his death. He devised the Spring Detent Chronometer Escapement.

Eddington, Sir Arthur.

4 Bennett Park, SE3
Sir Arthur Eddington OM (1882–1944) mathematician and astrophysicist lived here (GLC 1974).

Arthur Eddington took rooms in 4 Bennett Park when he was appointed chief assistant to the Astronomer Royal at Greenwich Observatory in 1906. He spent the next seven years studying the motion of 'star streams' and established a mathematical method of analysing their motion. He left Bennett Park in 1914 after becoming Plumian Professor of Astronomy at Cambridge and director of the University Observatory. That year he published his first major work, *Stellar Movements and the Structure of the Universe*.

Edwards, Edward.

11 Idol Lane, EC3
Edward Edwards pioneer of Public Libraries lived as a boy in a house on this site 1825–c.1830 (City of London).

Edward Edwards was born in London but there is little information about his childhood. He became a popular authority on libraries and assisted William Ewart, whose committee on free libraries resulted in legislation in 1850. Two years later Edwards became the first librarian of Manchester Free Library but he was forced to resign. The rest of his life was devoted to literary and bibliographical pursuits.

Eisenhower, Dwight.

31 St James's Square, Norfolk House, SW1
In this building 24 June 1942 – 8 November 1942 General of the Army Dwight D Eisenhower Supreme Allied Commander formed the First Allied Force Headquarters and in conjunction with the commanders of the fighting services of the Allied nations and the authorities in Washington and London planned and launched operation 'Torch' for the liberation of North Africa and later January 1944 – 6 June 1944 as Supreme Allied Commander Allied Expeditionary Force in conjunction with the commanders of the fighting services of the Allied nations and the authorities in Washington and London he planned and launched Operation 'Overlord' for the liberation of North West Europe (private).

20 Grosvenor Square, W1
In this building were located the Headquarters of General of the Army Dwight D. Eisenhower Commander in Chief Allied Force June–November 1942 Supreme Commander Allied Expeditionary Force January–March 1944

General Dwight Eisenhower went to London in January 1944 as Supreme Commander of the Allied Expeditionary Forces. After his return to the USA he entered politics and became the 34th president.

Eldon, Lord.

6 Bedford Square, WC1
Lord Eldon (1751–1838) Lord Chancellor lived here (LCC 1954).

John Scott lived at 6 Bedford Square from 1798, the year before he was made Lord Chief Justice of the Common Pleas, to 1818. He was created baron (1799) and, on Pitt's retirement, became Lord Chancellor. Except for a short break during Grenville's ministry of 'All the Talents' he continued as Lord Chancellor until 1827. Lord Eldon was a deeply conservative man, opposed to innovation of any kind, and his work with repressive legislation made him extremely unpopular.

Elen, Gus.

3 Thurleigh Avenue, SW12
Gus Elen (1862-1940) music hall comedian lived here (GLC 1979).

Gus Elen lived in the plain brick semi-detached 19th-century house at 3 Thurleigh Avenue for the last six years of his life. He was a music-hall comedian who brought to perfection the cockney character style, singing many songs by George Le Brunn and Edgar Bateman.

Elgar, Sir Edward.

51 Avonmore Road, W14
Sir Edward Elgar (1857-1934) composer lived here 1890-1891 (LCC 1962).

42 Netherhall Gardens, NW3
Edward Elgar composer lived in a house on this site 1911-1921 (Heath and Old Hampstead Society).

Edward Elgar went to London shortly after his marriage in 1889 and lived at 51 Avonmore Road from March 1890 until June 1891. The Elgars spent the next 20 years in Malvern and Hereford but returned to London in 1912, moving into Severn House in Netherhall Gardens. It was the second of two houses Norman Shaw designed for the affluent Royal Academician Edward Long in 1887.

Though Elgar spent only 15 months at Avonmore Road he composed there the concert overture *Froissart* which received its first performance at the Worcester Festival in 1890. In 1911 Elgar became the first musician to be appointed a member of the Order of Merit. His Cello Concerto and the symphonic study *Falstaff* were both composed while he was at Netherhall Gardens.

Severn House was demolished in 1938 and the position of the plaque erected on its site has been criticised. Both 42 and 44 Netherhall Gardens have been built since Norman Shaw's house was demolished but no.44 really occupies the site, using the old foundations of the entrance section of Shaw's house.

Eliot, George.

Holly Lodge, 31 Wimbledon Park Road, SW18
George Eliot (1819–1880) novelist lived here (LCC 1905).

4 Cheyne Walk, SW3
George Eliot (1819–1880) novelist died here (LCC 1949).

George Eliot lived at Holly Lodge from February 1859 to September 1860. It was a difficult time for her. She was living with a married man, the critic George Henry Lewes, and was a social outcast, unable to appear in public with him. She found London 'full of demons' but she described Holly Lodge as 'very comfortable. . .a tall cake, with a low garnish of holly and laurel', and she wrote *The Mill on the Floss* there.

Lewes died in 1878 and in 1880 George Eliot married John Cross who, though 20 years her junior, had been an intimate friend of Lewes and herself. Cross took the lease of 4 Cheyne Walk (nos.3–6 were built 1717–18) before they were married but the couple only spent a short time together in the house. George Eliot died on 22 December 1880. She had become a wealthy woman in the 1870s after the success of *Middlemarch* and was acknowledged as one of the greatest novelists of the age.

Elizabeth II.

Lombard North Central Bank Building, (site of) 17 Bruton Street, W1
This plaque was dedicated in the Silver Jubilee of her reign to Her Majesty the Queen who was born here on April 21st 1926 (private).

Engels, Friedrich.

121 Regent's Park Road, NW1
Friedrich Engels (1820–1895) political philosopher lived here 1870–1894 (GLC 1972).

Friedrich Engels's Victorian terrace house, 121 Regent's Park Road, was not far from the home of Karl Marx in Maitland Park Road and the two friends were able to work together, Engels devoting the last 12 years of his life to editing and translating Marx's work. Engels first came to England as agent for the Manchester branch of his father's German textile firm. He was converted to communism by Moses Hess and published his indictment of capitalist society, *The Condition of the Working Classes in England*, in 1844. His association with Marx began in 1845 when they collaborated in Brussels on the organisation of underground revolutionary groups and, in 1848, published the

Communist Manifesto. Engels fled to England after the suppression of the revolution in Baden and returned to his father's Manchester firm. His salary helped to support Marx through years of poverty in London.

Epstein, Sir Jacob.

18 Hyde Park Gate, SW7
   The house of Sir Jacob Epstein sculptor. Lived and died here 1929–1959 (private).

Epstein first began carving his unorthodox sculptures in Paris where he worked from 1902 to 1905. The common practice of the times was to 'farm out' clay and plaster models to be carved in stone, but Epstein preferred direct carving. Neither the public nor the critics could see any merit in his works. He went to London in 1905; nearly all his major works, including the stone reliefs for the British Medical Association building (1907–8) and 'Rock-Drill', directly inspired by the Vorticists and their praise of the machine, attracted hostility and derision. He took the studio in Hyde Park Gate in 1929.

Essex Street.

Essex Hall, Essex Street, WC2
   Essex Street was laid out in the grounds of Essex House by Nicholas Barbon in 1675. Among many famous lawyers who lived here were Sir Orlando Bridgeman (c.1606–1674) Lord Keeper; Henry Fielding (1707–1754) novelist; and Brass Crosby (1725–1793), Lord Mayor of London. James Savage (1779–1852) architect had his office here. Prince Charles Edward Stuart stayed at a house in the street in 1750. Rev. Theophilus Lindsey (1723–1808) Unitarian minister founded Essex Street Chapel here in 1774. Dr Samuel Johnson established an evening club at the 'Essex Head' in 1783 (LCC 1962).

Essex Street was named after Essex House, the town mansion of the Earl of Essex, which was bought and demolished by Nicholas Barbon towards the end of the 17th century. In a year Barbon had built a street of houses 'for taverns, alehouses, cookshops and vaulting schools', but most of them have now gone. Barbon, called in his time, 'rogue, knave and damned', was destined, in the words of Sir John Summerson, 'to become not merely the most daring speculative builder of his day but the virtual founder of fire insurance and an economist of prophetic perspicacity'. Only a part of Essex House survived Barbon's rebuilding, and Sir Orlando Bridgeman, Lord Chief Justice and Lord Keeper of the Great Seal, died there in 1674.

Henry Fielding lived at 24 Essex Street for a year before he was called to the Bar in 1740. Brass Crosby lived at no.17 from 1773 to 1780; he was Lord Mayor of London in 1770 and campaigned successfully for the unrestricted reporting of parliamentary debates. Prince Charles, the Young Pretender, stayed in Essex Street in 1750 during a revival of Jacobite activity. His visit was meant to be secret but George II is said to have known.

When Samuel Johnson established his club in 1783 the Essex Head was 'a little ale-house'; it was replaced by a late 19th-century building. James Savage, the architect who designed St Luke's, Chelsea, had his office in the street from 1827 to 1852.

Etty, William. *See* PEPYS, SAMUEL.

Ewart, William.

16 Eaton Place, SW1
William Ewart (1798–1869) reformer, lived here (LCC 1963).

When William Ewart moved into 16 Eaton Place in 1830, shortly after his marriage, the house had just been built. He remained there until 1838 when his wife died. Ewart was called to the Bar in 1827 and became an MP. Throughout his parliamentary career he put forward liberal and progressive views. He was responsible for the first Public Libraries Act of 1850 which led to the foundation of free libraries supported by local rates.

Ewart was the first person to propose a scheme of commemorating houses of the famous in London (*see* INTRODUCTION).

Faraday, Michael.

48 Blandford Street, W1
Michael Faraday man of science, apprentice here, b.1791, d.1867
(RSA 1876).

Michael Faraday was errand boy to Mr Riebau who kept a stationer's shop in Blandford Street. In 1804 he became apprentice to Riebau and lived at Blandford Street for the next eight years. In 1812 he attended four lectures by Sir Humphrey Davy at the Royal Institution and after sending his notes of the lectures to Davy he was employed by the eminent scientist. Faraday's great discovery, magneto electricity, was made in 1831 and for the rest of his life he devoted himself to investigating the new source of power and inventing a vocabulary to describe it.

Fawcett, Dame Millicent.

2 Gower Street, WC1
Dame Millicent Fawcett (1847-1929) pioneer of women's suffrage lived and died here (LCC 1954).

Millicent Fawcett and her sister Elizabeth, later Mrs Garrett Anderson, were two of the most influential figures in the campaign for women's rights. Millicent left school at the age of 15 but she obtained a wide knowledge of politics and economics through marrying Henry

Fawcett, the blind professor of economics at Cambridge. Inspired by her sister and encouraged by her husband, Millicent devoted herself to the cause of women's freedom, particularly to obtaining the vote for women. She preferred the constitutional to the militant approach and was a restraining influence during World War I.

Ferrier, Kathleen.

97 Frognal, NW3
Kathleen Ferrier (1912–1953) contralto lived here (GLC 1979).

Kathleen Ferrier lived at Flat 2, Frognal Mansions, from 1942 to 1953, virtually the whole of her international career. In 1937 she accepted her husband's wager to enter Carlisle Festival and won both piano and vocal competitions. She then began serious vocal training and moved to London in 1942. Many concerts followed and her last public appearance was in February 1953 when she sang in *Orfeo*, conducted by Sir John Barbirolli at Covent Garden. She had to withdraw, however, and died soon afterwards.

Fielding, Henry.

Milbourne House, Station Road, Barnes
Henry Fielding (1707–1754) novelist lived here (GLC 1978).

The outside of Milbourne House is of the late 17th and 18th centuries but there are internal features of an earlier date. It was named after William Milbourne, whose family occupied it until the reign of Henry VIII. Henry Fielding lived there from about 1748 to 1752 and probably wrote *Amelia* there. He had been appointed to the Bow Street magistrates' office in 1747 but his health broke down after his energetic administration of law and pursuit of social reform. He died in Lisbon. Fielding's most popular and greatest work, *The History of Tom Jones, a Foundling*, was published in 1749 while Fielding was living in Barnes.

Fielding, Sir John. *See* BOW STREET.

Fildes, Sir Luke.

11 Melbury Road, W14
Sir Luke Fildes (1844–1927) lived here 1878–1927 (LCC 1959).

Sir Luke Fildes was a highly successful and fashionable artist during his lifetime. His son recalls his father's decision in 1875 to build a house and to 'put into it all the money he had. The house would be designed

Henry Fielding, Milbourne House, Barnes

by Norman Shaw, the most fashionable "domestic" architect of the day'. Melbury Road was a new and extremely desirable site for houses: Norman Shaw called it 'delicious'. G.F. Watts was to live at no.6 and Sir Hamo Thornycroft at no.2a. The artist Val Prinsep had commissioned Philip Webb to design his house and studio in nearby Holland Park Road.

Fildes and his family moved into no.11 in October 1877 (the plaque is incorrect, according to his son). Every day at milking time cows came along the country lane from Holland House, through the gates by the side entrance of no.11 into Melbury Road and on to the dairy in Kensington High Road. Fildes's son recalls the William Morris wallpaper in the day and night nurseries and Morris's 'black spindly-legged chairs with rush seats'.

Fisher, John Arbuthnot, Lord.

16 Queen Anne's Gate, SW7
Admiral of the Fleet Lord Fisher OM (1841–1920) lived here as First Sea Lord 1905–10 (GLC 1975).

16 Queen Anne's Gate is one of a terrace of seven houses built *c*1775–8. John Arbuthnot Fisher lived there while he was serving as First Sea Lord. He entered the navy in 1854; by 1901 he was a full admiral and during his period commanding the Mediterranean fleet he won great popularity on the lower deck and among his junior officers through his professionalism coupled with a dislike of pointless routine. Fisher was responsible for building eight of the fast heavily-armed Dreadnought cruisers between 1909 and 1910.

Fitzroy, Robert.

38 Onslow Square, SW7
Admiral Robert Fitzroy (1805–1865) hydrographer and meteorologist lived here (GLC *c*1981).

Robert Fitzroy entered the navy in 1819 and nine years later was given command of *HMS Beagle*. The *Beagle*'s second voyage, 1831–6, was to become one of the most famous ever made: Charles Darwin was on board and his research, particularly on the Galapagos Islands, led ultimately to his theory of evolution.

After retiring from active service Fitzroy moved to 38 Onslow Square in 1854, remaining there until his death. The house is part of a complete listed terrace on the south side of the square, built in 1849 by the South Kensington developer Charles James Freake. Fitzroy designed a cheap and serviceable portable barometer and instituted a system of storm warnings for sailors which has developed into the daily weather forecast. A devout man, he never really recovered from his part in what he saw as Darwin's outright attack on the Bible; he committed suicide.

Fleming, Sir Alexander.

20*a* Danvers Street, SW3

Sir Alexander Fleming (1881–1955) discoverer of penicillin lived here (GLC *c*1981).

Alexander Fleming lived in a flat within 20 Danvers Street from 1929 until his death. He was appalled at the number of deaths in World War I caused by infections which invariably followed wounds. His search for a substance to kill the bacteria without harming the patient led to the discovery of penicillin notatum in 1928. The significance of his discovery was not fully realised until two other scientists, Dr E.B. Chain and Sir Howard Florey, succeeded in making pure penicillin in usable quantities in 1940. Fleming, Chain and Florey received the Nobel Prize for Medicine in 1945.

Fleming, Sir Ambrose.

9 Clifton Gardens, W9

Sir Ambrose Fleming (1849–1945) scientist and electrical engineer lived here (GLC 1971).

John Ambrose Fleming lived at 9 Clifton Gardens (now part of a hotel) in the 1890s when he was teaching at University College London. In 1885 he was appointed professor of electrical engineering, a position he held for over 40 years. He acted as consultant to the Edison Bell and Swan concerns, to the London Electricity Supply and Marconi's and for 25 years was closely connected with the development of all the major applications of electrical science.

Flinders, Matthew.

56 Fitzroy Street, W1

Captain Matthew Flinders RN (1774–1814) explorer and navigator lived here (GLC 1973).

Matthew Flinders lived at 56 Fitzroy Street from 1813 to 1814. He joined his first ship in 1790 and sailed to the West Indies with Captain Bligh. He made a voyage to New South Wales (1795–1800), surveying the coast from Hervey Bay in the north to the circuit of Van Diemen's

Land in the south. His survey of New Holland was begun in 1801 and still forms the basis of modern Admiralty charts. He was detained in Mauritius from 1803 to 1810, suspected of spying against the French.

Flint, Sir **William Russell.**

Peel Cottage, 80 Peel Street, W8
   Sir William Russell Flint RA, PRWS. Artist. Born 1880 Died 1969 Lived here 1925–1969 (private).

William Russell Flint was born in Edinburgh and first went to London in 1900 as a medical illustrator. After two years he took up magazine illustrating and commercial designing and was on the staff of the *Illustrated London News* from 1903 to 1907. Flint moved into Peel Cottage shortly after being elected an associate of the Royal Academy. He is best known for his paintings of half-naked women.

Forbes, Vivian. *See* RICKETTS, CHARLES.

Forbes-Robertson, Sir **Johnston.**

22 Bedford Square, WC1
   Sir Johnston Forbes-Robertson actor, lived here. Born 1853 Died 1937 (Duke of Bedford).

When Forbes-Robertson played Hamlet in 1897 it was acclaimed the greatest performance of the time and, by some critics, the greatest of all time. His 'noble bearing and saintly character' were fully exploited under the guidance of Henry Irving, whose company he joined at the Lyceum. From the 1890s the theatre was changing: actor-managers and playwrights were being knighted and melodrama was making way for serious drama. Forbes-Robertson did much to raise theatrical standards, both as an actor and manager.

Ford, Ford Madox.

80 Campden Hill Road, W8
   Ford Madox Ford (1873–1939) novelist and critic lived here (GLC 1973).

Ford Madox Ford was born Ford Hermann Hueffer on 17 December 1873 at Merton, Surrey. His grandfather was the Pre-Raphaelite painter Ford Madox Brown and his father was Francis Hueffer, a well-known music critic. He changed his surname to Ford in 1919. Ford moved to

South Lodge, 80 Campden Hill Road, in 1913. For most of the war he was fighting in France, but the house remained his home until 1919.

Ford had published several biographies before moving to South Lodge, and in 1908 he founded the *English Review*, whose early contributors included H.G. Wells, Henry James and Galsworthy. Ford's writing room on the first floor of South Lodge was decorated in a violent shade of red by his friend Wyndham Lewis and known as the 'Futurist's Room'. From December 1913 he worked there on *The Good Soldier* which was published in 1915, the year he obtained his commission in the Reserve of Officers and went to France.

Forster, Edward Morgan.

9 Arlington Park Mansions, Turnham Green Common, W4
  E.M. Forster (1879–1970) novelist lived here (GLC c1981).

In 1939 E.M. Forster moved to Arlington Park Mansions, a block built in 1905 on the west side of Turnham Green. He watched the bombing raid on the Surrey Docks in 1940 from his top floor flat (no.9): 'London Burning!. . .the Surrey Docks were ablaze at the back with towers and spires outlined against them, greenish yellow search-lights swept the sky in futile agony, crimson shells burst behind the spire of Turnham Green church'.

Forster wrote some of the finest novels in English this century, including *Howards End* (1910) and *A Passage to India* (1924); he was also a distinguished broadcaster, essayist and literary critic, short story writer, librettist (Britten's *Billy Budd*) and above all a great liberal thinker.

Fox, Charles James.

46 Clarges Street, W1
  Charles James Fox (1749–1806) statesman lived here (LCC 1950).

Clarges Street was built by the politician Sir Thomas Clarges and laid out in 1718. Fox lived at no.46 towards the end of his life, 1803–4. He was extremely extravagant in his dress when young, leading the fashion among the 'macaroni' fops. But he was a cultured and liberal politician and a friend of both Samuel Johnson and Voltaire. His coalition government of 1783–4 brought in 22 years of Conservative rule and his return to office in 1806 as Foreign Secretary and virtual leader of the government was an extraordinary achievement.

Frampton, George.

32 Queen's Grove, NW8
George Frampton (1860–1928) sculptor lived and worked here 1894–1908 (GLC 1977).

Frampton adorned many public buildings with his sculptures, including Lloyd's Register and the Constitutional Club. His statues of Queen Victoria may be seen throughout Britain and in Calcutta and Winnipeg. He designed the commemorative medal for the Coronation of Edward VII and after such devoted service to the monarchy he was knighted in 1908.

Franklin, Benjamin.

36 Craven Street, Strand, WC2
Benjamin Franklin (1706–1790) lived here (LCC 1914).

Benjamin Franklin was sent to England in 1757 as the London agent to the General Assembly of Pennsylvania. He returned to America briefly in 1762 but continued to live in London until 1775, spending 13 years in Craven Street and involving himself in the intellectual life of London's coffee houses. No.36 was built in about 1730 and Franklin wrote his speeches and reports in the panelled parlour on the first floor. Franklin was the living embodiment to Europeans of the American self-made man; the son of a Boston candle maker, he was apprenticed as a printer and rose to be colonial negotiator and ambassador to France (1776–84).

Freake, Sir **Charles James.**

21 Cromwell Road, SW5
Sir Charles James Freake (1814–1884) Builder and Patron of the Arts lived here (GLC c1981).

Charles Freake, 'the cleverest of all the speculating Builders', lived from 1860 in the imposing residence that he built for himself at 21 Cromwell Road. His wife and daughter, three female relations, a butler, two footmen and seven other servants lived there too. Musical and theatrical performances were staged in the great ballroom at the back of the house and sometimes the Prince of Wales attended. The son of a coal merchant and publican, Freake was granted a baronetcy in 1882 and died leaving an estate worth some £718,000.

In 1874–5 he built the National Training School for Music (now the Royal College of Organists) at his own cost. The Prince of Wales was particularly interested in the school and, according to Gladstone's political secretary, had 'persistently and somewhat questionably (if not "fishily") pressed Freake's name on the Prime Minister'.

Freud, Sigmund.

20 Maresfield Gardens, NW3
Sigmund Freud (1856–1939) founder of psycho-analysis lived here in 1938–1939 (LCC 1956).

Freud's home for 79 years was Vienna but he was forced to flee Hitler in 1938. His books had been publicly burnt in Berlin and four of his sisters were to be killed by the Nazis in 1944. Freud, his wife and daughter Anna found refuge in the Hampstead house which he considered 'too good for someone who would not tenant it for long' (he had first visited England in 1875). Freud was already seriously ill with cancer but he conducted four analyses daily until near death and spent a lot of time in the secluded garden that led from his consulting room at the back of the house. He completed *Moses and Monotheism* before his death on 23 September 1939; *The Outline of Psycho-Analysis* was published posthumously in 1940.

Friese-Greene, William.

136 Maida Vale, W9
William Friese-Greene (1855–1921) pioneer of cinematography lived here (LCC 1954).

William Friese-Greene went to London from Bristol in 1885 and rented an underground studio at 92 Piccadilly, where he experimented in making moving pictures and two years later succeeded in producing a film of a dancing skeleton. He took his wife and child to London and they rented 136 Maida Vale, 1888–91. From 1887 Friese-Green had been trying to solve the problem of making the right film for his camera: paper tore too easily and it was difficult to make celluloid of sufficiently even quality. However, in 1889 he made an even strip of celluloid 50 feet long and took a film of Londoners enjoying a leisurely Sunday in Hyde Park. Success did not bring Friese-Green financial reward and he died in poverty.

Frith, William Powell.

114 Clifton Hill, NW8
W.P. Frith (1818–1909) painter, lived and died here (GLC 1973).

95

Sigmund Freud, 20 Maresfield Gardens

Although W.P. Frith was virtually forced to become an artist by his innkeeper father, he was to become one of the most successful painters of contemporary life in the second half of the 19th century — so popular that barriers had to be erected at the Royal Academy to protect paintings such as 'Derby Day' and 'The Railway Station' from the crowds. By the end of the century, however, his reputation had dwindled and though he was said not to care himself, harsh criticism pained his family. Frith moved to 114 Clifton Hill in 1896 and lived there until his death in 1909.

Frobisher, Sir Martin. *See* WILLOUGHBY, Sir HUGH.

Froude, James Anthony.

5 Onslow Gardens, SW7
James Anthony Froude (1818-1894) historian and man of letters lived here (LCC 1934).

James Anthony Froude first met Thomas Carlyle in 1849 and became a frequent visitor to his Chelsea home; he shared Carlyle's ideas: 'If I wrote anything', Froude confessed, 'I fancied myself writing it to him, reflecting at each word on what he would think of it as a check on affectations'. He was Carlyle's literary executor and wrote a full and frank biography of him (1882-4). From 1860 until 1874 Froude edited *Fraser's Magazine*. His reputation as one of the great masters of English prose in the 19th century was firmly established with the publication in 12 volumes (1856-70) of his *A History of England from the Fall of Wolsey to the Death of Elizabeth*. The success of the *History* brought Froude to the attention of London society and from 1865 until 1892 he made his home at 5 Onslow Gardens.

Fry, Charles Burgess.

8 Moreland Court, Finchley Road, NW2
C.B. Fry scholar and sportsman lived at 8 Moreland Court from 1950-1956 (Hendon Corporation).

C.B. Fry has been described, somewhat incredibly, as 'probably the most variously gifted Englishman of any age'. As an undergraduate at Oxford he was an exceptionally skilful sportsman and broke the world long-jump record by clearing 23 feet 5 inches: a jump during which he was said to have reached five and a half feet above the ground. He taught, then took up sporting journalism and first-class cricket. Sport even took him into politics. He was substitute delegate on the

Indian delegation to the League of Nations in Geneva in 1920 accompanying his fellow cricketer Prince Ranjitsinhji.

Fry, Elizabeth.

Entrance to St Mildred's Court, Poultry, EC2
Mrs Elizabeth Fry (1780–1845) Prison reformer lived here 1800–1809 (City of London).

Elizabeth Gurney, a member of an old Quaker family, married Joseph Fry at the age of 20. For the first nine years of her marriage she lived at St Mildred's Court. She first took a practical interest in prison conditions in 1813 and was appalled by the suffering of nearly 300 women and their children huddled together in two wards and two cells in Newgate. The American ambassador of the time described her at work: '2 days ago I saw the greatest curiosity in London, aye and in England too. . . . I have seen Elizabeth Fry in Newgate, and I have witnessed there the miraculous effect of true Christianity upon the most depraved of human beings'. Her philanthropic work was restricted by the bankruptcy of her husband in 1828. She died at Ramsgate in 1845.

Fuseli, Henry.

37 Foley Street, W1
Henry Fuseli (1741–1825) artist lived here 1788–1803 (LCC 1961).

Henry Fuseli was born in Zurich and went to London in 1764. By the time he moved to 72 Queen Anne Street East (now 37 Foley Street) his paintings (the best known are of scenes from Shakespeare and the supernatural) had earned him the title of the 'wild Swiss' and the 'painter in ordinary to the Devil'.

Fuseli married just before moving to Queen Anne Street and the same year he began a friendship with the feminist Mary Wollstonecraft. She fell in love with him and pursued him until his wife Sophia refused her entrance to their house. In 1804 Fuseli moved to Somerset House where, as keeper of the Royal Academy, he lived in official apartments until his death.

Gainsborough, Thomas.

82 Pall Mall, SW1
Thomas Gainsborough (1727-1788) artist lived here (LCC 1951).

Thomas Gainsborough lived in the west part of Schomberg House (now no.82) Pall Mall from 1774 until his death. In 1768 he had been invited to become a founder-member of the Royal Academy but soon disagreed with the Academy over the hanging of his pictures. After a final disagreement in 1784 Gainsborough withdrew all his pictures and never exhibited there again. Instead, he had an annual exhibition in Schomberg House. His prosperity had already been assured by the patronage of George III and he was one of the most sought-after portraitists of the day. His chief rival Joshua Reynolds paid tribute to his technique in an obituary lecture: 'all those odd scratches and marks which, on a close examination, are so observable. . .and which even to experienced painters appear rather the effect of accident than design; this chaos, this uncouth and shapeless appearance, by a kind of magic, at a certain distance assumes form'.

Galsworthy, John.

Grove Lodge, Hampstead Grove, NW3
John Galsworthy (1867-1933) novelist and playwright lived here 1918-1933 (LCC 1950).

Success came to John Galsworthy in 1906 with his first play *The Silver Box*, and *The Man of Property*, which was to be the first part of the popular *Forsyte Saga*. Galsworthy was apolitical and chiefly concerned with expressing sympathy for the underdog. Joseph Conrad, who became a close friend after they met on board a merchant ship in the Far East, described him as a humanitarian moralist. Galsworthy won the Nobel Prize for Literature in 1932.

Galton, Sir Francis.

42 Rutland Gate, SW7
Sir Francis Galton (1822-1911) explorer statistician and founder of eugenics lived here for fifty years (private; LCC 1959).

Francis Galton lived at Rutland Gate from 1858 until six months before his death. His scientific and exploratory work covered many areas. As a meteorologist Galton was responsible for introducing the term 'anti-cyclone' into descriptions of the weather. His methods for recording weather were published in *Meteographica; or Methods of Mapping the Weather* (1863). Galton was also in the forefront of anthropology. He examined the hereditary characteristics of sections of the population and developed the concept of eugenics. His work was particularly important for its modification of Charles Darwin's theory of evolution.

Gandhi, Mahatma.

Kingsley Hall, Powis Road, E3
Mahatma Gandhi (1869-1948) stayed here in 1931 (LCC 1954).

Mahatma Gandhi first went to London to study law (1887-91). He returned in 1931 to represent the Indian Congress at talks in London about a constitutional government and stayed at Kingsley Hall for three months. However, his voice was lost at the conference in the clamour of conflicting interests: Muslim, Sikh, Christian, untouchables, princes. When he returned to India later in the year, a harsher viceroy, Lord Willingdon, had been appointed and the repression of Indians had increased. In 1932 Gandhi himself was arrested and detained without trial. He was not to become a major political force until 1940.

Garrett Anderson, Elizabeth.

20 Upper Berkeley Street, W1
Elizabeth Garrett Anderson (1836-1917) the first woman to qualify as a doctor in Britain lived here (LCC 1962).

Mahatma Gandhi, Kingsway Hall, Powis Road

Elizabeth Garrett Anderson lived at 20 Upper Berkeley Street from about 1860 to 1874, the period in which she won some of her greatest victories in the medical world. She became the first woman to qualify as a doctor in Britain in 1865 and the following year opened a dispensary (now the Elizabeth Garrett Anderson Hospital) for women and children in Marylebone. Because of her work and her example women were able to enter the medical profession: the London School of Medicine for Women was founded in 1874 and the Royal Free Hospital allowed women to gain practical experience in the wards.

Garrick, David.

27 Southampton Street, WC2
David Garrick lived here 1750–1772 (Duke of Bedford 1900).

Garrick's Villa, Hampton Court Road, Richmond
David Garrick (1717–1779) actor lived here (GLC 1970).

David Garrick became manager of the Drury Lane Theatre in 1747 where he was equally successful acting in tragedy, comedy and farce. His town residences were in Southampton Street and in the Adelphi, where he died in 1779.

Garrick acquired his villa on the Thames in 1754 and entertained lavishly there, giving memorable 'night fêtes'. Dr Johnson remarked of the house: 'Ah, David, it is the leaving of *such* places as these that makes a death bed terrible'. Garrick made many alterations and additions to the house and built the new front after a design by the Adam brothers. A visitor recorded his impressions: 'Nothing can be neater or fitted up with more decent elegance than this little box; every room shows the true taste and genius of the owner. . . . The drawing-room is hung with canvas painted in all greens in the most beautiful colours imaginable, and decorated with carvings of the same colour. The garden is laid out in the modern taste, with a passage cut under the road to a lawn, where, close by the water-side, stands the Temple of Shakespeare'.

Gaskell, Elizabeth Cleghorn.

93 Cheyne Walk, SW3
Mrs Gaskell (1810–1865) novelist born here (LCC 1913).

Elizabeth Cleghorn Stevenson was born at 93 Cheyne Walk but went to live with her aunt in Knutsford when her mother died soon after her birth. She stayed with her father in London for about two years until

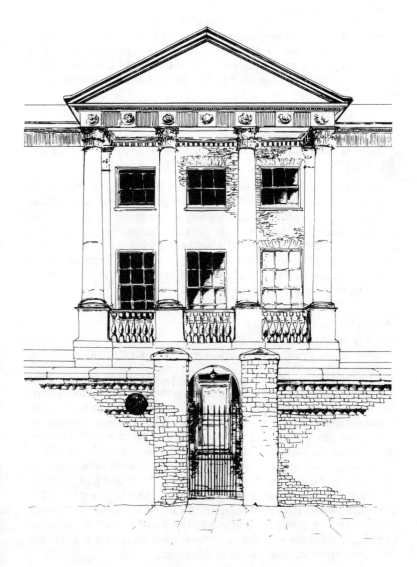

David Garrick, Garrick's Villa, Hampton Court Road

his death in 1829 but the north of England remained her home and when she married the Rev. William Gaskell, a Unitarian minister, in 1832 they settled in Manchester.

Elizabeth gained much experience of the life of the poor and deprived visiting her husband's congregation. Her first successful and controversial novel was *Mary Barton* (1848) in which she attempted to offer a humane approach to labour and class relations. In *Cranford* (1853) she explored country town life based on her childhood in Knutsford.

Gaudier-Brzeska, Henri.

454 Fulham Road, SW6
Henri Gaudier-Brzeska (1891–1915) sculptor and artist worked here (GLC 1977).

Henri Gaudier joined his name to Sophie Brzeska's after they met in Paris in 1910. In his short artistic life he was one of the most creative members of the Vorticists, contributing to the group's magazine *Blast* and becoming close friends with the poet Ezra Pound. He took Studio 5 at the rear of 454 Fulham Road from late in 1912 until his departure for France in 1914 and produced some of his most important work there. He began carving a head of Pound in 1914 but at the outbreak of war he enlisted in the French army and was killed in 1915.

Gertler, Mark.

32 Elder Street, E1
Mark Gertler (1891–1939) painter lived here (GLC 1975).

32 Elder Street, Spitalfields, is a listed three-storey house built in the late 1720s. Mark Gertler lived there with his eldest brother and his family from 1911 to 1915. Though the Gertlers were extremely poor, Mark was given art materials when he showed an interest in drawing; his first works were done on the paving stones of their yard in Whitechapel. He attended the Slade School and joined the New English Art Club in 1912. With his obvious talent and exotic appearance he was quickly taken up by patrons of the arts — Edward Marsh and Lady Ottoline Morrell — and became friends with leading artists of the day — D.H. Lawrence (who based the character of Loerke in *Women in Love* on him), Roger Fry, Virginia Woolf and Lytton Strachey. Gertler continued to paint between the wars but he suffered from depression and ill-health and committed suicide at his home in Highgate.

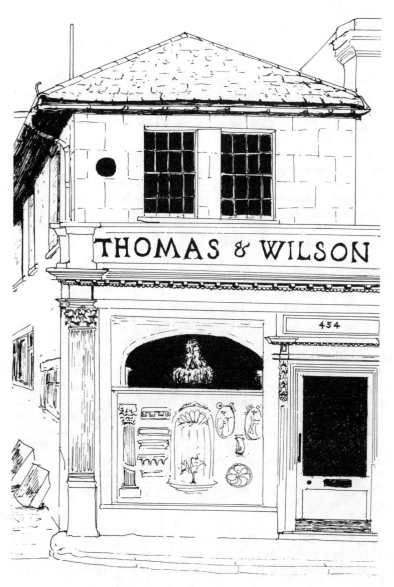

Henri Gaudier-Brezska, 454 Fulham Road

105

Gibbon, Edward.

7 Bentinck Street, W1
Edward Gibbon (1737–1792) historian lived in a house on this site 1773–1783 (GLC 1964).

When Edward Gibbon's father died in 1770 he left his son in comfortable financial circumstances enabling him to settle at 7 Bentinck Street. Gibbon was elected professor of ancient history at the Royal Academy and began work on *Decline and Fall of the Roman Empire*. The idea for the study came to him while he was musing among the ruins of the Capitol in Rome; the first volume appeared in 1776. Meanwhile Gibbon had joined Samuel Johnson's club, become an MP and Commissioner of Trade and Plantations. In 1783 he moved permanently to Lausanne, seeking more seclusion to write the last three volumes of *Decline and Fall* (1788).

Gibbons, Grinling. *See* BOW STREET.

Gilbert, Sir **William Schwenck.**

39 Harrington Gardens, SW7
Sir W.S. Gilbert (1836–1911) dramatist lived here (LCC 1929).

William Schwenck Gilbert lived at 39 Harrington Gardens from 1883 to 1890, during which time he wrote *The Mikado, The Yeomen of the Guard* and *The Gondoliers*. The house was built specially for him, designed by George and Peto, and equipped with unusual amenities such as central heating, a bathroom on every floor and a telephone. The collaboration of Gilbert and Sullivan, notably in the musical *Patience* in 1881 which ran for 578 performances, brought both men great wealth and fame. Gilbert and his wife were childless but they enjoyed the company of children and held many parties for them at Harrington Gardens. Later they adopted the American singer Nancy McIntosh as their daughter. In 1890 the Gilberts moved to Grimsdyke in the Harrow Weald, a house built for the painter Frederick Goodall by Shaw. (*See also* R. Norman Shaw.)

Gissing, George.

33 Oakley Gardens, SW3
George Gissing (1857–1903) novelist lived here 1882–1884 (GLC 1975).

George Gissing lived at over 13 different addresses in the 14 years he spent in London. One of his longer periods of residence was at 33 Oakley Gardens. Gissing lived in sometimes shabby, sometimes 'genteel' poverty all his life — his novel *New Grub Street* (1891) reveals his struggles as an unsuccessful novelist — and in the 1880s Chelsea provided inexpensive lodging for artists.

Gissing was dogged by ill-fortune, often of his own making. He first married a prostitute (who died), then another working-class girl, and he spent the last five years of his life living with Gabrielle Fleury, who translated his novels into French. He died in France in 1903.

Gissing's first novel *Workers in the Dawn* was written at one of his London residences that still remains intact, 60 Noel Road, Islington. When he moved to Chelsea he decided to earn his living solely by writing novels rather than magazine articles. He wrote *The Unclassed*, a novel about exiles from society, a group with which he strongly identified.

Gladstone, William Ewart.

11 Carlton House Terrace, SW1
William Ewart Gladstone (1809–1898) statesman lived here (LCC 1925).

Eglinton Road School, Plumstead, SE18
W.E. Gladstone delivered his last speech to his Greenwich constituents 30 November 1873 on the site of this plaque (private).

During his time at Carlton House Terrace (1856–75) Gladstone was Chancellor of the Exchequer (1859–66,), Leader of the Opposition (1867–8) and Prime Minister (1868–74). He also found time to pursue his literary studies and published *Studies in Homer and the Homeric Age* in 1858. Gladstone was the longest serving-public figure in Victorian times, with the exception of Victoria herself. He retired when he was 83 and was affectionately known as the GOM, 'Grand Old Man' (*see also* Sir CHARLES LYELL and WILLIAM PITT [Earl of Chatham]).

Glaisher, James.

20 Dartmouth Hill, SE10
James Glaisher (1809–1903) astronomer meteorologist and pioneer of weather forecasting lived here (GLC 1974).

James Glaisher lived at 20 Dartmouth Hill from about 1863 until 1894 or later. He was chief of the newly established magnetic and meteorological department at Greenwich Observatory from 1838 until his retirement in 1874 and he organised the system of precise daily observation and recording of the weather in Britain that is still used. Glaisher made some spectacular balloon ascents and in 1862 he risked his life by ascending to 37,000 feet without breathing apparatus.

Godley, John Robert.

48 Gloucester Place, W1
   John Robert Godley (1814-1861) founder of Canterbury New Zealand lived and died here (LCC 1951).

   John Robert Godley was managing director of the Canterbury Association, an organisation founded to establish a colony of Church of England people, representing all classes of English society in New Zealand, who would govern themselves right from the beginning. Godley was the chief architect of the scheme and after the first settlers began to arrive in December 1850 he was virtual governor of the colony for the next two years. He returned to England in 1852 and took a position in the war office.

Godwin, George.

24 Alexander Square, SW7
   George Godwin (1813-1888) architect journalist and social reformer lived here (GLC 1969).

   George Godwin lived at 24 Alexander Square from about 1850 to 1873. He designed several local churches, St Jude's, Collingham Road, and St Luke's, Redcliffe Square, and the layout of the Boltons. In the pages of *The Builder*, which he edited from 1844 to 1883, he expressed his concern to use architecture as a means towards affecting essential social reforms; he campaigned in particular to improve sanitary conditions in working-class dwellings.

Goldschmidt, Madame. *See* LIND, JENNY.

Goodall, Frederick. *See* SHAW, R. NORMAN.

Gounod, Charles.

15 Morden Road, SE3
   Charles Gounod (1818-1893) composer stayed here in 1870 (LCC 1961).

Charles Gounod stayed in the mid-Victorian detached house, 15 Morden Road, from the beginning of October until 10 November 1870. He left France with his family after war was declared on Russia and remained in London until 1874. In France he had concentrated on writing opera: *Faust* (1859) and *Roméo et Juliette* (1867). In London he became addicted to oratorios, considered at that time to represent the highest form of musical expression in England, and when he later returned to France he wrote *The Redemption* (1882) and *Mors et vita* (1885).

Grace, W.G.

Fairmount, Mottingham Lane, Bromley
  W.G. Grace (1848–1915) cricketer lived here (GLC 1966).

W.G. Grace practised in Bristol as a surgeon for most of his working life and only went to London when he was made manager of cricket at the Crystal Palace in 1899. He lived at Fairmount from 1909 to 1915. Grace started the Gloucestershire County XI with two of his brothers in 1870 and played for them until 1899, the year he played for England for the last time. In his cricketing career of 43 years he took nearly 3000 wickets and scored over 50,000 runs. He played his last game in 1914.

Grahame, Kenneth.

16 Phillimore Place, W8
  Kenneth Grahame (1859–1932) author of 'Wind in the Willows' lived here 1901–1908 (LCC 1959).

Kenneth Grahame took a long lease of 16 Durham Villas (now Phillimore Place) after his marriage to Elspeth Thomson in 1899 and lived on Campden Hill until 1908 when he moved permanently to Cookham Dean, near Marlow. Writing was not his full-time occupation: he worked for the Bank of England but retired in 1908, the year *The Wind in the Willows* was published.

Grahame was already well known as the author of *The Golden Age* (1895) and *Dream Days* (1898) when he moved to Durham Villas. He charmed his readers by re-creating the world of childhood in the English countryside.

Gray, Henry.

8 Wilton Street, SW1
Henry Gray (1827–1861) anatomist lived here (LCC 1947).

Henry Gray lived in Wilton Street for the greater part of his life. He became a student at St George's Hospital in 1845 and when he was only 25 he was elected a Fellow of the Royal Society. In 1853 his most famous work, *Anatomy*, was published. It has remained the standard textbook for medical students ever since, no other work being as detailed or well illustrated. Gray contracted smallpox from his nephew and died in 1861 when he was 34 years old.

Gray, Thomas.

39 Cornhill, EC3
Thomas Gray (1716–1771) poet was born in a house on this site. 'The curfew tolls the knell of parting day' (tablet portrait given by Alderman Sir Edward E. Cooper 1918).

Thomas Gray was the surviving child of a mentally unbalanced 'money scrivener' in the City of London. Through the efforts of his mother and an uncle, Gray was sent to Eton where he became friends with Horace Walpole. After a period of estrangement (they quarrelled while on the Grand Tour together) they resumed their friendship and Gray was a frequent visitor to Strawberry Hill. His *Ode on the Death of a Favourite Cat* (1747) described Walpole's pet cat. When he completed his best-known poem, *Elegy Written in a Country Churchyard* (1742–50), Gray sent it to Walpole, who persuaded him to publish it. It was an instant success and four editions were printed in two months.

Greaves, Walter.

104 Cheyne Walk, SW3
Walter Greaves (1846–1930) artist lived here 1855–1897 (GLC 1973).

Walter Greaves's father was a boatbuilder and was employed by J.M.W. Turner to row him across the river. His two sons, Walter and Henry, were to become close friends with Whistler who was a near neighbour. Whistler influenced Walter's paintings, though as Walter pointed out there was a basic difference in their attitudes to boats: 'Mr Whistler put his boats in wherever he wanted them, but we left them just where they were. . .to Mr Whistler a boat was a tone, but to us it was always a boat'. Greaves spent most of his life in virtual obscurity:

'Chelsea Regatta' and 'Boat Race Day, Hammersmith Bridge' are two of his better-known paintings.

Green, John Richard.

St Philip's Vicarage, Newark Street, E1
John Richard Green (1837–1883) historian of the English people lived here 1866–1869 (LCC 1910).

4 Beaumont Street, W1
John Richard Green (1837–1883) historian of the English people lived here (LCC 1964).

After taking holy orders Green was appointed to St Philip's, Stepney, in November 1865. But the anxieties of his East End parish, pressures from writing reviews and literary papers, and his increasingly liberal views on theological matters made Green give up his clerical career and accept the senior librarianship at Lambeth. He moved to 4 Beaumont Street in 1869, remaining there until 1876, and began work almost immediately on the project which first brought him success as a historian, his *Short History of the English People* (1874).

Green's house in Beaumont Street was demolished in 1924 and the unusual interior decorations created by a Pre-Raphaelite friend were lost: 'the result is wonderful. The end of my room reminds me of a conflagration — beneath, heaven; above a brilliant red! The doors are in the sea-sickness style, green picked out with a sickly blue! My poor old writing-desk, dear from many an association, had been clothed in light blue with lines of red. When I re-entered my rooms for the first time, my artistic friend had just begun covering it with black dragons'.

Greenaway, Kate.

39 Frognal, NW3
Kate Greenaway (1846–1901) artist lived and died here (LCC 1949).

Opinions of the sweetly innocent children Kate Greenaway created in her children's books, alphabets and almanacks, with their ribbons and mob-caps, have ranged from accusation (that she created 'a false and degenerate race of children in art') to rapture (her works are like a 'Midsummer Day's Dream in Modern England'). She moved to Frognal in 1885, to a house Norman Shaw designed for her. One of her closest friends was John Ruskin, who was shocked by her move to Frognal and particularly disliked the name of the area.

Greenwood, John. *See* CLINK PRISON.

Greet, Sir **Philip Benjamin.**

160 Lambeth Road, SE1
   Sir Philip Ben Greet (1857–1936) actor-manager lived here 1920–1936 (LCC 1961).

Philip Benjamin Greet took up theatre management in London in 1886 and was particularly keen to promote open-air performances of Shakespeare. From 1914 he worked in collaboration with Lilian Baylis at the Old Vic. Ben Greet never married and lived with the Keys family at 160 Lambeth Road. He was knighted for his services 'to drama and to education' in 1929: he had formed a company for the presentation of Shakespeare in LCC schools and educational centres in 1918.

Gresham, Sir **Thomas.**

Gresham House, 24 Old Broad Street, EC2
   In a house on this site lived Sir Thomas Gresham (1519–1579) (City of London).

Thomas Gresham built Gresham House in about 1560 when he was at the height of his distinguished career as agent to the Crown supervising the royal finances. He entertained lavishly at Gresham House; Sir Robert Cecil, a close friend, was a frequent guest and Queen Elizabeth dined there on a progress through the City of London. He made a large private fortune out of his work as a government financier and in 1565 he offered to build an exchange for the merchants of London, at his own expense, if the City provided a site. The site chosen was on the north side of Cornhill (where the present Royal Exchange is) and it was built, like Gresham House, over piazzas supported by marble pillars and forming covered walks opening into an inner courtyard.

Grey, Sir **Edward.**

1–3 Queen Anne's Gate, SW7
   Viscount Grey of Falloden Sir Edward Grey (1862–1933) Foreign Secretary lived here (GLC c1981).

Edward Grey lived at 3 Queen Anne's Gate from 1906 to 1912, during which time he was Foreign Secretary under Campbell-Bannerman and Asquith. Sir Henry Newbolt described an evening spent with Grey in the house: 'last night we talked birds, gardens and music during dinner, and I was attracted by Grey's account of the Horticultural Society. His whole smoking room was full of the scent of flowers'. Grey was largely responsible for constructing agreements between Britain, France and Russia for their mutual defence in case of German attack; this eventually brought Britain into World War I.

Grossmith, George (i).

28 Dorset Square, NW1
   George Grossmith (1847-1912) actor and author lived here (LCC 1963).

The elder George Grossmith moved to 28 Dorset Square in 1885 and remained there for over 15 years. His father was a police reporter for *The Times* and George acted as deputy at Bow Street police court until he was engaged by Richard D'Oyly Carte to take the part of John Wellington Wells in Gilbert and Sullivan's *The Sorcerer*. He appeared in Gilbert and Sullivan operas for the next 12 years, creating many famous roles. With his brother Walter Weedon Grossmith he wrote *The Diary of a Nobody* (1894), ostensibly written by a pompous London clerk; it was first published in *Punch* and has become a classic of English comic fiction.

Grossmith, George (ii).

3 Spanish Place, W1
   George Grossmith (1874-1935) actor-manager lived here (LCC 1963).

The younger George Grossmith's first stage appearance was in 1892 in *Haste to the Wedding*, a musical play adapted by Gilbert and with music by Grossmith's father. He acted in the USA as well as London, appearing in a succession of popular musicals. In 1909 he moved to 3 Spanish Place, where he lived until his death. Grossmith was manager of several London theatres and in 1925 he appeared in one of his greatest successes *No! No! Nanette*. He was also involved in the beginnings of the cinema.

Grote, George.

12 Savile Row, W1
   George Grote (1894-1871) historian died here (LCC 1905).

The Grotes moved to Savile Row in May 1848. *Plato and the Other Companions of Sokrates* was published in 1865 and Grote's greatest

113

Grote, George

historical work, *The History of Greece*, was published in 12 volumes between 1846 and 1856. Grote was an active liberal reformer and a major force in the founding of London University. After Brougham's death Grote became chancellor of the university in 1868.

Haggard, Sir Henry Rider.

69 Gunterstone Road, W14
Sir Henry Rider Haggard (1856–1925) novelist lived here 1885–1888 (GLC 1977).

After working as secretary to Sir Henry Bulwer, Governor of Natal, and attempting to farm ostriches in the Transvaal, Rider Haggard was called to the Bar in January 1885. He moved to Gunterstone Road the same year, just after the house was built, and began writing novels to relieve the monotony of his legal practice. *King Solomon's Mines* was published in September 1885 and was a great success. *Allan Quatermain* and *She* followed in 1887 and Haggard was able to give up his legal practice. He settled down to the life of a country gentleman on his wife's estate at Ditchingham Hall, Norfolk, and became an authority on the conditions of agriculture and the rural population; he was knighted for this work in 1912.

Haldane, Richard Burdon, Lord.

28 Queen Anne's Gate, SW7
Lord Haldane (1856–1928) statesman lawyer and philosopher lived here (LCC 1954).

28 Queen Anne's Gate was built in about 1704. Lord Haldane lived in the street from 1907 until 1928. He served as Secretary of State for

115

War (1905-12) in Asquith's Liberal government, but Asquith excluded him from the Cabinet in 1915 and Haldane found more sympathy for his progressive ideas, particularly in education, among leaders of the socialist party. He helped to found the London School of Economics with the Webbs and was also a supporter of the working-class education movement. From 1925 to his death he was leader of the Labour peers in the House of Lords.

Hallam, Henry.

67 Wimpole Street, W1
   Henry Hallam (1777-1859) historian lived here (LCC 1904).

Henry Hallam practised as a barrister but after the death of his father he was able to retire from the law and devote himself to studying history. His reputation was established with *A View of the State of Europe during the Middle Ages* (1818) and he moved to 67 Wimpole Street the year after its publication, remaining there until 1841. The most famous of his children (more famous now than his father) was Arthur Henry Hallam, the close friend of Tennyson. His early death in 1833 at the age of 22 inspired *In Memoriam* in which Tennyson referred to Wimpole Street as the 'long unlovely street'. Mr Barrett, father of Elizabeth Barrett Browning, lived at no.50 from 1838 to 1846.

Hammond, John Laurence; Hammond, Barbara.

Hollycot, Vale of Health, NW3
   J.L. and Barbara Hammond social historians lived here 1906-1913 (GLC 1972).

John Laurence Hammond began his career in journalism in 1885 as editor of *The Speaker*, a new liberal weekly. This became *The Nation* in 1907. H.W. Massingham took over the editorship and Hammond remained as a regular leader writer. He had married Lucy Barbara Bradby in 1901 and together they produced important pioneering studies of labour history, including *The Village Labourer 1760-1832* (1911), *The Town Labourer 1760-1832* (1917) and *The Skilled Labourer 1760-1832* (1919).

Handel, George Frideric.

25 Brook Street, W1
   George Frideric Handel (1865-1759) musician lived and died here (LCC 1952).

116

Handel first went to London early in 1710. He returned in 1712 and remained for the rest of his life, except for visits to the Continent. When George I succeeded to the throne in 1714, Handel, as a self-imposed exile from Germany, found himself out of favour with the Hanoverian court. On 22 August 1715 the royal family travelled by water from Whitehall to Limehouse and Handel, in a bid to restore his fortunes, it is said, wrote the *Water Music* which was played in a barge following the king's. The king was so impressed that he awarded Handel a pension for life.

Handley, Tommy.

34 Craven Road, W2
Tommy Handley (1892-1949) radio comedian lived here (GLC 1979).

Tommy Handley kept a flat in the four-storey mid-19th-century block near Paddington throughout World War II and until his death. He started working with the BBC in 1925, appearing in revues, vaudeville, operetta and pantomime. Lasting fame came with the absurd weekly show 'ITMA' ('It's that Man Again') which Handley wrote with Ted Kavanagh and Francis Worsley and which was broadcast throughout the war.

Hansom, Joseph Aloysius.

27 Sumner Place, SW7
Joseph Aloysius Hansom (1803-1882) architect founder-editor of 'The Builder' and inventor of the Hansom Cab lived here (GLC c1981).

Joseph Hansom set up in practice as an architect in Halifax. He won a competition to design Birmingham Town Hall in 1831, but he was forced to stand bond for the contractors and as a result was declared bankrupt. In order to recoup his fortune he patented a design for a 'safety cab' in 1836; this was to become the Hansom cab. He made no money from the enterprise and in 1842 he started *The Builder*, a periodical for the architectural trades. Hansom returned to architecture and designed churches. He lived at Sumner Place from 1873 to 1877.

Hardy, Thomas.

172 Trinity Road, SW17
Thomas Hardy (1840-1928) poet and novelist lived here 1878-1881 (LCC 1940).

Thomas Hardy, 172 Trinity Road

Thomas Hardy moved to 1 Arundel Terrace (now 172 Trinity Road) when *The Return of the Native* was two-thirds finished. He spent his days in the British Museum doing research into naval and military practice in the reign of George III for *The Trumpet-Major*. He described the view from the bedroom window of the unassuming mid-Victorian house in Tooting: 'daybreak: just past three. A golden light behind the horizon; within it are the Four Millions. The roofs are damp grey; streets are still filled with night as with a dark stagnant flood whose surface brims to the top of the houses. Above, the air is light. A fire or two glares within the mass. Behind are Highgate Hills. On the Crystal Palace hills in the other direction a lamp is still burning up in the daylight. The lamps are also still flickering in the street and one police-man walks down it as if it were noon'.

Hardy fell ill in October 1880 and was forced to stay in bed and dictate his next work *A Laodicean* to his wife Emma — a trying task as their marriage was already burdensome to him. The Hardys returned to Dorset the following year.

Harley, Robert [Earl of Oxford]. *See* PEPYS, SAMUEL.

Harmsworth, Alfred.

Hunt Cottage, Vale of Health, NW3
   From 1870 to 1873 this cottage was the home of Alfred and Geraldine Mary Harmsworth the parents of Viscount Northcliffe, Viscount Rothermere, Lord Harmsworth and of Sir Leicester and Sir Hildebrand Harmsworth (Hampstead Plaque Fund).

31 Pandora Road, NW6
   Alfred Harmsworth Viscount Northcliffe (1865–1922) journalist and newspaper proprietor lived here (GLC 1979).

The plaque to Alfred Harmsworth was unveiled by his nephew Sir Geoffrey Harmsworth who recalled the establishing of his uncle's first weekly papers while in Pandora Road: '*Comic Cuts* and *Answers to Correspondents* were conceived in the attic and led to bigger things'. They achieved large circulations and were the foundation of his fortune. Harmsworth moved to Pandora Road in 1888 and remained in the red-brick Victorian house until 1891. He was to acquire the *Evening News* (1894), to found the *Daily Mail* (1896) and the *Daily Mirror* (1903) and to own both *The Times* and the *Observer*.

Harrison, John.

Summit House, Red Lion Square, WC1
John Harrison (1693–1776) inventor of the marine chronometer lived and died in a house on this site (LCC 1954).

An Act of Parliament in 1713 offered rewards to inventors of an accurate method of determining longitude. John Harrison built five chronometers and after severe tests, two Acts of Parliament and the personal intervention of the king, he received his reward. From 1752 to 1776 he occupied a house at the corner of Red Lion Square and Dane Street which has been replaced by an office block.

Harte, Francis Bret.

74 Lancaster Gate, W2
Francis Bret Harte (1836–1902) American writer lived and died here (GLC 1977).

Francis Bret Harte wrote his most successful stories of life in the American West, including *The Ballad of the Heathen Chinee* (1868) and *The Luck of Roaring Camp* (1870), early in his writing career. When he went to London in 1885 he made a living selling revamped Californian tales to British magazines. 74 Lancaster Gate was designed by Sancton Wood and built in 1887; Harte lived there from 1895 to 1902.

Hawkins, Sir **Anthony Hope.** *See* HOPE, Sir ANTHONY.

Hawthorne, Nathaniel.

4 Pond Road, SE3
Nathaniel Hawthorne (1804–1864) American author stayed here in 1856 (LCC 1953).

Nathaniel Hawthorne was appointed US consul in Liverpool in 1853 and from July to September 1856 he and his family stayed in the house of the journalist Francis Bennock, now 4 Pond Street, Blackheath. He wrote of his stay as 'some of the happiest hours that I have known since we left our American home'. Hawthorne began writing in his early 20s but his publications received little attention until 1850, when *The Scarlet Letter* was published. This was followed by *The House of the Seven Gables* (1851). Hawthorne was one of America's earliest major novelists; one of his recurrent themes was moral ambiguity in American society.

Haydon, Benjamin.

116 Lisson Grove, NW8
Benjamin Haydon (1786–1846) painter and Charles Rossi (1762–1839) sculptor lived here (LCC 1959).

Charles Rossi bought land from a Colonel Eyre in 1808 and built the house that is now 116 Lisson Grove. Benjamin Haydon's health was poor because of the foul air of his previous studio; he moved into part of Rossi's house in 1817. The house became a meeting-place for Romantic writers and artists. Keats and Wordsworth first met at a dinner given by Haydon: 'an immortal evening. Wordsworth's fine intonation as he quoted Milton and Virgil, Keats' eager inspired look, Lamb's quaint sparkle of lambent humour, so speeded the stream of conversation, that in my life I never passed a more delightful time'.

Haydon was not as financially successful as his landlord. His large paintings of scenes from the Bible attracted much attention but few buyers. Rossi, however, was employed by the prince regent to decorate Buckingham Palace and in 1819 he and his son Henry decorated the new church of St Pancras and carved its eight colossal caryatids. Haydon left Lisson Grove in 1820 and committed suicide in 1846.

Hazlitt, William.

6 Bouverie Street, EC4
In a house on this site lived William Hazlitt 1829 (City of London).

6 Frith Street, W1
William Hazlitt (1778–1830) essayist died here (LCC 1905).

William Hazlitt took lodgings at 6 Frith Street early in 1830. The street was named after Richard Frith, citizen and bricklayer, and no.6 was built in 1718. Hazlitt wrote his last essays, including *The Sick Chamber*, in his lodgings and died there on 18 September: his last words were 'Well, I've had a happy life'.

The French Revolution was an inspiration to the young Hazlitt and, unlike many of his fellow Romantics, he maintained his early enthusiasm for it, criticising Coleridge for turning from radical to conservative. Hazlitt's important place in 19th-century thought was earned by his critical writing and lectures and particularly his attempts to write a history of English literature based on the development of ideas.

Heath Robinson, William.

75 Moss Lane, Pinner
W. Heath Robinson (1872–1944) illustrator and comic artist lived here 1913–1918 (GLC 1976).

Heath Robinson invented Uncle Lubin, his 'good genius', in 1902; the drawings for the *Adventures of Uncle Lubin* became the forerunners of his familiar ramshackle, complicated contraptions which have made his name a common adjective. He first moved to Pinner in 1905 but in 1913 he moved to 75 Moss Lane. During the war Heath Robinson was commissioned to make humorous drawings for the US army in France and he was arrested for sketching in St Nazaire harbour.

Heine, Heinrich.

32 Craven Street, WC2
Heinrich Heine (1799–1856) German poet and essayist lived here 1827 (LCC 1912).

Heinrich Heine made one visit to England: in 1827 he stayed from April to July in Craven Street. He spoke no English and found conditions in London wretched: 'it is snowing outside, and there is no fire in my chimney. . . . I am very peevish and ill to boot. . . . It is so fearfully damp and uncomfortable here, and no-one understands me, and no-one understands German'. He decided London was no place for a poet: 'the mere seriousness of everything, the colossal uniformity, the machine-like movement, the shrillness even of joy — this over-driven London oppresses fancy and rends the heart'. Paris became Heine's home from 1831 until his death. He spent the last eight years of his life confined to a 'mattress grave' by a spinal disease.

Heine is best known for his early poems, combining Romantic melody and satire; many were published in *Buch der Lieder* (1827).

Henderson, Arthur.

13 Rodenhurst Road, SW4
Arthur Henderson (1863–1935) statesman lived here (GLC 1980).

Arthur Henderson first became an MP in 1903 and formed the leadership of the new Labour Party with Ramsay MacDonald and Keir Hardie. The period he spent at 13 Rodenhurst Road (1909–21) was when he made his greatest contribution to the party's organisation. He was its secretary from 1911 to 1934 and, with MacDonald and Sidney Webb, he was responsible for establishing an internationalist and democratic labour party standing apart from the communism which attracted many European socialist parties. Henderson won the Nobel Peace Prize in 1934 for his work with the League of Nations.

Henty, George Alfred.

33 Lavender Gardens, SW11
G.A. Henty (1832-1902) author lived here (LCC 1953).

When George Alfred Henty lived at Lavender Gardens between 1894 and 1902 he was writing three or four adventure stories for boys a year. His favourite themes were colonial and military history. Henty led an adventurous life as a journalist before he took up story-writing full time. He accompanied Lord Napier to Abyssinia; starved in Paris during the Commune; witnessed the Russian conquest of Khiva; followed Lord Wolseley's expedition to Ashanti and experienced hand-to-hand fighting in the Turco-Servian War.

Herlan, Hugh.

24/25 Upper Thames Street, EC4
In a house on this site Hugh Herlan Chief Carpenter to Edward III, Richard II, Henry IV, Designer of Westminster Hall Roof (City of London).

Herzen, Alexander.

1 Orsett Terrace, W2
Alexander Herzen (1812-1870) Russian political thinker lived here 1860-1863 (GLC 1970).

Alexander Herzen came to England in 1852 and remained for nearly 12 years, becoming one of the most influential figures in Russian political thinking. He had left Russia in 1847 after years of conflict with the authorities and periods of imprisonment and banishment. Herzen established the Free Russian Press in Regent Square in 1853; the review *The Polar Star* began to appear in 1855 and *The Bell* in 1857. *The Bell* was issued at least once a month for ten years and smuggled into Russia. It achieved a wide circulation and advocated many reforms.

Russian visitors to England invariably went to Herzen's home in Orsett Terrace. They included Tolstoy (1861), Dostoyevsky (July 1862) and Bakunin (December 1861). Dostoyevsky described Herzen as 'an artist, a thinker, a brilliant writer, an extraordinarily well-read man, a wit [and] and wonderful conversationalist'.

Hill, Sir **Rowland.**

1 Orme Square, WC2
   Sir Rowland Hill (1795–1879) postal reformer lived here (LCC 1907).

Royal Free Hospital, Pond Street, NW3
   Sir Rowland Hill KCB originator of the penny post lived here 1849–1879. Born 1795, died 1879 (RSA 1892; re-erected on new building by GLC 1978).

Rowland Hill first planned his penny post while working as secretary to the South Australian Commission; two years later he sent a pamphlet, *Post Office Reform: its Importance and Practicability*, to the government, which was against his idea but was forced to yield to popular demand: the penny post was included in the Budget for 1839.

Rowland Hill lived at 1 Orme Square from 1839 to 1844. He moved to Hampstead in 1848. Bertram House, 'a large square brick house' (on the site of the new Royal Free Hospital), remained his home until his death. Gladstone said of his postal reform that it 'had run like wildfire through the civilized world'.

Hogarth, William.

Hogarth House, Hogarth Lane, W4
   William Hogarth (1697–1764) painter and engraver lived here for 15 years (Middlesex County Council *c*1904).

William Hogarth bought his villa in Chiswick in September 1749. He had been living in Leicester Fields for 15 years, becoming increasingly prosperous and famous, and he needed a country residence. Hogarth's house still looks much as it did when he was a resident. His studio, with its large window, was above the stable (which has been demolished): 'his paintings. . .would be let down through this window, for transmission, in his carriage, to town'. The mulberry tree from which Hogarth is supposed to have fed the village children is still in the garden. A visitor to the garden in 1780 found 'a rude and shapeless stone, placed upright against the wall' carved by Hogarth in memory of his pet bullfinch: 'ALAS POOR DICK! O.B.1760 AGED ELEVEN'. Hogarth is buried in the nearby church of St Nicholas, his tomb shaped like a teacaddy. Hogarth House is a museum and open to the public.

William Hogarth, Hogarth House, Hogarth Lane

Hogg, Quintin.

5 Cavendish Square, W1

Quintin Hogg (1845–1903) founder of the Polytechnic Regent Street lived here 1885–1898 (LCC 1965).

Quintin Hogg was the son of a wealthy East India merchant and worked for a firm of sugar merchants until his retirement in 1898. At the same time he pursued various schemes for educating poor children in London, starting a 'Ragged School' and the Youths' Christian Institute. In 1882 the institute opened with 2000 members at its new premises in Regent Street which Hogg had bought and renovated; it was renamed the Polytechnic of Regent Street. Hogg described his aims: 'what we wanted to develop our institute into was a place which should recognise that God has given man more than one side to his character, and where we could gratify any personal taste, whether athletic, intellectual, spiritual, or social'.

Holman-Hunt, William.

18 Melbury Road, W14

William Holman-Hunt, OM (1827–1910) painter lived and died here (LCC 1923).

William Holman-Hunt was the most forceful proponent of Pre-Raphaelitism and he first achieved popular success in 1854 with two paintings, 'The Light of the World' and 'The Awakening Conscience'. He thought of his role in life as a holy mission and made several journeys to the Holy Land to paint biblical subjects in their settings. This desire for authenticity created many problems: returning to his house in Melbury Road (where he had moved in the 1880s) after working on 'The Triumph of the Innocents' in Palestine, he was dissatisfied with the anatomy of an ass. His granddaughter Diana described the delivery of a dead tail-less horse from the knacker's yard: 'the carcass was cut into huge red joints which we carried through the drawingroom, down the steps, and laid on the grass in the garden'.

Hood, Thomas.

Midland Bank, 31 Poultry, EC2

In a house on this site Thomas Hood was born 23rd May 1799 (City of London).

59 Vicars Moor Lane, Winchmore Hill, N21

Site of Rose Cottage residence of Thomas Hood 1829–32 (private).

Devonshire Lodge, 28 Finchley Road, NW8
Thomas Hood (1799–1845) poet died here (LCC 1912).

Thomas Hood was born in the Poultry, in the house where his father kept a bookseller's shop. He began work in a counting-house but was forced to leave because of ill-health, so he took up engraving and journalism. After his marriage in 1824 he lived at 2 Robert Street remaining until 1829 (*see* ROBERT ADAM). He was often in financial trouble and spent much of his short life engaged in hackwork, editing and contributing to magazines. While living in Winchmore Hill he wrote one of his best-known serious poems, *The Dream of Eugene Aram*. *The Song of the Shirt* (1843), his bitter protest against sweated labour, appeared in *Punch*, making it a successful periodical.

Hood was the first occupant of Devonshire Lodge, which was built in 1843. His health broke down soon after moving in and his wife confessed: 'we fear the clay soil of this neighbourhood does not agree with him'. Hood died before he could move to a more sympathetic environment.

Hope [Hawkins], Sir **Anthony.**

41 Bedford Square, WC1
Sir Anthony Hope Hawkins (Antony Hope) (1863–1933) novelist lived here 1903–1917 (GLC 1976).

Anthony Hope first qualified as a barrister but he wrote novels in his spare moments. After the amazing success of *The Prisoner of Zenda* in 1894 he decided to devote himself to writing. *Rupert of Hentzau* was published in 1898. During World War I and while he was living in Bedford Square, Hope turned from writing fiction to working in the Ministry of Information.

Hopkins, Gerard Manley.

Gatepost, Manresa House, Roehampton, SW15
Gerard Manley Hopkins (1844–1889) priest and poet lived and studied at Manresa House (GLC 1979).

Gerard Manley Hopkins entered the Jesuit order as a novitiate in 1868 and spent the next two years studying at Manresa House, a Catholic seminary. He returned to the house as a teacher (1873–4) and to serve his tertianship (1881–2).

When Hopkins became a Jesuit he burnt his youthful verse as an act of renunciation, but at the request of his superiors produced one of his finest poems, *The Wreck of the Deutschland*, to commemorate the death of five Franciscan nuns in a shipwreck on the Goodwin Sands. He continued to write but almost nothing was published until after his death when his friend Robert Bridges produced a collected volume in 1918. Hopkins was a great technical innovator, coining the term 'sprung rhythm' to describe his verse. *The Windhover* is one of his best-known poems.

Manresa House was designed by Sir William Chambers and built for Lord Bessborough (1762-7).

Hore-Belisha, Leslie, Lord.

16 Stafford Place, SW1
Lord Hore-Belisha (1893-1957) statesman lived here (GLC 1980).

During his time as Minister of Transport (1934-7) Leslie Hore-Belisha gave his name to 'Belisha beacons', which he introduced as part of a campaign to reduce road accidents. He bought 16 Stafford Place in 1936 and moved the following year after the house had been altered for him by Edward Lutyens. He moved to the War Office in 1937 but made many enemies among the older service officials by being in favour of developing a small-scale mechanised expeditionary force of high quality rather than a large army on the lines of that of World War I. Hore-Belisha resigned rather than abandoning his principles.

Horsley, John Callcott. *See* CLEMENTI, MUZIO.

Housman, Alfred Edward.

17 North Road, N6
A.E. Housman (1859-1936) poet and scholar wrote 'A Shropshire Lad' while living here (GLC 1969).

Byron Cottage, 17 North Road, was built early in the 18th century. A.E. Housman wrote 'while at University College, which is not residential, I lived alone in lodgings in the environs of London. *A Shropshire Lad* was written at Byron Cottage...where I lived from 1886 to 1905'. Housman was a shy and retiring scholar, deeply pessimistic and sensitive. He was professor of Latin at University College London from 1892 to 1911 and published his finest collection of poetry *A Shropshire Lad* in 1896. His wistful, melancholy poems were inspired by the English countryside, particularly Worcestershire (where he was born), and his love of young men.

Howard, Sir Ebenezer.

Moor House, London Wall, EC2

Near this spot at 62 Fore Street on the 29th January 1850 was born Sir Ebenezer Howard, Founder of the Garden City Movement (City of London).

Ebenezer Howard's interest in improving the living standards of his contemporaries and encouraging service to the community rather than self-interest came after reading the American Edward Bellamy's *Looking Backward*, a vision of an ideal civilisation in the year 2000. His own version, *Tomorrow. A Peaceful Path to Real Reform*, was published in 1898 and advocated 'garden cities', newly built municipally owned towns of mixed residential and industrial buildings surrounded by rural belts. A year later he founded the Garden City Association and the planning of Letchworth, the first garden city, was begun in 1903.

Howard, John.

23 Great Ormond Street, WC1

John Howard (1726?–1790) prison reformer lived here (LCC 1908).

John Howard lived in Great Ormond Street from 1777 to 1790 but he maintained a country seat in Bedfordshire where he served as high sheriff from 1773.

He was often abroad, inspecting the prisons of Europe and supplementing his great work *The State of the Prisons in England and Wales, with Preliminary Observations, and an Account of some Foreign Prisons*. His reforming work was directed towards the county jails of England, and he obtained Acts of Parliament for the abolition of jailers' fees and for sanitary improvements. His final work, *An Account of the Principal Lazarettos in Europe*, was published in 1789.

Hudson, William Henry.

40 St Luke's Road, W10

W.H. Hudson's friends' Society of Quilmes, near Buenos Aires, where the great writer was born on August 4th, 1841, and where he spent his youth, has placed this bronze plaque at 40 St. Luke's Road, London, the house in which Hudson lived his last years, and died on August 18th, 1922 (LCC 1938).

'I'm not one of your damned writers', said W.H. Hudson, 'I'm a naturalist from La Plata.' Hudson spent his childhood roaming the pampas of Argentina and did not leave South America until 1869. He settled in London, lonely and extremely poor, and struggled to keep himself and his wife alive with hack-writing after their first boarding-house failed. He achieved some success with *Green Mansions* (1904) with its haunting heroine, Rima, the bird-girl. Hudson's fortune further improved when, as Ford Madox Ford recounted: 'his wife inherited a fantastically gloomy house in the most sooty neighbourhood of London and a small sum of money with which she set up a boarding-house that this time did not fail'. This was 40 St Luke's Road and its position close to Paddington Station was particularly suitable for the Hudsons: 'they could slip away from there to the country...going away towards English greennesses, through the most lugubrious streets the world could imagine'.

Hughes, Mary.

71 Vallance Road, E1
Mary Hughes (1860–1941) friend of all in need, lived and worked here 1926–1941 (LCC 1961).

When Mary Hughes bought 71 Vallance Road in 1926 it was a notorious public house. She renamed it 'The Dewdrop Inn', a centre for 'education and joy', and took in lodgers, held trade-union meetings during the week and Christian Socialist gatherings on Sundays. Financially independent (her father Thomas Hughes wrote *Tom Brown's Schooldays*), she devoted her energies to helping the East End poor as philanthropist and enlightened JP. She was an invalid for the last years of her life after being knocked down by a tram while taking part in a march for the unemployed.

Hunt, James Henry Leigh.

Vale of Health, NW3
Leigh Hunt poet lived in a cottage on this site (1816–1821) (LCC 1905).

22 Upper Cheyne Row, SW3
Leigh Hunt (1784–1859) essayist and poet lived here (LCC 1905).

16 Rowan Road, W6
Leigh Hunt (1784–1859) lived here (private).

James Henry Leigh Hunt is now better known for his friendship with the young Romantic poets, particularly Lamb, Shelley and Byron, than for his poetry and essays. In his youth he shared their rebellious attitudes and was imprisoned for two years for calling the prince regent a fat Adonis of 50. He travelled in Italy with Byron and

Shelley and was present at Shelley's cremation. He founded *The Examiner* with his brother John, editing the paper for 13 years. He not only raised the standards of newspaper writing but produced an independent radical paper which consistently demanded parliamentary reform, even though he and his brother were prosecuted three times for political offences.

Leigh Hunt, his wife and their seven children lived at 4 (now 22) Upper Cheyne Row from 1833 to 1840. He enjoyed Chelsea: 'the end of the world. The air of the neighbouring river so refreshing and the quiet of the "no thoroughfare" so full of repose that although our fortunes were at their worst, and my health almost of a piece with them, I felt for some weeks as if I could sit still for ever, embalmed in silence'. Carlyle was living nearby, at 24 Cheyne Row, but found the Hunts' house far from peaceful: 'his house excels all you have ever read of a political Tinkerdom, without parallel even in literature. In his family room where are a sickly large wife and a whole school of well-conditioned wild children, you will find half-a-dozen different hucksters and all seeming engaged, and just pausing, in a violent horn-pipe. On these and around them and over the dusty table and ragged carpet lie all kinds of litter-books, papers, egg-shells, scissors and last night when I was there, the torn heart of a quartern loaf'.

The Leigh Hunts had many homes in London; the last was at 16 Rowan Road, Hammersmith.

Hunter, John.

31 Golden Square, W1
 John Hunter (1728–1793) surgeon lived here (LCC 1907; refixed 1931 after premises rebuilt).

John Hunter lived in Golden Square from 1763 to 1770, when he moved to the house in Jermyn Street vacated by his brother William (who had moved to Great Windmill Street). Though he was already a doctor of some reputation the period he spent in Golden Square was not easy: 'years of waiting for practice'. His brother-in-law Sir Evelyn Hone described his work: 'not finding the emoluments from his half-pay and private practice sufficient to support him, he taught practical anatomy and operative surgery for several winters'. In 1767 recognition came when he was elected a Fellow of the Royal Society.

Hunter, 'the founder of comparative anatomy', began his extensive collection of creatures from all parts of the world when he moved to a house in Earl's Court in 1772, and this became the basis of his Museum of Comparative and Pathological Anatomy.

Hunter, William.

Lyric Theatre (rear portion), Great Windmill Street, WC1
   This was the home and museum of Dr William Hunter anatomist (1718-1783) (LCC 1952).

When William Hunter moved to Great Windmill Street in 1770 he was recognised as the leading anatomist and obstetrician of the day. He established a medical school there at which he and his younger brother John Hunter taught, and he built a lecture theatre, dissecting room and museum. Hunter's museum was not limited to his scientific interests but included many fine paintings, with works by Rembrandt, Rubens and Stubbs and a valuable library of incunabula. The Hunterian Collection was bequeathed to Glasgow University.

Huskisson, William.

28 St James's Place, SW1
   William Huskisson (1770-1830) statesman lived here (LCC 1962).

28 St James's Place was built in about 1790. William Huskisson lived there from about 1804 to 1806, the period when he served in Pitt's government as Secretary to the Treasury. He resigned in 1806 and joined the Conservatives, becoming, in 1822, Treasurer of the Navy and President of the Board of Trade. Grenville described him as 'tall, slovenly, and ignoble-looking' but he possessed the invaluable gift of being able to win the new industrialists' support. His career ended tragically in 1830 when he was killed by a train while attending the ceremonial opening of the Liverpool and Manchester Railway.

Hutchinson, Sir Jonathan.

15 Cavendish Square, W1
   Sir Jonathan Hutchinson (1828-1913) surgeon scientist and teacher lived here (GLC c1981).

Jonathan Hutchinson lived at Cavendish Square from 1874 for most of the rest of his life. A student described him lecturing in 1906: 'what we saw that day was a tall, bent old man with a great dome of a head, dark eyes looking benevolently through steel-rimmed spectacles, and a long straggling white beard that came down well over his chest. . .he held us completely'. Naturalist, pathologist, surgeon, ophthalmologist, syphilographist and neurologist, Hutchinson achieved many of the highest positions in the medical profession. He is reported to have seen over a million cases of syphilis and one of his greatest contributions was his description of the notched, peg-shaped incisor teeth in congenital syphilis, which together with keratitis and middle-ear disease are now designated 'Hutchinson's triad'.

Huxley, Sir Julian.

31 Pond Street, NW3
Sir Julian Huxley FRS lived here 1943–1975 (private).

The grandson of Thomas Henry Huxley and son of Leonard, Julian Huxley was a biologist, scientific administrator, rationalist and philosopher of science. As professor of zoology at King's College London he studied hormones, developmental processes, ornithology and ecology. As secretary to the Zoological Society of London he transformed the London Zoo in Regent's Park and was involved in the development of Whipsnade. He was highly regarded internationally in both scientific and literary circles and he became the first director-general of UNESCO. Huxley wrote many distinguished scientific and philosophical works. While living in Hampstead he published *Soviet Genetics and World Science* (1949), *Evolution in Action* (1953), *The Human Crisis* (1963) and *Essays of a Humanist* (1964).

Huxley, Thomas Henry.

38 Marlborough Place, NW8
Thomas Henry Huxley (1825–1895) biologist lived here (LCC 1910).

4 Marlborough Place (now 38) was T.H. Huxley's home from 1872 to 1890. His son Leonard has described it: 'the irregular front of the house, with the original cottage, white-painted and deep-eaved, joined by a big porch to the new uncompromising square face of yellow brick, distinguished only by its extremely large windows, was screened from the road by a high oak paling, and a well-grown row of young lime trees. Taken as a whole, it was not without character, and certainly was unlike most London houses. It was built for comfort, not beauty'.

Huxley was one of the most brilliant intellectuals of his day: a preeminent Victorian. His distinguished career began as a naturalist serving on *HMS Rattlesnake* (1846–50). Ten years later he defended Darwin, securing a fair trial for the revolutionary theories in Darwin's *Origin of Species* (1859). The years he spent in St John's Wood were filled with official duties. Huxley was secretary (1871–80) of the Royal Society and its president (1883–5). His *Anatomy of Invertebrated Animals* and *Physiography* were published in 1877.

Thomas Henry Huxley, 38 Marlborough Place

Hyndman, Henry Mayers.

13 Well Walk, NW3

Henry Mayers Hyndman (1842–1921) Socialist leader lived and died here (GLC 1972).

H.M. Hyndman came from a privileged upper-class background but in 1880, after reading *Das Kapital*, he became a dedicated follower of Marx and in 1884 established the Socialist Democratic Federation, the first avowedly socialist political party in England. Lenin described Hyndman as 'a bourgeois philistine, who belonging to the best of his class, eventually struggles through to Socialism but never quite sheds his bourgeois conceptions and prejudices'. For all his dictatorial methods, opportunism and love of intrigue, Hyndman was largely responsible for introducing Marx's ideas to the labour movement in Britain. In 1916 he moved to 13 Well Walk, previously the home of the poet John Masefield, and died there.

Innes, John.

Manor House, Watery Lane, SW20
John Innes (1829–1904) founder of the John Innes Horticultural Institution lived here (GLC 1978).

John Innes bought the Merton Park Estate in 1867 and spent the next 30 years transforming the small farmhouse into a country gentleman's residence. He was a businessman and property developer and he left his estate for charitable purposes with special provision for a public park (the garden of the house is now the John Innes Park). The bulk of his fortune was used for promoting horticultural instruction, experiment and research. The John Innes Horticultural Institution was established at Manor House in 1909 (remaining there until 1946) and has specialised in the study of genetics.

Irving, Sir Henry.

15*a* Grafton Street, W1
Sir Henry Irving (1838–1905) actor lived here from 1872–1899 (LCC 1950).

Henry Irving lived on the first and second floors of 15a Grafton Street in 'the confusion and neglect of order in which the artistic mind delights'. Engravings of the art of fencing hung over the dark, winding staircase which led to his rooms. His study was kept in

Henry Irving, 15a Grafton Street

perpetual twilight, with curtained windows and stained and leaded glass. The block, at the corner of Bond Street and Grafton Street, was owned (and still is) by Messrs Asprey.

Irving's first great success was in the part of Matthias, the haunted murderer of the melodrama *The Bells*, which he performed at the Lyceum in 1871. He was not afraid to cut Shakespeare and rewrite parts but he did restore the reputation of the acting profession. Acting was a serious discipline for him. He initiated the device of lowering the auditorium lights to focus attention on the stage during performances, and he continued to use gas lighting for subtle effects after electricity was available.

Isaacs, Rufus [1st Marquess of Reading].

32 Curzon Street, W1

Rufus Isaacs 1st Marquess of Reading (1860–1935) lawyer and statesman lived and died here (GLC 1971).

Rufus Isaacs's father was a fruit merchant but Rufus turned to the law. He was called to the Bar in 1887 and quickly established a successful practice, becoming Attorney-General in 1910, the year he moved to Curzon Street, and Lord Chief Justice in 1913. After his elevation to the Lords Isaacs played a major part in securing the cooperation of the USA in the Allied war effort. He was Viceroy of India (1921–6) and a leading figure in the conference on the Indian constitution (1930).

J

Jackson, John Hughlings.

3 Manchester Square, W1
John Hughlings Jackson (1835–1911) physician lived here (LCC 1932).

John Hughlings Jackson lived at 3 Manchester Square from 1871 to his death. Through investigating epilepsy and speech defects caused by brain disease Jackson was able to identify the portions of the brain controlling the voluntary movements of the body. His work received little public recognition: although he contributed important papers to medical journals he was very retiring by nature.

James, Henry.

34 De Vere Gardens, W8
Henry James (1843–1916) writer lived here 1886–1902 (LCC 1949).

James was American by birth but Europe always held a fascination for him. He made his first visit to London from 1877 to 1881 but he said: 'my interest in London is chiefly that of an observer, in a place where there is most in the world to observe'. However, on returning to the USA he realised he had to choose between the continents: 'my work lies there — and with this vast new world je n'ai que faire'.

The period James spent in De Vere Gardens coincides with his turning from a popular, easily accessible novelist, famous for *The Portrait of a Lady* (1881), to one admired by a small circle of readers willing to pursue his attempts, in novels such as *The Golden Bowl* (1904) and *What Maisie Knew* (1897), to present 'what "goes on" irreconcilably, subversively beneath the vast smug surface'. James found his increasing isolation far from comforting: 'I have felt for a long time past, that I have fallen upon evil days — every sign or symbol of one's being in the least bit *wanted*, anywhere or by anyone, having so utterly failed'.

Jellicoe, John Rushworth, Earl.

25 Draycott Place, SW3
Admiral of the Fleet Earl Jellicoe OM (1859-1935) lived here (GLC 1975).

Jellicoe worked with John Fisher on the design of the new Dreadnought class of battleship. As First Lord of the Admiralty, Fisher thought highly of Jellicoe's abilities as a commander and through his influence Jellicoe was appointed commander-in-chief of the fleet at the outbreak of World War I. Jellicoe has been blamed for the uncertain outcome of the Battle of Jutland, but he succeeded in forcing the German high sea fleet to remain in their home base for the duration of the war. After a difficult year combating the menace of submarines Jellicoe resigned in December 1917. He lived at 25 Draycott Place, a large red brick and terracotta house built in the 1890s, from between about 1906 and 1908.

Jessop, Gilbert Laird.

3 Sunnydale Gardens, NW7
Gilbert Jessop cricketer lived here 1924-1936 (Hendon Corporation).

Gilbert Laird Jessop played for Gloucestershire as captain from 1900 to 1913. He was nicknamed 'The Croucher' for his huddled posture at the wicket and was a brilliant fieldsman, fast bowler and skilled batsman. He played in 18 test matches but by the time he lived in north London he was spending more time writing about cricket than playing. *Cricket and How to Play it* was written in 1925.

Jinnah, Mohammed Ali [Quaid i Azam].

35 Russell Road, W14
Mohammed Ali Jinnah Quaid i Azam (1876-1948) founder of Pakistan stayed here in 1895 (LCC 1955).

Mohammed Ali Jinnah was born in Karachi. He came to England in 1892 to study law and was called to the Bar in 1896, living in lodgings in Russell Road for some of the time. When he returned to Bombay he was already a convinced nationalist. In 1909 he was elected as the Bombay Muslims' representative on the imperial legislative council and in 1913 he joined the All India Muslim League. Jinnah was losing sympathy with the ideas of his fellow nationalist Gandhi; the break between Muslims and Hindus came in 1940 when Jinnah inspired the passing of a resolution in the Muslim League meeting at Lahore demanding the formation of Pakistan. The British government reluctantly accepted the principle of Pakistan in 1947 and Jinnah became the first governor-general. His title Quaid i Azam means 'the great leader'.

John, Augustus.

28 Mallord Street, SW3
   This house was built for Augustus John (1878–1961) painter (GLC c1981).

The house at 28 Mallord Street was built for Augustus John by the architect Robert Van t'Hoff, a founding member of De Stijl which had a marked influence on the architecture of the Bauhaus movement. John was the epitomy of English bohemianism, defying social conventions in his dress, behaviour and way of life. He joined the New England Art Club in 1903 where he quickly gained a reputation for his superb draughtsmanship. He owned the Mallord Street house from 1914 until the 1930s when it was sold to Gracie Fields.

Johnson, Samuel.

17 Gough Square, EC4
   Dr Samuel Johnson author lived here. Born 1709. Died 1784 (City of London).

Johnson's Court, Fleet Street, EC4
   In a house on this site Dr. Samuel Johnson lived between 1765–1776 (City of London).

Anchor Brewery, Southwark Bridge Road, SE1
   Dr Samuel Johnson once occupied a room near the gatehouse

Samuel Johnson is probably most famous for his dictionary, published in two volumes in 1755. The work on it took place at 17 Gough Square where Johnson lived from 1749 to 1759. The house was bought for the nation in 1910 by Cecil Harmsworth when it was 'perhaps the most

Samuel Johnson, 17 Gough Square

dilapidated and forlorn tenement in London' and is now open to the public.

The dictionary was not a financial success and in 1756 Johnson was arrested for a debt of £5.13s. Samuel Richardson lent him six guineas but Johnson gave up the Gough Square house and moved into 'indolent poverty' in Inner Temple Lane. However, in 1762, he was granted a pension of £300 a year and accepted it, even though his dictionary definition for a pension was 'generally understood to mean pay given to state hireling for treason to his country'. He moved to rooms in Johnson's Court and lived in comparative comfort, writing little, for, as he had himself observed, 'no man but a blockhead ever wrote except for money'.

Two of Johnson's closest friends were Henry and Hesther Thrale. Johnson frequently stayed at their large house, Streatham Park, and he also had a room in their Southwark house (now commemorated on the Anchor Brewery). The thatched summer house in which Johnson sat in the grounds of Streatham Park is now on the Kenwood House estate (*see also* ESSEX STREET).

Johnston, Edward.

3 Hammersmith Terrace, W8

Edward Johnston (1872-1944) master calligrapher lived here 1905-1912 (GLC 1977).

Edward Johnston began teaching illumination at the Central School of Arts and Crafts in 1899 and his classes were attended by leading members of the Arts and Crafts movement, including Cobden Sanderson and Eric Gill. When Emery Walker moved from 3 Hammersmith Terrace to no.7, Johnston moved in with his expanding family. He described the move and area to a friend: 'we have for some time thought of leaving Gray's Inn, and, a delightful house offering itself, we suddenly flitted on the 31st of March. . . . If you should want a house having the advantages of country (very nearly) and town combined there are one or two to let in the Terrace at about £60 per annum. They are old houses on the river and you can keep a boat or be content with watching the LCC historical steamboats passing up and down'.

While he was at Hammersmith Terrace Johnston wrote *Writing, Lettering and Illuminating*, still the most valuable book on the subject, and designed the typeface used by the London Transport underground railway network.

Jones, Adrian.

147 Old Church Street, SW3
   Captain Adrian Jones (1890–1937) M.V.O. Sculptor lived here (private 1947).

Adrian Jones lived at 147 Old Church Street from 1892 until his death. His best-known work is probably the Peace Quadriga on the Constitution Hill arch at Hyde Park Corner.

Jordan [Bland], **Dorothy.**

30 Cadogan Place, SW1
   Mrs Jordan (Dorothy Bland) (1762–1816) actress lived here (GLC 1975).

Dorothy Bland began her acting career in Dublin when she was only 15; she was to become one of the best comedy actresses of the time. Hazlitt found her irresistible: 'her smile had the effect of sunshine, and her laugh did one good to hear it. . . . She was all gaiety, openness and good nature. She rioted in her fine animal spirits, and gave more pleasure than any other actress, because she had the greatest spirit of enjoyment in herself'. Her charms not only furthered her stage career but won her a series of influential lovers, among them William, Duke of Clarence, the third son of George III, and William IV. She had already produced five children by various liaisons when she established a home with William in 1790. In the 21 years of their relationship they had ten illegitimate Fitzclarences.

The government made a generous settlement on Mrs Jordan and the Fitzclarences when William broke up the relationship in 1811 so that he was free to marry and produce an heir to the throne. From about 1812 to 1814 the family lived at 30 Cadogan Place. In 1815 Mrs Jordan was forced to move to France to escape her creditors. The government allowance was insufficient to cover her generosity to dependents and friends. She was also suffering from mental delusions; she died at St Cloud.

143

Keats, John.

Moorgate Public House, 85 Moorgate, EC2
In a house on this site 'The Swan and Hoop' John Keats poet was born 1795 (City of London).

Enfield Town Station Booking Hall, Enfield
John Keats' first school was in a house on this site, demolished 1872

7 Keats Parade, Church Street, Edmonton
(Site of) cottage of Thomas Hammond, surgeon, where John Keats served his apprenticeship 1811–1815

Keats's House, Wentworth Place, Keats Grove, NW3
John Keats, Poet, lived in this house, b.1795, d.1821 (RSA 1896).

John Keats's father Thomas ran livery stables at the sign of the 'Swan and Hoop', where Keats was born. When he was about eight Keats was sent to a school in Enfield run by John Clarke. Keats was then apprenticed to Thomas Hammond, a surgeon at Edmonton: a fellow student called him 'an idle loafing fellow, always writing poetry', and Keats left his apprenticeship a year early to continue surgical studies in London. There, Charles Cowden Clarke (son of John Clarke) introduced him to Leigh Hunt, editor of *The Examiner*, and Keats found himself in the centre of the young artists and writers of the time.

144

John Keats, 'Keats House', Keats Grove

Keats moved into Wentworth Place in December 1818. The house was built by two of his friends, Charles Wentworth Dilke and Charles Armitage Brown. Keats paid Brown £5 a month for board and lodging and had his own small sitting-room at the back of the house with a bedroom above. He wrote some of his finest poetry there: *La belle dame sans merci*, the odes and *Lamia*. The *Ode to a Nightingale* was composed in a single morning.

Keats met Coleridge when he was out walking on the Heath — as the older poet recalled with additions of hindsight after his death: 'a loose, slack, not well-dressed youth. . . . He was introduced to me, and stayed a minute or so. After he had left us a little way, he came back and said: "let me carry away the memory, Coleridge, of having pressed your hand!" — "There is death in that hand" I said'.

The love-affair of Keats and Fanny Brawne flourished during his stay at Wentworth Place. Mrs Brawne and her three children moved into Charles Dilke's half of the house in May 1819 and Keats began writing love-letters to Fanny in July: 'I almost wish we were butter-flies and liv'd but three summer days — three such days with you I could fill with more delight than 50 common years could ever contain'. They became engaged but Keats's fatal disease ended their relationship. He died in Rome of tuberculosis less than a year after leaving Hampstead.

Kedleston, Marquess of. *See* CURZON, GEORGE NATHANIEL.

Keene, Charles Samuel.

Cadby Hall, (site of) 82 Hammersmith Road, W6
Charles Samuel Keene (1823–1891) artist lived in a house on this site from 1865 to 1891 (LCC 1937).

Charles Keene was largely self-taught and the turning-point in his career as an artist came when he joined *Punch* in 1851. The magazine was then ten years old and edited by Mark Lemon; its contributing artists and writers included Thackeray, Tenniel and John Leech.

Keene never married but lived with his mother and sisters at 5 Brook Green Terrace, Hammersmith, later renamed 82 Hammersmith Road. He also kept a studio in Chelsea.

Keith, Sir Arthur.

17 Aubert Park, N5

Sir Arthur Keith (1866–1955) anthropologist lived here 1908–1933 (London Borough of Islington).

Arthur Keith's interest in the comparative anatomy of primates and the evolution of man was first aroused among the monkeys and gibbons of Siam, where he went as a medical officer to a mining company in 1889. On returning to England, he became conservationist of the Hunterian Museum of the Royal College of Surgeons, and, under his inspired direction, the museum came to possess one of the finest records of the structure and history of the human body.

Aubert Park was named after Alexander Aubert, Fellow of the Royal Society and a keen astronomer, who lived at Highbury House (demolished 1938) from 1788 to 1805. The park is a mixture of bow-fronted cottages and grand villas and no.17 is distinguished by the eagles on its gateposts.

Kennedy, John Fitzgerald.

14 Prince's Gate, SW7
John Fitzgerald Kennedy President United States of America 1961–1963 lived here (College of General Practitioners 1967).

J.F. Kennedy is supposed to have stayed at 14 Prince's Gate during his father's residence. Joseph P. Kennedy, shipbuilder, motion-picture tycoon, supporter of the US Democratic party and millionaire was made US ambassador to Great Britain in 1937. He lived at Prince's Gate until he resigned in 1940, convinced that Britain was to be invaded by Germany and that the USA's best policy was isolationism.

14 Prince's Gate was built in 1850 as two houses but J. Pierpoint Morgan (another American millionaire) combined them early in the 20th century.

Keynes, John Maynard.

46 Gordon Square, WC1
John Maynard Keynes (1883–1946) economist lived here 1916–1946 (GLC 1975).

46 Gordon Square is part of a terrace built in the 1820s which now houses part of the University of London's Institute of Computer Science. An affable and enthusiastic host, Keynes made no.46 a centre for the Bloomsbury artists and writers who were his friends and relatives. In the 1920s his neighbours in Gordon Square included Vanessa and Clive Bell, Duncan Grant, Adrian Stephen and Lytton Strachey; the Woolfs were in Tavistock Square and E.M. Forster in Brunswick Square. At a typical party at Keynes's house on Twelfth Night 1923, Marjorie Strachey (Lytton's sister) sang obscene comic versions of nursery

rhymes, Sickert acted Hamlet and Lydia Lopokova danced; she was a member of Diaghilev's ballet company and became Keynes's wife in 1925.

As a teacher and writer Keynes established himself as the leading economist between the wars. *A Treatise on Money* (1930) and *A General Theory of Employment, Interest and Money* (1936) have, until recently, been standard economic texts. In 1944-5 Keynes played an important part in the negotiations leading to the founding of the International Monetary Fund.

Kingsley, Charles.

56 Old Church Street, SW3
Charles Kingsley (1819-1875) writer lived here (GLC 1979).

St Luke's Rectory, 56 Old Church Street, was built in about 1725. Charles Kingsley's father was rector of St Luke's from 1836 and Charles spent his adolescence at the rectory.

Kingsley was influenced in his thinking by F.D. Maurice and Thomas Carlyle: an ardent Christian Socialist, he believed in the reconciliation between religion and science. Many of his novels are propagandist, attempting to interest the middle class in the sufferings of the poor but advocating moral persuasion rather than violent revolution to effect change. *Alton Locke*, described by Carlyle as a 'fervid creation still left half chaotic', was published in 1850 and Kingsley's popular children's allegory *The Water Babies* was published in 1863.

Kingsley, Mary.

22 Southwood Lane, N6
Mary Kingsley (1862-1900) traveller and ethnologist lived here as a girl (GLC 1975).

Mary Kingsley (niece of Charles and Henry Kingsley) was born in Islington. In 1863 her parents moved to 22 Southwood Lane, where they remained until 1879. She had little formal education but was allowed to read widely. Between 1893 and 1895 she travelled in Africa: she climbed the highest peak in the Cameroons, lived in the villages of the Fan headhunters and made important collections for the Natural History Museum. She died of typhoid while nursing Boer War prisoners at Simonstown.

Kipling, Rudyard.

43 Villiers Street, WC2
Rudyard Kipling (1865-1936) poet and story writer lived here 1889-1891 (LCC 1957).

Rudyard Kipling arrived in London in September 1889 'with fewer pounds in his pocket than he cared to remember' and took three rooms on the second floor of 43 Villiers Street. He recalled the street in his autobiography *Something of Myself*: 'primitive and passionate in its habits and population. My rooms were small, not overclean or well-kept, but from my desk I could look out of my window through the fan-light of Gatti's Music-Hall entrance, across the street, almost on to its stage. The Charing Cross trains rumbled through my dreams on one side, the boom of the Strand on the other, while, before my windows, Father Thames under the Shot Tower walked up and down with his traffic'.

At Villiers Street Kipling wrote his *Barrack Room Ballads* and his novel *The Light that Failed*. He found it difficult to adjust to English weather and in 1891 his 'Indian microbes joined hands and sang for a month in the darkness of Villiers Street'. He left England to recuperate in warmer climates, returning in 1896 with an American wife. They settled in Sussex where Kipling pursued the life of a country gentleman and wrote some of his finest works: *Just So Stories* (1902), *Puck of Pook's Hill* (1906), *Rewards and Fairies* (1910).

Kirk, Sir John.

32 John Street, WC1
Sir John Kirk J.P. Christian Philanthropist. The Children's Friend (1847-1922) (Shaftesbury Society).

John Kirk began work for the Ragged School Union in 1867 and was appointed secretary 12 years later. During his period as director of the union its annual income increased from £6000 to £60,000. In 1914 it became the Shaftesbury Society and Ragged School Union and its headquarters were at 32 John Street.

Kitchener, Horatio Herbert, Earl.

2 Carlton Gardens, SW1
Field-Marshal Earl Kitchener of Khartoum KG (1850-1916) lived here 1914-1915 (LCC 1924).

After a distinguished military career in which he rose to the rank of field-marshal, Kitchener was appointed British agent and consul-general in Egypt (1911–14). He was knighted for his services and was about to return to Egypt when war became imminent and the Prime Minister H.H. Asquith, appointed him Secretary of State for War.

Kitchener was one of the few statesmen and soldiers who considered the war might last even as long as three years and that it might be possible to raise large new armies. As a result of his work three million men volunteered. He was only reluctantly involved in the Dardanelles campaign and offered his resignation after the expedition had to be abandoned. He was sent to Russia to establish cooperation between the Allied armies of eastern and western Europe; shortly after leaving Scapa Flow *HMS Hampshire* struck a mine and went down with the loss of practically all on board, including Kitchener.

Kossuth, Louis.

39 Chepstow Villas, W11
  Louis Kossuth (1802–1894) Hungarian patriot stayed here (LCC 1959).

Louis Kossuth led the struggle for independence in Hungary in 1848. Using his brilliant powers as journalist and orator, he helped to found a new republic, free from the repressive control of the Hapsburg Emperor. The republic was short-lived, however, as Russian and Imperial troops together defeated the Hungarians at Vilagos in August 1849 and a new era of repression began. Kossuth fled the country, and came to England in 1851. He gave public lectures and visited the United States, trying to enlist help for the Hungarian cause.

Lamb, Charles.

2 Crown Office Row, Temple, EC4
Charles Lamb was born in the chamber which formerly stood here 10 February 1775 'Cheerful Crown Office Row (place of my kindly engendure). . . a man would give something to have been born in such places' (private).

Colebrook Cottage, 64 Duncan Terrace, N1
Charles Lamb (1775–1834) essayist lived here (LCC 1907).

Clarendon Cottage, 85 Chase Side, Enfield
This house was occupied by Charles Lamb September 1827 to October 1829

Westwood Cottage, Chase Side, Enfield
This house was occupied by Charles Lamb October 1829 to May 1833

Walden Cottage, Edmonton
Charles Lamb (1775–1834) lived here

Charles Lamb was born at 2 Crown Office Row and spent part of his childhood there, in the house of Samuel Salt, lawyer and employer of his father. He is most famous for the essays he wrote under the pseudonym of 'Elia'. These were published as a book in 1823, the year Lamb and his sister Mary moved to Islington. Charles had looked after

Charles Lamb, 64 Duncan Terrace

his sister since she had stabbed their mother to death in a fit of insanity in 1796. They collaborated on *Tales from Shakespeare* (1807), written for children.

In a letter to Bernard Barton Lamb described Colebrook Cottage: 'a white house with six good rooms; the New River (rather elderly by this time) runs. . .close to the foot of the house; and behind is a spacious garden with vines (I assure you). . . . You enter without passage into a cheerful diningroom, all studded over and rough with old Books, and above is a lightsome Drawing room, three windows, full of choice prints. I feel like a great Lord, never having had a house before'.

Lamb was never well off and for many years he had to work as a clerk for East India House. Islington was not an expensive area in the 1820s and Duncan Terrace is reputed to have been its red-light district. The Lambs left in 1827, moving to Clarendon House and Westwood Cottage in Chase Side, Enfield, then to Walden Cottage near the Lower Edmonton railway bridge. Charles Lamb is buried in Edmonton.

Lang, Andrew.

1 Marloes Road, W8
   Andrew Lang (1844–1912) man of letters, lived here 1876–1912 (LCC 1959).

Although Andrew Lang is probably best known for his anthologies of fairy stories and his translation, in collaboration with S.H. Butcher, of the *Odyssey* (1879), his most influential work was as an anthropologist. While living in Marloes Road he wrote *Custom and Myth* (1884), *Myth, Ritual and Religion* (1887) and *The Making of Religion* (1898), combining Greek scholarship with his literary sensibility and interest in the sociology of religion.

Langtry, Lillie.

21 Pont Street, SW1
   Lillie Langtry (1852–1929) actress lived here (GLC 1980).

The Prince of Wales first met Lillie Langtry, who was to become his mistress, in 1877. Her father was the Dean of Jersey and she became known as the 'Jersey Lily' because of her exceptional beauty. She first appeared on stage as Kate Hardcastle at the Haymarket in 1881 but it was her appearance rather than her acting ability which enraptured her audiences. She lived at 21 Pont Street (now the Cadogan Hotel) from 1892 to 1897.

153

Laski, Harold.

5 Addison Bridge Place, W14
*Harold Laski (1893–1950) teacher and political philosopher lived
here 1926–1950* (GLC 1974).

Harold Laski became professor of political science at the London
School of Economics in 1926. That year he moved into 5 Addison Bridge
Place (Coleridge's brief stay at no.7 is also commemorated by a plaque).
He was elected to the national executive of the Labour Party in 1936,
becoming chairman in 1945. Although he considered the Russian
example of revolution undesirable in a Western democracy, the
depression of the 1930s made him adopt a Marxist interpretation of
history. During World War II he wrote of the opportunity that war
offered to the working classes to achieve 'revolution by consent'. His
best-known works include *1931 and After* (1932), *Democracy in
Crisis* (1933) and *Parliamentary Government in England* (1938).

Lauder, Sir Harry.

46 Longley Road, SW17
*Sir Harry Lauder (1870–1950) music hall artiste, lived here 1903–
1911* (GLC 1969).

Harry Lauder lived in London from 1900 to 1911, the period when he
established his reputation as one of the most popular music-hall performers of the day. He wore Scottish dress and carried a crooked walking
stick, and he wrote the words and music of some of his most famous
songs: *Keep Right on to the End of the Road, Roamin' in the Gloamin'*
and *I Love a Lassie*.
24 (now 46) Longley Road was Lauder's only permanent residence
in London. He described the house in his reminiscences: 'A Scotsman's
house, they say, is his castle. My castle is a very modest villa out Tooting
way. I'm never so truly happy as when at home in the bosom of my
wife and "me family"'.

Lavery, Sir John.

5 Cromwell Place, SW7
Sir John Lavery (1856–1941) painter lived here 1899–1940 (GLC
1966).

John Lavery achieved popularity as a painter after his 'Tennis Party'
was hung at the Royal Academy in 1886 and bought for a Munich
gallery. Two years later he was commissioned to paint the state visit

of Queen Victoria to the Glasgow Exhibition and thereafter painted society portraits and contemporary scenes.

Lawrence, David Herbert.

1 Byron Villas, Vale of Health, NW3
   David Herbert Lawrence (1885–1930) novelist and poet lived here in 1915 (GLC 1969).

The few months D.H. Lawrence spent in Hampstead, from August until just before Christmas 1915, were disastrous for him, and in letters of the period he referred to London as his image of hell. He described his situation to Bertrand Russell: 'very dislocated and unhappy in these new circumstances. . .delivered up to chaos and tables and doormats'. *The Rainbow* was published in September but suppressed after being declared obscene at a hearing in Bow Street on 13 November.

The magazine *Signature* was launched in October by Lawrence and his friends J. Middleton Murry and Katherine Mansfield. Lawrence published 'The Crown', his defence of *The Rainbow*, in *Signature*. Only three issues of the magazine appeared, however, because of insufficient subscribers and funds.

Lawrence's position was made worse through his opposition to the war and his wife's German nationality. The couple witnessed the first Zeppelin attack on London on 8 September as they walked across the Heath: 'a long-ovate, gleaming central luminary, calm and drifting in a glow of light, like a new moon, with its light bursting in flashes on the earth, to burst away the earth also. So it is the end — our world is gone, and we are like dust in the air'.

Lawrence, John Laird Mair, Baron.

Southgate House (Minchenden School), High Street, Southgate
   The residence was here 1861–64 of Baron Lawrence who raised the siege of Delhi (private).

When John Lawrence arrived in England in 1859 he was a popular hero. Lord Canning wrote of his services in India, 'But for him the hold of England over Upper India would have had to be recovered at a cost of English blood and treasure which defies calculation. It is difficult to exaggerate the value of such ability, vigilance, and energy, at such a time'. Lawrence continued to work at the India Office but lived a country life at Southgate House until his return to India as viceroy in 1864.

Lawrence, Thomas Edward.

14 Barton Street, SW1
   T.E. Lawrence (1888–1935) 'Lawrence of Arabia' lived here (GLC 1966).

   T.E. Lawrence learnt the Arabic language and customs working for Sir Leonard Woolley excavating the Hittite city of Carchemish. He enlisted in 1914 and was appointed liaison officer and adviser to Prince Faisal. He led a dramatic campaign against the Turks culminating in the capture of Damascus in October 1918 and became a popular hero, his fame increased by the publication of his memoirs, *The Seven Pillars of Wisdom*.

   Lawrence lived at 14 Barton Street in 1922; occasionally, in 1923 and 1929, he used it as a forwarding address. The architect Sir Herbert Baker occupied the building and wrote that Lawrence 'found a haven of peace in the attic of my office in quiet secluded Barton Street. . . when he was being mercilessly hunted by the hounds of Press and Film'. To escape publicity, Lawrence changed his name in August 1922 to J.H. Ross and enlisted in the ranks of the RAF. After his identity was discovered he changed his name to T.E. Shaw but was discharged when he was again discovered. After a short period in the tank corps he returned to the RAF in 1928. Retiring in February 1935, Lawrence sought a secluded life at his cottage in Dorset but he died in a motor-cycle accident in May.

Lear, Edward.

30 Seymour Street, W1
   Edward Lear (1812–1888) artist and writer lived here (LCC 1960).

   Edward Lear's nonsense books have remained popular since the first was published in 1845. Lear was also a talented landscape painter and spent most of his life travelling throughout southern Europe and the Middle East, painting and drawing. From 1871 until his death he lived in San Remo. He did, however, come back to England for brief visits, although warmer climates were better for his health. In 1845 he returned to give drawing lessons to Queen Victoria, and from 1857 to 1858 he occupied rooms at 16 Upper Seymour Street (no.30 Seymour Street).

Lecky, William Edward Hartpole.

38 Onslow Gardens, SW7
   W.E.H. Lecky (1838–1903) historian and essayist lived and died here (LCC 1955).

W.E.H. Lecky was a controversial historian, treating the development of civilization in an 'evolutionary' manner. His eight-volume *A History of England in the 18th Century* was published between 1878 and 1890. Lecky was elected MP for Dublin University in 1895 and was praised for his impartial handling of Irish problems both in Parliament and in his writings. 38 Onslow Gardens was his home from about 1874 until his death.

Leighton, Frederick, Lord.

Leighton House, 12 Holland Park Road, W14
Lord Leighton (1830–1896) painter lived and died here (LCC 1958).

Frederick Leighton introduced a classical revival into Victorian painting and employed George Aitchison to build Leighton House in 1866 to reflect his unusual and exotic tastes. The Arab hall was an authentic copy of a hall in Moorish Spain, the dome inlaid with stained glass and the walls faced with tiles collected by Leighton and his friends from the Middle East, Rhodes and Persia. Contemporary artists added to the decorations, Walter Crane designing the mosaic frieze, William de Morgan the Damascus tiles on the inner hall and the walls of the white stone staircase leading to the domed landing, Randolph Caldecott the birds on the marble columns supporting the dome. The house is now a museum. Leighton was one of the most successful Victorian artists, becoming president of the Royal Academy in 1878. He died the day after he was raised to the peerage.

Lenin, Vladimir Ilyich.

Royal Scot Hotel, 100 King's Cross Road, WC1
Vladimir Ilyich Ulyanov Lenin (1870–1924) founder of the USSR stayed in 1905 at Percy Circus which stood on this site (private c1972).

Lenin stayed at 16 Percy Circus during the Third Congress of the Russian Social Democratic Labour Party which was held in London from 25 April to 10 May 1905. Lenin first went to London in 1902 when he lived in Holford Square, also near King's Cross. He worked in the British Museum and was a frequent visitor to the 'Pindar of Wakefield' public house in the Gray's Inn Road. He edited the newspaper *Iskra* at the building which is now the Marx Memorial Library in Clerkenwell Green.

Leno, Dan.

56 Akerman Road, SW19
Dan Leno (1860–1904) music hall comedian lived here 1898–1901 (LCC 1962).

Dan Leno was born in Holborn and made his first stage appearance when he was four as a tumbler and contortionist, trained by his parents who were music-hall performers. When he moved to Brixton in 1898 Leno was nearing the end of a triumphant career as a comedian. His portrayals of Widow Twankey and Mother Goose in pantomimes at Drury Lane were particularly successful and in 1901 he became the first music-hall comedian to give a royal command performance before Edward VIII at Sandringham.

Lethaby, William Richard.

20 Calthorpe Street, WC1
William Richard Lethaby (1857–1931) Architect lived here 1880–1891 (GLC 1979).

Central School of Art and Design, Southampton Row, WC1
William Richard Lethaby (1857–1931) Architect and first principal of this school in 1896 to 1911 (LCC 1957).

Lethaby went to London in 1879 to work under the architect Norman Shaw. He became his chief assistant and remained in his offices until 1891. During this period Lethaby lived in humble lodgings at 20 Calthorpe Street, part of a terrace of plain early 19th-century yellow stock brick houses.

He began his independent career as an architect in 1891 and in 1896 he and George Frampton were appointed joint principals of the new Central School of Arts and Crafts which had been set up 'to encourage the industrial application of decorative design'. He became sole principal in 1902 and when the present building in Southampton Row was opened in 1908 he was responsible for 1200 evening students and over 250 day students and had an eminent staff including Eric Gill, Edward Johnston and T.J. Cobden-Sanderson.

Lethaby resigned from the Central School in 1911 to concentrate on teaching at the Royal College of Art. He was Master of the Art Workers' Guild from 1906 to 1928 and author of several influential books on arts and crafts, including *Form in Civilization* (1922).

William Richard Lethaby, Central School of Art and Design

Leybourne, George.

136 Englefield Road, N1

George Leybourne (1842–1884) music hall comedian 'Champagne Charlie' lived and died here (GLC 1970).

George Leybourne trained as a mechanic in Gateshead but, on realising he could entertain audiences with his singing voice, he went to London to seek fame and fortune. He found both and is now considered one of the first music-hall 'stars'. 'Champagne Charlie' was his most popular stage name. He would appear as an immaculately dressed man about town, with monocle, whiskers and a fur collar singing of the delights of dissipation. But he shared the faults of his character, drinking excessively in private, and spent his last years in Englefield Road disillusioned and sick, dying at the age of 42.

Linacre, Thomas.

Wall at rear of GPO (Faraday Building), Knightrider Street, EC4

In a house on this site lived Thomas Linacre Physician (1460–1524) (City of London).

Thomas Linacre lived in London from about 1500 when he was made tutor to Prince Arthur and, in 1509, king's physician. He was physician not only to Henry VII and Cardinal Wolsey but to his own eminent friends, including Erasmus and Sir Thomas More. In 1520 Linacre took holy orders and gave up medical practice, to concentrate on literary pursuits. His most important public service was founding the College of Physicians in 1518. He was its first president and meetings were held in his house in Knightrider Street.

Lind [Goldschmidt] , **Jenny.**

189 Old Brompton Road, SW5

Jenny Lind : Madame Goldschmidt (1820–1887) singer lived here (LCC 1909).

Jenny Lind, the 'Swedish Nightingale', was born in Stockholm and became one of the most glamorous prima donnas of the 19th century. She joined the Berlin Opera, through Meyerbeer's influence, and caused a sensation in 1844 singing in the première of his opera *Ein Feldlager in Schlesien* which he wrote for her. She was idolised in London after her appearance in *Robert le diable* in 1849. She married her concert conductor Otto Goldschmidt and they moved to 1 Moreton Gardens (now 189 Old Brompton Road) in 1876. Jenny

Lind taught at the Royal College of Music while living there and trained the sopranos of the Bach Choir, which her husband founded.

Lindsey, Theophilus. *See* ESSEX STREET.

Linnean Society. *See* BANKS, Sir JOSEPH.

Linnell, John.

Old Wyldes, North End Road, Hampstead Way, NW11
John Linnell (1792-1882) painter lived here. William Blake (1757-1827) poet and artist stayed here as his guest (GLC 1975).

When John Linnell rented part of Old Wyldes in 1824 it was known as Collins Farm, on the Wyldes' estate, and was the property of Eton College. He was by this time a successful artist, painting portraits and landscapes. He is best known, however, for the friendship and financial help he gave to William Blake. He helped to get Blake a grant of £25 from the Royal Academy in 1822 and commissioned Blake's greatest achievement as an engraver, *The Book of Job* (1826). Although Blake enjoyed visiting Linnell and his family (Linnell was one of the few acquaintances who never thought Blake mad) he did not like the location of the farm and was convinced the area was bad for his health. Blake influenced many of the artists whom he met at Old Wyldes, including Samuel Palmer, John Varley, William Mulready and George Richmond. (*See also* Sir RAYMOND UNWIN.)

Lister, Joseph, Lord.

12 Park Crescent, W1
Lord Lister (1827-1912) surgeon lived here (LCC 1915).

Park Crescent was one of the earliest terraces built by John Nash as part of his plan for Regent's Park. It was completely demolished in 1961 after the effects of bomb damage and general deterioration, but was rebuilt behind a façade almost identical to the original.

Lister was appointed to the chair of clinical surgery at King's College Hospital in 1877 on the strength of his work in Glasgow originating antiseptic treatment during operations. He lived at Park Crescent from 1877 to 1902 in great simplicity, carrying out experiments in the early hours of the morning with the assistance of a devoted wife. He retired from active surgical work in 1893, the year his wife died, and suffered from physical and mental exhaustion until his death. A pioneer of bacteriology, Lister was president of the Royal Society and was awarded the Order of Merit.

John Linnell, 'Old Wyldes', North End Road

Little Tich. *See* RELPH, HARRY.

Little, William John.

Old Red Lion, Leman Street, E1
   William J. Little (1810–1894) physician and pioneer in Orthopaedics was born here (London Hospital 1961).

William Little was born at the Red Lion Inn, Red Lion Street (now Leman Street), where his father was landlord. He became assistant physician to the London Hospital in 1839 and in 1861 his investigation into the cause of spastic rigidity of the limbs of newborn children was published. It was the first such investigation and led to the worldwide use of the term 'Little's disease' or spastic diplegia. Little was the founder of British orthopaedic surgery and in 1840 he established the first orthopaedic hospital for the study and treatment of the limbs and spine, in Bloomsbury Square.

Lloyd, Marie.

55 Graham Road, E8
   Marie Lloyd (1870–1922) music hall artiste lived here (GLC 1977).

Marie Lloyd's real name was Matilda Wood. She first appeared at the Royal Eagle Music Hall in 1885 where her father was a waiter. Her first hit song was *The Boy I Love Sits up in the Gallery*, and she soon became notorious for her risqué lyrics. In an interview in 1895 she revealed that out of her music-hall earnings she was paying for 150 beds each night for London's homeless and destitute. She died soon after falling on the stage of the Edmonton Empire, playing the part of a drunken woman so realistically that the audience never realized her fall was not part of the act.

Lloyd George, David.

3 Routh Road, SW18
   David Lloyd George (1865–1945) Prime Minister lived here (GLC 1967).

Lloyd George entered Parliament in 1890 at the age of 27, as Liberal MP for Caernarvon, a constituency he was to represent for the next 54 years. He lived with his wife Margaret in various London flats in the City and Kensington until they bought their first house at 179 Trinity Road, Wandsworth. From there they moved to 3 Routh Road, a large detached late Victorian house, staying from 1904 to 1908.

Marie Lloyd, 55 Graham Road

The end of the Boer War brought a revival of British radicalism and the period when Lloyd George lived at Routh Road was when his political fortunes were in the ascendant. He was President of the Board of Trade in the new Liberal government from 1906 to 1908, showing himself to be a firm and resilient administrator with tact and drive. He was able to charm the House of Commons as well as deputations of industrialists and businessmen, confessing to Charles Masterman 'I found them *children*'.

Lloyd George's residence at Routh Road was also a time of personal grief: his eldest daughter died of appendicitis in 1907 at the age of 17. The loss affected his marriage and his wife remained for longer periods in their Welsh home at Criccieth. By the time time Lloyd George became Prime Minister in 1916, Frances Stevenson, his private secretary, was his mistress; in 1943 she became his second wife.

Loudon, John; Loudon, Jane.

3 Porchester Terrace, W2
   Here lived John and Jane Loudon (1783–1843 and 1807–1858) Their horticultural work gave new beauty to London squares (LCC 1953).

When John Loudon signed the building contract for 3 and 5 Porchester Terrace in 1823 he had published his *Encyclopedia of Gardening* and was well known as a horticulturalist and designer of conservatories and hot-houses. Full details of his design of the 'double-detached villa' appeared in *The Suburban Garden and Villa Companion* (1838). 'The object was to build two small houses, which should appear as one, and have some pretensions to architectural design; being at the same time calculated for invalids, and, therefore, furnished with verandas extending nearly round the whole building for taking exercise in during inclement weather.'

Loudon married Jane Webb in 1830 and when they became increasingly oppressed by debts and illness, Jane took up writing on horticultural subjects. Her best-known works were *The Ladies Companion to the Flower Garden* (1841) and *How to Enjoy a Country Life Rationally* (1845).

Lubbock, Sir John [Baron Avebury].

29 Eaton Place, SW1
   Baron Avebury : Sir John Lubbock (1834–1913) born here (LCC 1935).

John and Jane Loudon, 3 Porchester Terrace

John Lubbock lived at Eaton Place until 1840 when his family moved to High Elms, Downe, Kent, his country home for most of his life. He left Eton to join the family banking firm of Robarts, Lubbock & Co. in 1849 with which he had an eminent career. He was a notable public figure and served as Liberal MP from 1870 to 1900. While in Parliament he drew up the Bank Holidays Act of 1871.

Lubbock's early interest in natural history was encouraged by Darwin (a neighbour of his father's), with whom he studied in the evenings after working at the bank. Lubbock became a pioneer in the experimental study of animal behaviour and particularly in the social life of ants.

Lucan, Arthur.

11 Forty Lane, Wembley
Arthur Lucan (Arthur Towle) (1887–1954) entertainer and creator of Old Mother Riley lived here (GLC 1978).

11 Forty Lane, a rather ponderous house of red brick with a red tile roof built soon after World War I, was Lucan's home when he died in 1954. He named himself after the Lucan Dairy in Dublin. When he married in 1913 he and his wife Kathleen performed a double act calling themselves 'Lucan and McShane' or 'Old Mother Riley and her daughter Kitty'. Their signature tune was *The Kerry Dances* and they recounted homely adventures of the naive 'mother' and her sophisticated daughter, adding strong draughts of Irish humour. The act became a favourite with music halls and on the radio and after 1937 they began making successful films.

Lugard, Frederick John Dealtry, Baron.

51 Rutland Gate, SW7
Lord Lugard (1858–1945) Colonial Administrator lived here 1912–1919 (GLC 1972).

Lugard joined the 2nd Battallion of the 9th Foot (the Norfolk Regiment) in India in 1878 and had an active career as soldier, big-game hunter and colonial administrator. He was High Commissioner of Nigeria (1900–06), Governor of Hong Kong (1907–12) and Governor of Nigeria (1912–19, when he lived at Rutland Gate).

Lutyens, Sir Edwin Landseer. *See* PEARSON, JOHN LOUGHBOROUGH.

Lyell, Sir Charles.

73 Harley Street, W1

In a house on this site lived from 1854 to 1875 Sir Charles Lyell (1797–1875) geologist and from 1876 to 1882 W.E. Gladstone (1809–1898) statesman (LCC 1908).

Lyell's most famous book *The Principles of Geology* was first published in 1830 and sold more copies, according to Harriet Martineau, than the most popular contemporary fiction. It was to provide Darwin with geological evidence to support the theory of natural selection. When Lyell lived in Harley Street he published *The Antiquity of Man* (1863). His health and eyesight were beginning to fail, however, and the death in 1873 of his wife (12 years his junior) greatly affected him.

A year after Lyell's death Gladstone moved into Harley Street while he was leader of the Opposition. His attack on Beaconsfield's Turkish policy culminated in the general election of 1880 and his return to power as Prime Minister. A visitor described Gladstone at home: 'I found him sitting at a plain writing table in a small room which contained very little furniture. The fireplace tiles bore Homeric subjects, and a toy figure of Lord Beaconsfield, something like a clown, hung from the bell'.

Macaulay, Thomas Babington, Lord.

Holly Lodge, now Atkins Buildings, Queen Elizabeth College, Campden Hill, W8

Lord Macaulay (1800–1859) historian and man of letters lived here (LCC 1903; GLC 1969).

Macaulay was eminent in both literature and politics. He began his *History of England* in 1839 and that year was elected Liberal MP for Edinburgh and made Secretary of War. In 1842 his *Lays of Ancient Rome* were published and sold 18,000 copies in ten years. After he lost his seat in Parliament in 1847 (he was too independent and outspoken for his constituents) he was able to spend more time writing and in 1849 the first two volumes of his history were published. Its considerable success led to his re-election as MP for Edinburgh in 1852. His health was damaged by the strain of such intensive activity, however, and he resigned from Parliament in 1856, retiring to Holly Lodge. The house was only a short walk from Holland House, headquarters of the Whig political coterie since the early 18th century, so he was able to keep in touch with politics. He died in the library of Holly Lodge. (*See also* ZACHARY MACAULAY.)

Macaulay, Zachary.

5 The Pavement, Clapham Common, SW4

Zachary Macaulay (1768–1838) philanthropist and his son Thomas Babington Macaulay afterwards Lord Macaulay (1800–1859) lived here (LCC 1930).

Zachary Macaulay lived at 5 The Pavement from 1805 to 1818. He had joined the Sierra Leone Company in 1792 after witnessing the appalling conditions of slaves while he was managing an estate in Jamaica, and he governed the company's colony of liberated slaves (1793–9). He returned to England as secretary of the company, marrying Selina Mills, daughter of a Quaker bookseller. Thomas was their eldest child, born in 1800.

For most of his time in Clapham, Zachary was editor of the *Christian Observer*, the organ of the 'Clapham sect', which was devoted to the abolition of the slave trade. The political agitation which he helped to create did much to encourage his son's interests. When Thomas was away at school his parents showered him with moral, religious and political advice; at home he was allowed the unusual freedom of walks on Sundays.

Macdonald, George.

Kelmscott House, 26 Upper Mall, W6

George Macdonald poet and novelist lived here 1867–1877 (private).

George Macdonald was appointed professor of English literature at Bedford College and settled in London in 1859. Born in Aberdeenshire, he had a strict Calvinist upbringing and was a Congregational minister until dismissed for heresy. His friends in London included F.D. Maurice, whose radical social and religious views he shared, and Lewis Carroll. *Alice's Adventures in Wonderland* were read to the 11 Macdonald children before Carroll decided to publish it. Macdonald's own children's books, *At the Back of the North Wind* (1871) and *The Princess and the Goblin* (1872), were written at 26 Upper Mall. (*See also* WILLIAM MORRIS and FRANCIS RONALDS.)

MacDonald, Ramsay.

9 Howitt Road, NW3

Ramsay MacDonald (1866–1937) Prime Minister lived here 1916–1925 (LCC 1963).

Soon after Ramsay MacDonald moved to Howitt Road he was

visited by M. Ivan Maisky who recorded his impressions of the statesman: 'he was then living. . .in one of those modest little villas favoured by middle-class English intelligentsia. . . . MacDonald was then about 50, but looked very young and vigorous. . . . Tall, upstanding and powerful, his dark hair beginning to be tinged with silver, he seemed the incarnation of health and energy'.

MacDonald first entered the Commons in 1906 as Labour MP for Leicester and became leader of his party in 1911. He was forced to resign at the outbreak of World War I as he was opposed to the war and denounced as pro-German. He resumed the leadership in 1922 and two years later formed the first Labour government, serving as both Foreign Secretary and Prime Minister. His government lasted only for a few months but returned to power in 1929 as the strongest party in the Commons.

MacDowell, Patrick.

20 Wood Lane, N6
Patrick MacDowell RA (1799–1870) eminent sculptor lived here for many years (private).

Patrick MacDowell, apprentice coachbuilder and self-taught artist, entered the Royal Academy Schools in 1830. He was elected RA in 1846 and one of his last works was the 'Europe' group for the Albert Memorial.

Macfarren, Sir George Alexander.

20 Hamilton Terrace, NW8
George Alexander Macfarren Knt. lived in this house and died here 1887 (Incorporated Society of Musicians 1895).

George Macfarren studied music at the Royal Academy where he became professor in 1834 and principal in 1876. He wrote several operas (*The Devil's Opera, The Adventures of Don Quixote, Robin Hood*) and oratorios and symphonies, but he was best known as a writer of music theory. His eyesight began to fail in the 1870s but he continued to work at composition and teaching even when he was blind.

In 1900 the painter William Strang went to live and work at no.20 and he too is commemorated with a plaque.

171

McGill, Donald.

5 Bennett Park, SE3
   Donald McGill (1875-1962) postcard cartoonist, lived here (GLC 1977).

Donald McGill lived at Bennett Park from 1931 to 1939. He first drew cartoons when working in the drawing office of a naval architect. The publisher Joseph Asher realised his potential and offered him 6s. for the copyright of any acceptable card, so McGill produced six a week from 1905 until the outbreak of World War I. During the war he designed cards for all occasions, but the seaside holiday season prompted a proliferation of cartoons of outsize women and undersize men. His heyday lasted until well after World War II. He produced some 12,000 designs and sold several hundred million cards.

Mackenzie, Sir James.

17 Bentinck Street, W1
   Sir James Mackenzie (1853-1925) lived here (College of General Practitioners).

James Mackenzie qualified as a doctor at Edinburgh University in 1882. He went to London in 1907 and became consulting physician to the London Hospital in 1913. He carried out extensive research into the rhythm of the heart, publishing *The Study of the Pulse* (1902) and *Diseases of the Heart* (1908), and was elected a Fellow of the Royal Society in 1915. He died of angina pectoris, a disease he had done much to elucidate.

Macklin, Charles. *See* BOW STREET.

McMillan, Margaret; McMillan, Rachel.

127 George Lane, SE13
   Margaret McMillan CH CBE (1860-1931) and Rachel McMillan (1859-1917) social reformers and educationists lived here 1910-1913 (Lewisham Borough Council).

After working in Bradford for the establishment of school medical inspections and earning the title of 'labour prophetess of the north', Margaret McMillan joined her sister Rachel in London in 1902. Their children's clinic in Deptford received grants from the LCC for dental, eye and ear treatment in 1911 and 1912. During World War I the McMillan sisters established open-air nursery schools and in 1930

Queen Mary opened the new building of the Rachel McMillan College at Deptford for training nursery-school teachers.

Mallarmé, Stéphane.

6 Brompton Square, SW3
  Stéphane Mallarmé (1842–1898) poet stayed here in 1863 (LCC 1959).

Stéphane Mallarmé went to London in 1862 to learn English. He stayed for two years and in 1863 lived in Brompton Square, where he married a German governess, Marie Gerhard. He taught English for the rest of his life and found it a constant struggle to compose poetry in conditions of poverty and discomfort. Mallarmé was influenced by the English Romantic poets, particularly Keats, Shelley and Coleridge, as well as by his countryman Baudelaire. Two of his best-known poems are *L'après-midi d'un faune* (1865) and *Hérodiade* (1864).

Malone, Edmond.

40 Langham Street, W1
  Edmond Malone (1741–1812) Shakespearian scholar lived here 1779–1812 (LCC 1962).

Malone settled in London in 1777; a substantial private income enabled him to lead a scholarly life devoted to literature. Friends who called at his house in Langham Street included Samuel Johnson and James Boswell, Joshua Reynolds (who painted his portrait), Edmund Burke, George Canning and Horace Walpole. Malone published his chronology of Shakespeare's plays in 1778 and, after seven years' work, published a ten-volume edition of the plays in 1790. An even larger edition of 21 volumes was completed by Boswell's son after Malone's death.

Malone raised literary criticism to a science, exploring early editions of Shakespeare, discovering new information about his life, and doing research into the history of the Elizabethan and Jacobean theatre. The Malone Society was founded in 1907 to further the study of early English drama by reprinting texts and documents.

Manby, Charles.

60 Westbourne Terrace, W2
  Charles Manby (1804–1884) civil engineer lived here (LCC 1961).

173

Manby joined his father's ironworks near Birmingham when he was a young boy, and in 1821 both father and son laid down the iron steamship, the *Aaron Munby*. Charles supervised the building of it at the Surrey Docks and in 1822 it became the first iron steamship to make a sea voyage.

Manby settled in London in 1835 and introduced a system of warming and ventilating buildings, known as Price and Manby's System. He was involved in the staging of the Great Exhibition (1851) and the planning of the Suez Canal, and was also business manager of the Adelphi and Haymarket Theatres. He lived at Westbourne Terrace from 1870 to 1876.

Manning, Cardinal.

22 Carlisle Place, SW1
Cardinal Manning (1808–1892) lived here (LCC 1914).

Henry Edward Manning was converted to Roman Catholicism in 1851 and settled in London after three years in Rome. He was made Archbishop of Westminster in 1865 and in 1873 moved to Carlisle Place, where he remained until his death. He enjoyed the bareness and austerity of his house. One of his biographers, Bodley, described the interior: 'a litter of books and papers made the upper room where he sat the least dreary in the cavernous house. The only object of piety discernible in the dim lamplight was a fine malachite crucifix which had always stood near him for 27 years. . . . Facing it Manning used to sit, in a low armchair. With his faded red skull-cap cocked over his eyebrow he looked like an old warrior of the days of his boyhood'.

During his residence in Carlisle Place Manning devoted himself to educating the poor and he was involved in establishing industrial and reformatory schools. He was also an active supporter of trade unions, helping Joseph Arch and Charles Bradlaugh to found the Agricultural Labourers' Union.

Mansbridge, Albert.

198 Windsor Road, Ilford.
Albert Mansbridge (1876–1952) founder of the Workers' Educational Association lived here (GLC 1967).

The Workers' Educational Association was founded by Albert Mansbridge in 1903, soon after he moved to Windsor Road. The university extension movement which had begun in 1873 had become predominantly middle-class and Mansbridge realised the need for a new organisation for workers. The scheme was an immediate success and, by 1914, 3234 students attended tutorial classes established by the WEA.

Mansfield, Katherine.

17 East Heath Road, NW3
Katherine Mansfield (1888–1923) writer and her husband John Middleton Murry (1889–1957) critic lived here (GLC 1969).

Katherine Mansfield and John Middleton Murry were married in May 1918 and moved into 17 East Heath Road in July. Murry wrote 'we agreed that I should look for a house in Hampstead, and I found a tall grey brick one, outwardly unprepossessing, but immediately over-looking the Heath. Because of its greyness and its size we christened it the Elephant'. Katherine was already seriously ill with tuberculosis. She spent the winter of 1919–20 in Italy and finally left Hampstead for France in autumn 1920, Murry joining her the following year.

The two writers met when Katherine sent some of her short stories to *Rhythm*, a review edited by Murry. She established her considerable reputation as a short-story writer with *Prelude* (1918) and *Bliss, and Other Stories* (1920). Murry founded *Adelphi* in 1923 and edited the magazine for 25 years. He also wrote critical studies; during World War I he was chief censor in the intelligence department of the War Office and during World War II he edited *Peace News*.

Marconi, Guglielmo.

71 Hereford Road, W2
Guglielmo Marconi (1874–1937) the pioneer of wireless communication lived here in 1896–1897 (LCC 1954).

General Post Office, Aldersgate Street, EC1
From the roof of this building Guglielmo Marconi made the first public transmission of wireless signals. Under the patronage of William Freece FRS Engineering Chief The General Post Office 27 July 1896 (private).

When Guglielmo Marconi failed to get support from the Italian government for his experiments in the electrical transmission of messages he went to London with his equipment. He remained there for about 18 months and patented his 'Improvements in Transmitting Electrical Impulses and Signals, and in Apparatus therefor', while living at Hereford Road. Marconi's Wireless Telegraph Company has described its founder as 'beyond question, the inventor of wireless. He was also the pioneer of broadcasting, and broadcast regular programmes from Writtle, Chelmsford. . .long before the British Broadcasting Company was formed. He also pioneered world wide communications before the first war and perfected them with the Empire beam system after the first war'.

Marryat, Frederick.

3 Spanish Place, W1

Captain Frederick Marryat (1792–1848) novelist lived here (LCC 1953).

Captain Marryat entered the navy when he was 14 and remained until 1830, when he resigned to devote the rest of his life to writing. Many of his novels, including *Mr Midshipman Easy* (1836) and *Masterman Ready* (1841), draw on his experiences at sea. He published an average of one book a year from 1830 until his death. He lived at Spanish Place from 1841 to 1843 when he left for his country estate in Norfolk. One of his last novels was the popular children's story *The Children of the New Forest* (1847).

Marvell, Andrew.

Outside wall of Waterlow Park, west side Highgate High Street, N6

Four feet below this spot is the stone step formerly the entrance to the cottage in which lived Andrew Marvell poet wit and satirist colleague with John Milton in the Foreign and Latin Secretaryship during the Commonwealth and for about twenty years MP for Hull Born at Winestead Yorkshire 31 March 1621 Died in London 18 August 1678 and buried in the church of St Giles-in-the-Fields (LCC 1898).

Though Marvell was a royalist sympathiser at the time of Charles I's execution, he was employed as tutor by both Lord Fairfax, the parliamentary general, and Oliver Cromwell; on the recommendation of Milton he was assistant Latin secretary to the government. He served as MP for Hull from 1859 until his death and by the Restoration he was sufficiently in royal favour to be able to plead for Milton's life. Marvell wrote many satires and political tracts but he is now best known for such love lyrics and pastoral poems as *To his Coy Mistress*, *The Garden* and *The Nymph Complaining for the Death of her Faun*.

Marx, Karl.

28 Dean Street, W1
Karl Marx (1818–1883) lived here 1851–1856 (GLC 1967).

Marx came to England with his family in August 1849 after the collapse of the revolutionary movement in the Rhineland the previous year. He lodged in Camberwell, Chelsea and a hotel in Leicester Square before moving to Dean Street in 1850. He spent a few months staying at no.64 (now demolished) and in 1851 he took two small rooms on the top floor of no.28. He shared the house with an Italian cook, an Italian confectioner and a language teacher. The five years in Dean Street were passed in poverty and sickness: three of his children died. His income came from contributions to the *People's Paper* and the *New York Tribune* and he spent most of the time studying in the British Museum, working on *Das Kapital* (1867). A Prussian agent described Marx's rooms after a visit: 'in one of the worst, therefore also the cheapest, quarters of London. He occupies two rooms...and in the whole apartment there is not one clean and good piece of furniture to be found; all is broken, tattered and torn, everywhere is the greatest disorder...his manuscripts, books and newspapers lie beside the children's toys, bits and pieces for his wife's work-basket, tea-cups with broken rims, dirty spoons, knives, forks, lamps, an inkwell, tumblers, Dutch clay-pipes, tobacco ash...all this on the same table...sitting down is a really hazardous business'. The house is now one of London's most expensive restaurants.

Masaryk, T.G.

21 Platts Lane, NW3
Here lived and worked during 1914–18 war T.G. Masaryk, President Liberator of Czechoslovakia (Czechoslovakia Colony 1950).

The Slovak nationalist T.G. Masaryk escaped to England during World War I to appeal to the Allies for help in liberating the Czechs and Slovaks from the domination of the Austrian Empire. He was joined by the Czech leader Edvard Benes and they impressed President Wilson to the extent that he included the establishment of a Czecho-Slovak republic among the war aims of the Allied powers. Masaryk became the first president of the new country: Benes became president in 1935.

Matthay, Tobias.

21 Arkwright Road, NW3
  Tobias Matthay (1858–1945) teacher and pianist lived here (GLC 1979).

Tobias Matthay lived in Arkwright Road from 1902 to 1909. He is best remembered for his work as a teacher. He devised a method of piano teaching that laid great stress on touch controlled by weight and relaxation; *The Art of Touch* was published in 1903. He established his own school in 1906 and his pupils included Myra Hess, Harriet Cohen and Ethel Kennedy.

Maugham, William Somerset.

6 Chesterfield Street, W1
  William Somerset Maugham (1874–1965) novelist and playwright lived here 1911–1919 (GLC 1975).

Somerset Maugham qualified as a doctor but never practised, making writing his career. His first novel, *Liza of Lambeth* (1897), was influenced by the French naturalistic novelists and describes London slums. While Maugham was living at Chesterfield Street the novels *Of Human Bondage* (1915) and *The Moon and Sixpence* (1919) were published, the latter based loosely on Gauguin's life. Maugham's comedies of manners were popular in the 1920s and included *The Circle* (1921) and *East of Suez* (1922). After a marriage that ended in divorce, Maugham moved permanently to Cap Ferrat in the south of France where he lived from 1930 until his death.

Maurice, Frederick Denison.

2 Upper Harley Street, NW1
  Frederick Denison Maurice (1805–1872) Christian philosopher and educationalist lived here 1862–1866 (GLC 1977).

As professor of English literature and history at King's College London (1840–46) and professor of theology (1846–53), F.D. Maurice became a well-known academic figure. He was particularly interested in further education and helped to found Queen's College (1848) and the Working Men's College (1854). He was also spiritual leader of the Christian Socialists, editing their journal *Politics for the People*. This brought the group into contact with some of the more radical Chartist leaders and the Christian Socialists were able to secure the 1852 Act legalising cooperative bodies. Maurice, however, was forced to resign from King's College for his radical activities. He became minister of St Peter's, Vere Street, in 1860, living in Upper Harley Street until he was elected to the Knightsbridge chair of moral philosophy at Cambridge in 1866.

Maxim, Sir **Hiram**.

57*d* Hatton Garden, EC1

Sir Hiram Maxim (1840–1916) inventor and engineer designed and manufactured the Maxim Gun in a workshop on these premises (GLC 1966).

Maxim went to London after receiving the Légion d'honneur at the 1881 Paris Exhibition for inventing the electrical current regulator. He rented a workshop at 57*d* Hatton Garden where he worked on his most famous invention, the Maxim gun, the first fully automatic machine-gun, which could discharge 600 rounds a minute with great accuracy. Maxim was knighted in 1901 after becoming a naturalised citizen (he was born in the USA). He died at Streatham.

Maxwell, James Clark.

16 Palace Gardens Terrace, W8

James Clark Maxwell (1831–1879) physicist lived here (LCC 1923).

James Clark Maxwell lived at 16 Palace Gardens Terrace from just after he was appointed professor of natural history at King's College London in 1860 until his resignation in 1865. He completed some of his most important papers there including *A Memoir on Colours* (1861), *A Dynamical Theory of the Electro-magnetic Field* (1864) and *A Dynamical Theory of Gases* (1866), carrying out experiments in the large garret running the length of the house. Sir Joseph Larmer wrote: 'by universal consent his ideas as the mathematical co-interpreter and continuator of Faraday, rank as the greatest advance in our understanding of the laws of the physical universe that has appeared since the time of Newton'. In 1871 Maxwell was appointed to a new chair of experimental physics at Cambridge and he supervised the planning of the Cavendish laboratory, which opened in 1874.

Mayhew, Henry.

55 Albany Street, NW1

Henry Mayhew (1812–1887) founder of 'Punch' and author of 'London Labour and the London Poor' lived here (LCC 1953).

Henry Mayhew was the son of a London attorney and he began his working life as a dramatist. He was the author of several successful comedies and farces, including *The Wandering Minstrel*. In middle age he became joint editor of the newly created *Punch*, at the same time writing novels, biographies and travel books. His main work, however, was *London Labour and the London Poor*, first published in 1851. It was pioneering in its detailed sociological studies of the poor of London as well as being immensely entertaining. With its mixture of comedy, warmth, horror and an intense interest in humanity it is reminiscent of the best novels of Dickens (who used it as source material). Mayhew lived at no.55 from about 1840 to 1851. The house was first owned by John Nash's plasterer, Nosworthy.

Mazzini, Guiseppe.

183 Gower Street, WC1
Guiseppe Mazzini (1805-1872) Italian patriot lived here (LCC 1950).

5 Hatton Garden, EC1
Dio e popolo. In this house Guiseppe Mazzini the apostle of modern democracy inspired young Italy with the idea of unity, independence and regeneration of his country (private 1912).

10 Laystall Street, EC1
Dio Populo Pensiero 1805-1872 In this country Guiseppe Mazzini the apostle of modern democracy inspired young Italy with the ideal of the independence unity and regeneration of his country (private 1922).

Mazzini arrived in London in January 1937, an exile from Italy, and settled at 183 Gower Street under the name of Hamilton. He remained there until 1840, writing for newspapers and journals and dabbling unprofitably in the fur and olive oil trades. He founded the Garibaldi and Mazzini Operatives' Society for Italian workers in London and the club met in Laystall Street. In a room on the second floor Garibaldi recruited volunteers and raised subscriptions for his Italian campaign. Mazzini also started a free elementary school in Hatton Garden in 1841. Italy was finally unified in 1861 but under Victor Emmanuel, King of Sardinia. Mazzini's dream of a free republican Italy was not fulfilled until 1946.

Menon, Krishna.

57 Camden Square, NW1
In this house from 1924 to 1947 lived V.K. Krishna Menon St Pancras Borough Councillor 1934-1957 Honorary Freeman 1955 High Commissioner for India 1947-1952 (Camden Borough Council).

Meredith, George.

7 Hobury Street, SW10
George Meredith OM (1828-1909) poet and novelist lived here (GLC 1976).

Meredith lived at 7 Hobury Street, a terrace house built in the mid-19th century, from 1857 to 1859. He married the widowed daughter of Thomas Love Peacock in 1849 but she left him for the painter Henry Wallis just before he moved to the house. Meredith had been trained as a solicitor but turned to journalism, creative writing and reading. His first characteristic novel, *The Ordeal of Richard Feverel*, describes an idyllic love-affair brought to a tragic end by the social and educational restrictions of the time; it was written in Hobury Street. His sonnet sequence *Modern Love*, based on his own unhappy marriage, caused a stir when it was published in 1862. Meredith rediscovered domestic happiness when he married Marie Vulliamy in 1864. They settled at Flint Cottage, Box Hill, where Meredith died. After the publication of *The Egoist, A Comedy in Narrative* (1879) he was an 'elder statesman' of English literature and Box Hill became a literary shrine visited by young aspiring writers. (*See also* DANTE GABRIEL ROSSETTI.)

Metternich, Prince.

44 Eaton Square, SW1
Prince Metternich (1773-1859) Austrian statesman lived here in 1848 (GLC 1970).

44 Eaton Square was built in 1826 by Seth Smith. Prince Metternich-Winneburg stayed at the house, owned by Lord Denbigh, from 6 May to 14 September. He had reached the climax of his diplomatic influence at the Congress of Vienna (1814-15). As Austrian chancellor he helped ensure stability in Europe for the next 30 years by suppressing nationalist movements. His system collapsed with the 1848 revolutions and he fled from Vienna. He did not return until 1851, spending the intervening years in London, Brighton and Brussels. At Eaton Square he received

visits from prominent Conservatives; the Duke of Wellington called every morning.

Meynell, Alice.

47 Palace Court, W2
Alice Meynell (1847–1922) poet and essayist lived here (LCC 1948).

47 Palace Court is part of a terrace built at the end of the 19th century by Leonard Stokes. Alice and Wilfrid Meynell lived there from 1890 to 1905. Wilfrid returned to the house in 1926. Alice Meynell's first book of verse *Preludes* was published in 1875, shortly after she became a Roman Catholic. Many contemporary writers visited the Meynells' house, including Coventry Patmore and George Meredith. The poet Francis Thompson was rescued from poverty and drug addiction by the Meynells' care.

Mill, John Stuart.

18 Kensington Square, W8
John Stuart Mill (1806–1873) philosopher lived here (LCC 1907).

John Stuart Mill lived with his mother and sisters in Kensington Square from 1837 to 1851. A visitor to no.18 described their surroundings: 'visited John Mill's charming library, and saw portions of his immense herbarium; the mother so anxious to show us everything, and her son so terribly afraid of boring us'. Mill was so depressed by the death of his father James, his brother Henry, and the loss of money in the American Repudiation in 1842 that he was forced for a time to take the omnibus (he usually walked) between his Kensington home and his work at India House (he joined the East India Company as a clerk in 1823).

Mill worked on two of his more influential books while in Kensington Square: the *System of Logic, Ratiocinative and Inductive* (1843) and his *Principles of Political Economy* (1848) in which he attempted to discuss the growth and increasing importance of the working class.

Millais, Sir John Everett.

2 Palace Gate, W8
Sir John Everett Millais Bt.PRA (1829–1896) painter lived and died here (LCC 1926).

Millais began his career as a painter as one of the revolutionary Pre-Raphaelite brotherhood. When 'The Carpenter's Shop' was exhibited

John Stuart Mill, Kensington Square

a critic for *The Times* was appalled by his radical moral and intellectual position: 'the attempt to associate the Holy Family with the meanest details of the carpenter's shop, with no conceivable omission of misery, of dirt, of even disease, all furnished with the same loathesome minuteness is disgusting'. Such criticism encouraged Millais's gradual change into an artist more interested in pleasing than in educating his public, and he became one of the wealthiest and most admired of Victorian painters. He paid Cubitts £8400 in March 1873 just for the site in Palace Gate on which his friend Philip Hardwick designed his mansion; the cost of the house was never disclosed. Sicilian marble covered the hall floors and on the landing water spouted from the mouth of a black marble seal within a marble basin, the fountain designed by J. Edgar Boehm. Millais's studio was 40 feet long.

Milne, Alan Alexander.

13 Mallord Street, SW3
A.A. Milne (1882-1956) author lived here (GLC 1979).

A.A. Milne took up freelance journalism after obtaining a mathematics degree at Cambridge. His light, witty style was at home in the pages of *Punch*, and in 1906 he became assistant editor. The stage comedies he wrote after the war, *Mr Pim Passes By* (1920) and *The Truth about Blayds* (1921), established his reputation as a writer.

Milne moved to Mallord Street in 1920, remaining there until 1939. His son Christopher Robin and his nursery toys inspired the world of *Winnie the Pooh* (1926) and its sequels.

Miranda, Francisco de.

58 Grafton Way, W1
Francisco de Miranda (1756-1816) lived in this house between 1803 and 1810 Born in Caracas Venezuela he was the forerunner of the independence of the republics of Latin America Here he met in 1810 the liberator Simon Bolivar (British Council 1942).

When Francisco de Miranda stayed in England he was encouraged by William Pitt to found a South American 'circle', and many of its members were later to become involved in the struggle for independence in Latin America. Miranda's attempt to seize power in Caracas in 1806 was unsuccessful, but in 1808, after Joseph Bonaparte was proclaimed king, the Venezuelans revolted. Miranda was declared dictator of the new independent republic in 1811 but only a year later he was defeated by a royalist counter-offensive. His former lieutenant Simon Bolivar arrested him and he died in prison in Cadiz.

Mondrian, Piet Cornelis.

60 Parkhill Road, NW3
Piet Cornelis Mondrian (1872–1944) painter lived here (GLC 1975).

Mondrian left Paris for London in 1938 and remained until summer 1940 when he moved to New York. He took a studio in Hampstead, a large room at the rear of 60 Parkhill Road. Hampstead was full of talented young artists including Henry Moore, Barbara Hepworth, Walter Gropius and Herbert Read. Ben Nicholson had a studio below Mondrian's. Hepworth wrote of Mondrian's time in Parkhill Road: 'for history's sake I think this period of Mondrian's life, which has not been so far appreciated sufficiently, should be recorded. . . . We were all extremely near each other and very much in touch with each other, Mondrian being, of course, a most important focus. He made his studio as exciting as the one in Montparnasse where he lived for so many years'.

Moore, George.

121 Ebury Street, SW1
George Moore (1852–1933) lived and died here (LCC 1936).

George Moore's most popular novel was *Esther Waters* (1894) which was influenced by Emile Zola. It exposed the Victorian attitude to illegitimacy among the working class and the existence of 'baby farms'. Moore was born in County Mayo and when he lived in Ireland at the turn of the century he was high sheriff for Mayo and involved in the Celtic revival with W.B. Yeats and Lady Gregory. He lived in Ebury Street from 1911 until his death, publishing *Conversations in Ebury Street* in 1924 and two historical novels — *The Brook Kerith* (1916) and *Heloise and Abelard* (1921).

Moore, Tom.

15 George Street, W1
Tom Moore (1779–1852) Irish poet lived here (LCC 1963).

Tom Moore went to London in 1799 to read for the Bar and took lodgings in George Street, remaining there for perhaps two years. His social success was ensured by the favour of the Prince of Wales, one of the subscribers to his first popular work — a translation of *Anacreon*. Moore was poet, satirist and musician and *Irish Melodies* became his most famous work, set to music by Macdonald. Moore is also remembered for his friendship with Byron and custody of the poet's memoirs which he allowed John Murray to burn.

Morris, William.

Kelmscott House, 26 Upper Mall, W6
William Morris Poet craftsman socialist lived here 1878–1896 (William Morris Society).

While house-hunting in 1878 William Morris discovered the 'Retreat', in the Upper Mall, Hammersmith. He declared 'the situation is certainly the prettiest in London' and moved his family there in October, undeterred by the damp or by Dante Gabriel Rossetti's criticisms of the decorations: 'made fearful to the eye with a blood-red flock paper and a ceiling of blue with gold stars'. Only a row of elms and a narrow towpath separated the rather plain late 18th-century house from the Thames, and Janey Morris complained that the noise of the river steamers kept her awake.

Morris pursued his political activities from his London home and Gustav Holst, who lived nearby, trained the choir of the Hammersmith branch of the Socialist Democratic Federation meeting in the house. Morris's manorial home near Lechlade was also called Kelmscott House and from there he ran the Kelmscott Press, designed and worked his tapestries, and wrote poetry and romantic novels. He died at his London home. He had always attempted to improve the living conditions and social rights of the underprivileged through his political and artistic activities, and almost his last words were 'I want to get mumbo-jumbo out of the world'. (*See also* RED HOUSE, GEORGE MACDONALD and FRANCIS RONALDS.)

Morrison, Herbert, Lord.

55 Archery Road, SE9
Herbert Morrison, Lord Morrison of Lambeth (1888–1965) cabinet minister and leader of the London County Council lived here (GLC 1977).

Herbert Morrison lived at the modest, semi-detached two-storey house in Eltham from 1929 to 1960. He was first elected a Labour member of the LCC in 1922 and after the Labour victory in 1934 he was leader of the council until 1940. His work with civil defence helped save much of London during World War II. In Parliament Morrison was Minister of Transport in Ramsay MacDonald's second Labour government and he set up the London Transport Passenger Board.

Morse, Samuel.

141 Cleveland Street, W1
Samuel Morse (1791-1872) American painter and inventor of the Morse Code lived here 1812-1815 (LCC 1962).

Samuel Morse, the 'American Leonardo', visited London to further his studies in art and worked with Benjamin West, exhibiting at the Royal Academy throughout the years he stayed in Cleveland Street. His letters home convey his surprise and annoyance at some London customs: 'the cries of London, of which you have doubtless heard, are very annoying to me, as indeed they are to all strangers. The noise of them is constantly in one's ears from morning till midnight and, with the exception of one or two, they all appear to be the cries of distress'.

Morse is perhaps better known for his inventions than for his painting although he is now recognised as one of the most important early American artists. He gave his name to the Morse code: the first Morse telegraph was opened between Baltimore and Washington in 1844.

Mozart, Wolfgang Amadeus.

180 Ebury Street, SW1
Wolfgang Amadeus Mozart (1756-1791) composed his first symphony here in 1764 (LCC 1939).

Leopold Mozart, the composer's father, took his children on a grand tour of Europe between June 1763 and November 1766 to find patronage for Wolfgang and enable him to hear the work of other musicians and composers. The family spent over a year in London, from April 1764 to July 1765, lodging in Ebury Street. They were well received by George III and Queen Charlotte and Mozart played music by Handel, the king's favourite composer. A spectator recorded: 'his execution was amazing, considering that his little fingers could scarcely reach a fifth on the harpsichord'. Mozart wrote two symphonies in London, K16 and K19, as well as his first vocal composition *God is our refuge* K20. This four-voice motet was written for a visit to the British Museum in what Mozart thought to be the 'antient' or Baroque style of Anglican

187

church music. His father also published his six sonatas for harpsichord and violin, K10–K15, and dedicated them to Queen Charlotte.

Muirhead, Alexander.

20 Church Road, Shortlands, Bromley
Alexander Muirhead (1848–1920) electrical engineer lived here (GLC *c*1981).

After graduating from London University in chemistry (1869) and with a doctorate in electricity (1872) Muirhead joined his father's telegraphy company. He invented duplex cables in 1875, creating a technique for sending more than one message, or messages, in different directions along the same cable simultaneously (the basis of the Post Office's telecommunications network). He established his own factory at Elmers End in the 1890s for manufacturing electrical instruments and moved to a house nearby, 20 Church Road, where he lived until his death. He was made a Fellow of the Royal Society in 1904.

Munnings, Sir Alfred.

96 Chelsea Park Gardens, SW3
Sir Alfred Munnings President of the Royal Academy lived here 1920–1959 (private 1960).

Alfred Munnings first achieved fame and financial success as a painter of gypsy families and he was able to build a large studio for himself in Chelsea Park Gardens. He loved the countryside and was passionate about horses, earning vast amounts for paintings of famous race horses. In 1944 he defeated Augustus John to become president of the Royal Academy and he was openly hostile towards all modern art.

Murray, Sir James A.H.

Sunnyside, Hammers Lane, Mill Hill, NW7
Sir James A.H. Murray schoolmaster philologist and editor of the New English Dictionary lived here 1870–1885 (Hendon Corporation).

J.A.H. Murray lived at Sunnyside, the whitewashed, slate-roofed house at the top of Hammers Lane near its junction with Mill Hill Ridgeway while he taught at Mill Hill School. He officially taught history, geography and English but a pupil recalled 'you learnt everything under the sun', and a teacher said 'he never had to keep order, he just kept their interest'. He began work on the New English

Dictionary in 1879 and was responsible for parts A–C, D, H–K, O, P and T. About three tons of paper bearing examples of word usage, quotations and their origins were sent to him while he lived at Sunnyside. In 1885, finding it impossible to teach and work on the dictionary, he moved to quieter surroundings in Oxford.

Murry, John Middleton. *See* MANSFIELD, KATHERINE.

Nabuco, Joaquim.

52 Cornwall Gardens, SW7
Joaquim Nabuco (1849–1910) eminent Brazilian statesman and diplomat lived here 1900–1905 (Brazilian Government).

Joaquim Nabuco devoted his political life to the abolition of African slavery in Brazil, finally achieving it in 1888. He lived at 52 Cornwall Gardens while he was Brazilian ambassador in London: 'I loved London above all other cities and places I visited. . . . If I had been born an Englishman, perhaps I would detest England; but as I was born a Brazilian, I adore it'. He was the last diplomat to be received by Queen Victoria before her death.

Napoleon III.

1c King Street, SW1
Napoleon III lived here 1848 (RSA 1875).

Louis Napoleon went into exile after the fall of his uncle the Emperor Napoleon Bonaparte. He moved into 1c King Street in December 1847, just after the house was built, and passed the time collecting books and family portraits. An acquaintance recalled him spending 'a great deal. Moreover he owns several houses. I will only mention the one he has bought in Berkeley Street. . .for Miss Howard'. The fortunate lady was later made Comtesse de Beauregard.

Louis Napoleon returned to France in 1848 as president of the Second Republic and four years later declared himself Emperor Napoleon III. He returned to England after the fall of his empire in 1870 and died at Chislehurst.

Nelson, Horatio, Lord.

147 New Bond Street, W1
Nelson lived here in 1797 Born 1758 fell at Trafalgar 1805 (RSA 1876).

103 New Bond Street, W1
Horatio Lord Nelson (1758-1805) lived here in 1798 (LCC 1958).

Nelson entered the navy at the age of 12 as a midshipman on the *Raisonnable* commanded by his uncle Maurice Suckling. His visits to England were brief. He spent only a few months (September 1797 to February 1798) at 147 New Bond Street (since demolished and rebuilt) and a month (February–March 1798) at no.103. He had returned to England a popular hero after defeating the Portuguese at the Battle of Cape St Vincent. However, he 'swallowed flattery like a child swallows pap', a failing which, when combined with his passion for Lady Emma Hamilton, antagonised both society and the Admiralty. Emma became his mistress while tending his wounds in Naples after the Battle of Aboukir Bay in 1798.

Newman, John Henry, Cardinal.

17 Southampton Place, WC1
Here in early life lived John Henry Cardinal Newman Born 1801 Died 1890 (Duke of Bedford 1908).

Grey Court, Ham Street, Ham, Richmond
In this house John Henry Newman (1801-1890) later Cardinal Newman spent some of his early years (GLC c1981).

About a year before Newman was born, his parents moved to 17 Southampton Place, the family home until 1822 (except for some brief intervals). There is a tradition that Newman and Benjamin Disraeli played together as children in the gardens of nearby Bloomsbury Square where the D'Israeli family lived. The Newmans owned Grey Court before John Henry's birth but gave it up in 1807. Newman visited the 18th-century house in 1861: 'I have been looking at the windows of our house at Ham, near Richmond, where I lay, aged 5, looking at the candles stuck in them in celebration of the Victory of Trafalgar. I have never seen the house since September 1807 — I know more about it than any other house I have been in since.... It has ever been in my dreams'.

Newman became an eminent theologian, a leading member of the Oxford Movement, a brilliant preacher and the author of the persuasive spiritual autobiography *Apologia pro vita sua* (1864). He became a Roman Catholic in 1845 and founded the oratories in Birmingham and in the Brompton Road, London, and also helped to found the Catholic University in Dublin.

Newton, Sir Isaac.

87 Jermyn Street, SW1
Sir Isaac Newton (1642–1727) lived here (LCC 1908; plaque refixed 1915 after premises rebuilt).

Jermyn Street was built in about 1667 and named after Henry Jermyn, Earl of St Albans. When Isaac Newton took up residence in 1697 the street was already fashionable and his neighbours included Lord Halifax, Sir George Rooke and the Duke of St Albans. Newton's reputation as a natural philosopher was firmly established by this time: his *Philosophiae naturalis principia mathematica* had been published in 1686-7. He was well off, receiving £1500 a year as Master of the Mint, and he 'lived in a very handsome style, and kept his carriage, with an establishment of three male and three female servants. In his own house he was hospitable and kind, and on proper occasions he gave splendid entertainments, though without ostentation or vanity. In his own diet he was frugal, and in all his habits temperate. When he was asked to take snuff or tobacco, he declined, remarking "that he would make no necessities to himself"'. Newton lived in two houses in Jermyn Street, no.88 (1697-1700) and no.87 (1700–09).

Nightingale, Florence.

10 South Street, W1
Florence Nightingale (1820–1910) lived and died in a house on this site (LCC 1955).

10 South Street was demolished in 1929 and replaced by an office block. Florence Nightingale settled there after her return in 1856 from the Crimea, where she had spent two years attempting to organise and improve the medical care offered to wounded soldiers. Her headquarters were at Scutari and conditions when she arrived were appalling. At

one point the death rate in the hospital rose to 42% as the patients contracted typhus, cholera and dysentery. When Florence Nightingale's entreaties to the War Office to introduce sanitary reforms were finally answered the rate fell to 2%. Her health was seriously affected by conditions in the Crimea and she led the life of an invalid in South Street. She was able to write, however, and *Notes on Nursing* (1860) was an immediate success. In 1907 Florence Nightingale became the first woman to receive the Order of Merit; in 1908 she received the freedom of the City of London.

Nollekens, Joseph.

44 Mortimer Street, W1
   Joseph Nollekens (1737–1823) sculptor lived and died in a house on this site (LCC 1954).

According to a contemporary, Nollekens's childhood was 'more remarkable for his fondness for ringing St James's church bells than for any more laudable exertions'. As a young man he went to Rome where he lived for ten years sculpting and dealing in antique fragments; on his return to London in 1770 he established a successful studio in Mortimer Street. He received commissions from the fashionable society of London and was able to amass a considerable fortune.

Norden, John.

Hendon Senior High School, The Crest, NW4
   Site of the residence of John Norden (1548–1625) antiquary and topographer mapmaker to Queen Elizabeth I (Hendon Corporation).

John Norden moved to Hendon during the reign of James I and built his 'poore house at Hendon' which remained the home of 'gentle-folk' until it was demolished early in the 20th century. Norden made extensive journeys through England and Wales from 1593 onwards as official mapmaker for Elizabeth I; the first of his works to be published, *Speculum Britanniae, first parte: Middlesex,* was the earliest county map to show roads. Of Hendon, Norden wrote 'it was called of the Saxons Highendune which signifieth Highwood, of the plentie of wood growing on the hills'.

Northcliffe, Viscount. *See* HARMSWORTH, ALFRED.

Novello, Ivor.

11 Aldwych, WC2

Ivor Novello (1893–1951) composer and actor-manager lived and died in a flat on the top floor of this building (GLC 1973).

The plaque to Ivor Novello was unveiled by Olive Gilbert, who appeared in all his productions. Novello was born in Cardiff and was encouraged in his interest in music and the theatre by his mother, who taught singing. Perhaps Novello's most famous song is *Keep the Home Fires Burning*, written at the beginning of World War I. After war service Novello made his début as an actor and took up theatre management. He wrote many musicials, from *Symphony in Two Flats* (1929) to *King's Rhapsody* (1949). Novello moved to the top-floor flat in the Aldwych with his mother in 1914 and died there in 1951.

Oates, Lawrence.

309 Upper Richmond Road, SW15
  Captain Lawrence Oates (1880–1912) Antarctic explorer lived here (GLC 1973).

309 Upper Richmond Road was Lawrence Oates's boyhood home from 1885 to 1891. It had a large walled garden with a sunny conservatory and a small separate coach house for the family's 'growler'. Oates served with the 6th Inniskilling Dragoon Guards in the Boer War and on the North West Frontier before being granted leave to join Robert Falcon Scott's expedition to the antarctic. The party reached the South Pole on 18 January 1912 but on the return journey Oates was suffering from severe frostbite and exhaustion: 'poor Oates' feet and hands were badly frost-bitten – and he constantly appealed to Wilson for advice. What should he do, what could he do? Poor gallant soldier, we thought such a world of him. Wilson could only answer, "Slog on – just slog on"'. Oates realised his crippled condition was endangering the lives of his comrades and on his 32nd birthday (17 March) left the tent saying 'I am just going outside and may be some time'. He walked out in a blizzard and his body was never recovered. The surviving three died only 11 miles from supplies of food on about 29 March.

Obradovich, Dositey.

27 Clements Lane, EC3
Here lived in 1784 Dositey Obradovich (1742–1811) eminent Serbian man of letters, First minister of education in Serbia (private).

Obradovich was closely involved in the Serbian struggle for independence from the Ottoman Empire between 1804 and 1813; he helped to shape the national culture of Serbia through his educational reforms and his work as a writer and translator.

Oliver, Percy Lane.

5 Colyton Road, SE22
Percy Lane Oliver (1878–1944) founder of the first voluntary blood donor service lived and worked here (GLC 1979).

Oliver and his wife were dedicated workers in the Red Cross and during World War I they provided European refugees with clothing, food and temporary shelter. In 1921, when Oliver was serving as honorary secretary of the Camberwell Red Cross, he received a telephone call from King's Cross Hospital who were trying to find a blood donor. This gave him the idea of establishing a panel of donors for the London area, at a time when giving blood was regarded as risky for the donor. The service was run from the Olivers' home and in 1928 they had to move to a larger house, at 5 Colyton Road, to accommodate the increased demand.

Onslow, Arthur.

20 Soho Square, W1
Arthur Onslow (1691–1768) Speaker of the House of Commons from 1728 to 1761 lived in a house on this site (LCC 1927).

Onslow lived at Fauconberg House, 20 Soho Square, from 1753 to 1761, when he retired as Speaker and moved to his last home in Great Russell Street. Samuel Richardson was a frequent visitor and, according to Dr Johnson: 'used to give large vaills [tips] to the Speaker Onslow's servants, that they might treat him with respect'. Onslow was opposed to late sittings in Parliament and wrote in 1759: 'this is shamefully grown of late, even to Two of the Clock. I have done all in my power to prevent it, and it has been one of the griefs and burdens of my life'.

Onslow sold the lease of his house to the 4th Duke of Argyll and in 1771 it passed to John Grant, Baron of the Scottish Exchequer. He employed Robert Adam to embellish the façade and decorate the interior. Crosse & Blackwell took over the house in the mid-19th century and used it for offices and bottling rooms; a jam and pickle factory occupied the back premises. In 1924 the firm demolished the 17th-century house and replaced it with a large office block with a Portland stone front which dominates the square.

Orford, Earl of. *See* RUSSELL, EDWARD.

Orpen, Sir William.

8 South Bolton Gardens, SW5
Sir William Orpen (1878–1931) painter lived here (GLC 1978).

The magnificent studio Orpen used in South Bolton Gardens reveals his wealth. Rolls-Royces were frequently to be seen in front of the paved forecourt. His financial success began when he was a student at the Slade, winning the £40 Slade Prize in 1899 for 'The Play Scene in Hamlet'. According to John Rothenstein (his nephew by marriage), however, this marked the culmination of his career as a painter, even though he went on to make a fortune. During the last 30 years of his life he suffered from a mental and physical decline caused by 'spiritual barrenness which he experienced as a consequence of harbouring deep emotions to which, as an artist, he was unable to give coherent expression'.

Orwell, George.

Promp Corner Coffee Bar, South End Road, NW3
George Orwell writer (1903–1950) lived and worked in a bookshop on this site 1934–35 (private).

50 Lawford Road, NW5
George Orwell (1903–1950) novelist and political essayist lived here (GLC 1980).

27 Canonbury Square, N1
George Orwell (1903–1950) novelist and essayist lived at 27B 1945 (London Borough of Islington).

George Orwell worked part-time in 'Booklover's Corner', South End Road, 1934–5. He described the shop in *Keep the Aspidistra Flying*: 'there were high brow, middle brow and low brow books, new and second-hand all jostling together, as befitted this intellectual and social borderland'. He worked in the afternoons, writing in the mornings and evenings in his flat over the shop. His developing political interests were encouraged by the owners of the bookshop: Myfanwy Westrope was a veteran of the women's rights movement; Francis Westrope had been imprisoned during World War I as a conscientious objector.

From August 1935 to the beginning of 1936 Orwell shared a flat at 50 Lawford Road with Rayner Heppenstall and Michael Sayers. He was the most conscientious of the three, cooking breakfast, washing up and always shaving and dressing before beginning to write; Heppenstall has described how Orwell's distaste for bohemianism led to considerable friction.

In 1945, having completed *Animal Farm*, Orwell and his wife Eileen and their adopted boy Richard moved to a two-bedroom flat in Canonbury Square. The square was not the elegant residential area it is now, but rather seedy and close to the depressed East End. A visitor to the Orwells' flat described how comfortable it was, especially at high tea time: 'a huge fire, the table crowded with marvellous things, Gentleman's Relish, and various jams, kippers, crumpets and toast. . . . He thought in terms of vintage tea and had the same attitude to bubble and squeak as a Frenchman has to Camembert. I'll swear he valued tea and roast beef above the OM and the Nobel Prize'.

His wife died while Orwell was acting as a war correspondent in France, and he returned to the Islington flat with Richard and a house-keeper. The winter of 1945/6 was so cold and Orwell so poor that he resorted to chopping up some of Richard's toys for firewood. For entertainment he took his young housekeeper to Collins's Music Hall on Islington Green. Orwell left the flat in 1947 for the island of Jura.

Ouida [Maria Louisa de la Ramée].

11 Ravenscourt Square, W6
  'Ouida' (1839–1908) novelist lived here (LCC 1952).

Louisa de la Ramee wrote a history of England when she was only 14. She used the name of Ouida, a childish corruption of Louisa. After the death of her father, Ouida and her mother went to London in 1857, living first in Kensington Park and then Bessborough House in Ravens-court Square. Her first long novel was published in 1863, *Granville de Vigue*, and her most famous, *Under Two Flags*, in 1867. Her novels are escapist and she was accused of being an emotional drug peddler by some of her critics but her readership was enormous and enthusiastic.

After 1866 she took apartments in the Langham Hotel, Welbeck Street, spending much of the time in Italy where she and her mother settled permanently in 1878.

Oxford and Asquith, 1st Earl of. *See* ASQUITH, HERBERT HENRY.

Page, Walter Hines.

6 Grosvenor Square, SW1
Here lived Walter Hines Page Ambassador of the United States of America to the Court of St James 1913–1918 (English Speaking Union).

Walter Hines Page was appointed US ambassador to Great Britain in 1913 by President Wilson. He worked to maintain close relations between the two countries while America remained neutral during World War I, expressing opposition to Wilson's non-interventionist policies. Before becoming ambassador, Page had been a publisher and journalist and while in London he was friendly with many literary figures.

Palgrave, Francis Taylor.

5 York Gate, NW1
Francis Taylor Palgrave (1824–1897) compiler of 'The Golden Treasury' lived here 1862–1875 (GLC 1976).

Palgrave's first married home was at 5 York Gate. John Nash designed the Gate in 1822 to provide an entrance to Regent's Park between the two halves of York Terrace. Palgrave was a gifted student, winning a scholarship to Balliol College, Oxford, and taking a first-class degree. He interrupted his university career to act as assistant private secretary to Gladstone. From 1855 to 1884 he worked in the Department of Education, becoming professor of poetry in 1884. The first of his well-known anthologies of poetry, *The Golden Treasury*, was published in 1861, just before he moved to York Gate. He worked out the scheme for the treasury while on holiday with the Tennysons and it became a formative influence on successive generations of children.

Palmer, Samuel.

6 Douro Place, W8
Samuel Palmer (1805-1881) artist lived here 1851-1861 (GLC 1972).

Samuel Palmer is best known for the paintings he produced during his 'visionary years' at Shoreham (1826-32). During the ten years he spent in Kensington and the 20 years (1862-81) at Furze Hill House, Mead Vale, Redhill, Palmer produced equally fine etchings and water-colours of the works of Milton and Virgil. He was always poor and had to accept the charity of his father-in-law, the more successful artist John Linnell. He resorted to wearing his wife's flannel petticoats when cold and was a subject of fun in the streets of London, with his hat so wide across the brim that it served as an umbrella in bad weather.

After the death of his son Thomas at the age of 19, Palmer could not bear to return to Douro Place. He was overcome with remorse for forcing Thomas to study too hard. He left London for Redhill after Linnell settled an income on his daughter Hannah.

The large, white-stuccoed house in Douro Place is hardly the 'hideous little semi-detached' Palmer's son Alfred later described. Alfred called it 'about the most complete antithesis to his ideal of a residence that could have been devised'.

Palmerston, Henry John Temple, 3rd Viscount.

20 Queen Anne's Gate, SW7
Henry John Temple, 3rd Viscount Palmerston (1784-1865) Prime Minister born here (LCC 1925).

4 Carlton Gardens, SW1
Henry John Temple, 3rd Viscount Palmerston (1784-1865) states-man lived here (LCC 1907).

Naval and Military Club, 94 Piccadilly
In this house formerly a Royal residence lived Lord Palmerston Prime Minister and Foreign Secretary (LCC 1961).

Palmerston's birth at 20 Queen Anne's Gate was recorded by his father in his diary: '19th October Dined at home. Lady P. ill. 20th October Lady P. brought to bed of a son at seven in the evening'.

Samuel Palmer, 6 Douro Place

Palmerston first entered the House of Commons as a Conservative MP at the age of 23 and served at the War Office. In 1828 he left the Conservatives to join the Whigs and became Foreign Secretary, Home Secretary and Prime Minister, the last Prime Minister to ride to the House of Commons on horseback. He personified the politics of jingoism, saying 'our desire for peace will never lead us to submit to affront either in language or act'.

Palmerston lived at 4 Carlton Gardens from 1846 to 1855. In 1857 he moved to 94 Piccadilly, having previously lived at no.144, and remained there until his death. No.94 was built about 1760 for Charles Wyndham, 2nd Earl of Egremont, and was probably designed by the architect William Chambers. A contemporary report described the new house: 'it is of stone, and tho' not much adorned, is elegant and well situated for a town house, having fine views over the Green Park'. The house was occupied from 1830 until his death in 1850 by Adolphus Frederick, Duke of Cambridge. Queen Victoria was attacked by a lunatic in the courtyard when visiting the duke in 1850. Appropriately, after Palmerston's death, the house was bought by the Naval and Military Club.

Park, Thomas; Park, John James.

18 Church Row, NW3
  Thomas Park FSA 'The Poetical Antiquary' B 1759 D 1834 and his son John James Park author of the first history of Hampstead B 1795 D 1833 (Hampstead Antiquary and Historical Society 1909).

Thomas Park trained as an engraver but turned to literature and antiquarian studies in 1797. He lived in Hampstead from about 1804 until his death and helped to organise local charities as well as assisting in the publication of Robert Bloomfield's poetry. His only son John James was called to the Bar in 1822 and nine years later appointed to the chair of English law at King's College London. But he died only a year later.

Parkinson, James.

1 Hoxton Square, N1
  James Parkinson (1755–1824) physician and geologist lived here (London Hospital 1961).

James Parkinson practised as a family doctor in his father's house at 1 Hoxton Square (since demolished). In 1817 he published *An Essay on the Shaking Palsy* which gave his unique description of paralysis agitans, now known as Parkinson's disease. He was a radical, political

Lord Palmerston, 94 Piccadilly

agitator and pamphleteer. As a geologist he worked on fossil remains, publishing *Organic Remains of a Former World* in 1804.

Parry, Sir Charles Hubert.

17 Kensington Square, W8
   Hubert Parry (1848-1918) musician lived here (LCC 1949).

   Hubert Parry moved into 17 Kensington Square in 1887, remaining there until his death. He came to public notice in 1880 when Dannreuther played his piano concerto at the Crystal Palace and his choral scenes from Shelley's *Prometheus Unbound* were performed at the Gloucester Festival. Parry taught at the Royal College of Music, succeeding George Grove as director in 1894.
   Parry helped to instil new life into English music, writing operas, choral works, symphonies and concertos, sonatas and songs. He frequently set the words of English poets to music and his setting of Blake's *Jerusalem* was written for the meeting of the 'Fight for Right' movement of the suffragettes in the Queen's Hall.

Patmore, Coventry.

14 Percy Street, W1
   Coventry Patmore (1823-1896) poet and essayist lived here 1863-1864 (LCC 1960).

   Patmore earned a meagre living from translating and contributing to periodicals until he found regular work at the British Museum Library. His first volume of poetry appeared in 1844 and attracted the attention of Rossetti and Holman Hunt, with whom be became friends, contributing to the Pre-Raphaelite magazine *The Germ. The Angel in the House* was published in four volumes (1854-62) and is a celebration of conjugal love, based on his courtship of and marriage to Emily Andres. After his wife's death Patmore travelled abroad. He became a Roman Catholic and much of his later poetry deals with religious subjects.

Pavlova, Anna.

Ivy House, North End Road, NW11
   Anna Pavlova lived here 1912-1931 (Hendon Corporation).

   Anna Pavlova first went to London in 1910 after touring Europe. She entered the Imperial Ballet School in St Petersburg when only ten, eventually becoming their prima ballerina. Anna bought Ivy

House in 1912; with its large lofty rooms and six acres of ground it attracted many artists, painters and sculptors who came to visit and work. Anna enjoyed working in clay, and dancers posed for her. She gave her last public performance at the Golder's Green Hippodrome in December 1930 and died at The Hague six weeks later.

An earlier resident of Ivy House was Charles Cockerell, professor of architecture at the Royal Academy, and J.M.W. Turner was a visitor.

Peabody, George.

80 Eaton Square, SW1
George Peabody (1795–1869) philanthropist died here (GLC 1976).

George Peabody was born to impoverished parents near Massachusetts and settled permanently in London in 1837, some eight years after he had established the firm of George Peabody & Company to deal in foreign exchange and American securities. Peabody amassed a large fortune, most of which he used for philanthropic purposes in the USA. In 1862 he established a trust fund 'to ameliorate the condition and augment the comforts of the poor who. . .form a recognised portion of the population of London'. The blocks of flats which were built throughout London set new standards of construction and accommodation for artisans. Peabody often stayed at 80 Eaton Square, the home of his friend Sir Curtis Miranda Lampson, a fellow American merchant and trustee of the Peabody Fund.

Pearson, John Loughborough.

13 Mansfield Street, W1
John Loughborough Pearson (1817–1897) and later Sir Edwin Landseer Lutyens (1869–1944) architects lived and died here (LCC 1962).

Mansfield Street was laid out by Robert Adam in 1770. Many of the houses were bought as pieds-à-terre by Adam's country-house patrons.

J.L. Pearson was born in Durham and his work was profoundly influenced by Durham Cathedral. He was to become the leading exponent of the Gothic revival in architectural forms. He went to London in 1842, working under Philip Hardwick, and supervised the building of the Tudor–Gothic hall and library at Lincoln's Inn. He set up on his own a year later and began his finest work, the church of St Augustine, Kilburn, in 1871.

Edwin Lutyens bought 13 Mansfield Street in 1919 with the help of a £5000 loan from Lady Sackville, who also gave him a Rolls-Royce complete with chauffeur. Lutyens had established his reputation at the turn of the century as an architect of domestic houses for the affluent middle class. While living in Mansfield Street he was employed as consultant architect to the Westminster estate and he spread neo-Georgian façades throughout Mayfair in a desperate attempt to keep his wife and family in gracious style (his father-in-law was Lord Lytton, Viceroy of India). He was the chief architect of New Delhi and designed the Cenotaph in Whitehall.

Peczenik, Charles Edmund.

48 Grosvenor Square, W1
Charles Edmund Peczenik (1877–1967) architect lived here (private).

Penry, John. *See* CLINK PRISON.

Pepys, Samuel.

Westminster Bank, Salisbury Court, EC4
In a house on this site Samuel Pepys Diarist was born (1632–1703) (City of London).

Seething Lane, Private Garden of PLA, EC3
Site of the Navy Office where Samuel Pepys lived and worked Destroyed by fire 1673 (City of London).

12 Buckingham Street, WC2
Samuel Pepys (1633–1703) diarist and Secretary of the Admiralty lived here 1679–1688 (LCC 1947).

14 Buckingham Street, WC2
In a house formerly standing on this site lived Samuel Pepys (1633–1703) diarist and Robert Harley Earl of Oxford (1667–1724) statesman and in this house lived William Etty (1787–1849) painter and Clarkson Stanfield (1793–1867) painter (LCC 1908).

When Charles II made Pepys Secretary of the Admiralty in 1673 it marked the height of his career in the navy office. His official residence was at Derby House, Cannon Row. He restored order to the chaotic state of the navy; 30 new vessels were built, pay, discipline and service conditions were improved and duties defined. With the election of an anti-Catholic and anti-French Parliament in 1679 Pepys found himself under attack and spent six weeks in the Tower accused of selling naval secrets to the French. On his release he lived with William

Hewer at 12 Buckingham Street. From 1684 to 1688 he enjoyed royal patronage and was an MP, president of the Royal Society, Master of Trinity College and Secretary for Admiralty Affairs. In 1688 he moved to 14 Buckingham Street, a splendid new mansion overlooking the Thames. After the Glorious Revolution of 1688 he was again out of favour and retired to Will Hewer's country house in Clapham. The diarist John Evelyn described his friend Pepys: 'universally beloved, hospitable, generous, learned in many things, skilled in music, a very great cherisher of learned men'.

Robert Harley lived at 14 Buckingham Street from 1700 to 1714, the most important years of his political career. He was elected Speaker of the Commons in 1701 and in 1703 obtained Daniel Defoe's freedom (he had been imprisoned for writing a pamphlet). In 1710 Harley became Chancellor of the Exchequer. He was an unpopular figure until a French refugee stabbed him with a penknife, whereupon he was raised to the peerage. Jonathan Swift, a close friend, commented 'this man has grown by persecutions, turnings out, and stabbing'.

William Etty moved into rooms on the first floor of 14 Buckingham Street in 1824. However 'the top-floor was the watch-tower for which our Artist sighed. On *its* falling vacant two years later, thither he ascended; getting rid of his lease at a loss' but surrounded by 'none but the Angels and the Catholics who had gone before him' (Alexander Gilchrist). He remained for 23 years achieving financial success with romantic studies of naked girls.

Clarkson Stanfield lived in Etty's first-floor rooms from 1826 to 1831.

Perceval, Spencer.

59–60 Lincoln's Inn Fields, WC1
   Spencer Perceval (1762–1812) Prime Minister lived here (LCC 1914).

Lindsey House, now 59–60 Lincoln's Inn Fields, was built as a mansion in 1641 by Sir David Cunningham and is thought to be a design of Inigo Jones. It was originally faced in brickwork with stone trim and a cornice of wood but is now covered with stucco. The years Perceval spent there were marked by his professional and political advancement. He was appointed deputy-recorder of Northampton in 1790 and, by 1796 when he took silk, his fees at the Bar amounted to £1014. He entered Parliament as MP for Northampton in 1796 and by 1807 he had become Chancellor of the Exchequer under the Duke of Portland. Two years later Perceval became Prime Minister but did not

Spencer Perceval, 59–60 Lincoln's Inn Fields

hold the position for long: he was assassinated in the lobby of the House of Commons on 11 May 1812.

Petrie, Sir William Matthew Flinders.

5 Cannon Place, NW3
  Sir Flinders Petrie (1853-1942) Egyptologist lived here (LCC 1954).

William Matthew Flinders Petrie, grandson of the explorer Matthew Flinders, lived at Cannon Place from 1919 to 1935. After working on Stonehenge he devoted himself to Egyptian archaeology, investigating the pyramids at Giza, the Tanis temple and Memphis. He raised archaeology to an accurate and specialised science and from 1892 to 1933 he was Edwards Professor of Egyptology at University College London.

Phelps, Samuel.

8 Canonbury Square, N1
  Samuel Phelps (1804-1878) tragedian lived here (LCC 1911).

Samuel Phelps lived at 8 Canonbury Square from the time when he took over the lease and management of Sadler's Wells Theatre in 1844 until the death of his wife in 1867. He wrote 'I took an obscure theatre in the north of London called Sadler's Wells, and nearly the whole of my brethren in the profession and many out of it, said it could not last a fortnight. It lasted 18 years and my stock-in-trade chiefly consisted of the plays of Shakespeare!' The theatre opened with a performance of *Macbeth* which Charles Dickens described: 'it was performed amidst the usual hideous medley of fights, foul language, catcalls, shrieks, yells, oaths, blasphemy, obscenity, apples, oranges, nuts, biscuits, ginger-beer, porter, and pipes — pipes of every description were at work in the gallery, and pipes of all sorts and sizes were in full blast in the pit'.

Philpot, Glyn. *See* RICKETTS, CHARLES.

Pick, Frank.

15 Wildwood Road, NW11
  Frank Pick (1878-1941) pioneer of good design for London Transport lived here (GLC c1981).

Frank Pick joined the London underground railway in 1906, rising to joint managing director in 1928. In 1933 he became vice-chairman and chief executive of the newly created London Passenger Transport

Board. He moved to 15 Wildwood Road in Hampstead Garden Suburb in 1914, remaining there until his death.

Pick changed public transport for the Londoner more than any other individual. He not only created the largest urban transport system in the world but employed designers of imagination to give the system a pleasing appearance. Edward Johnston designed a typeface for London Transport lettering, and artists like Frank Brangwyn, E. McKnight Kauffer, Graham Sutherland and Rex Whistler produced posters. Charles Holden designed stations on the Piccadilly and Northern lines which, for their functional versatility and efficiency, received international acclaim.

Pinero, Sir Arthur.

115*a* Harley Street, W1
Sir Arthur Pinero (1855-1934) playwright lived here 1909-1934 (GLC 1970).

Pinero's greatest success as a playwright was during the 1880s and 1890s; his reputation declined after World War I. His first full-length play, *The Money-Spinners*, was performed at St James's Theatre in 1881 and exposed gambling in polite society. Pinero continued to shock his audiences and in *The Second Mrs Tanqueray* (1893) presented a forthright treatment of the double standards of morality of the day. Mrs Patrick Campbell and George Alexander took the leading roles and the play established Pinero as one of the foremost dramatists of the period. Another popular play, *Trelawnay of the Wells*, traced the history of Old Sadler's Wells.

Pissarro, Lucien.

27 Stamford Brook Road, W6
Lucien Pissarro (1863-1944) painter printer wood engraver lived here (GLC 1976).

Lucien Pissarro first went to London in 1883 and lodged with his uncle in Holloway while working for the music publishers Weber & Co. He returned to France to exhibit in the last impressionist exhibition of 1886 with his father Camille, Gauguin, Dégas and other artists. England became his permanent home, however, and he first lived in Epping in 1890. With the founding of the Eragny Press, Pissarro became established as a leading artist-craftsman-printer, along with William Morris and Charles Ricketts.

Pissarro moved to The Brook, Stamford Brook Road, in 1900,

remaining there until his death. The Georgian house became a regular meeting-place for many young artists and writers including the poet Thomas Sturge Moore, Ethel Walker, William Rothenstein, Ricketts, Shannon and Sickert. They spent 'the second and fourth Sundays in every month. . .in serious talk and study of his excellent collection of prints and illustrated books'.

Pitt, William [Earl of Chatham].

10 St James's Square, SW1
Here lived three Prime Ministers William Pitt Earl of Chatham (1708–1778) Edward Geoffrey Stanley Earl of Derby (1799–1869) William Ewart Gladstone (1809–1898) (LCC 1910).

Pitt House, North End Avenue, NW3
William Pitt Earl of Chatham (1708-1778) Prime Minister lived in a house on this site (private).

The elder William Pitt lived at 10 St James's Square for about four years (1759–62). In the political chaos of 1757 he had boasted: 'I am sure that I can save this country, and that nobody else can'. Macaulay has described his achievement: 'in the space of three years [1758–61] the English had founded a mighty empire. The French had been defeated in every part of India. . .even on the Continent the energy of Pitt triumphed over all difficulties'.

When Pitt lived at North End, Hampstead (1766–7), he was often ill, suffering from 'suppressed gout falling on his nerves' and this had serious effects on his mental capacity for governing the country. During a particularly bad fit at North End: 'he sits all day leaning on his hands, which he supports on the table; does not permit any person to remain in the room: knocks when he wants anything'. He died at his last residence in Hayes, soon after falling backwards in a fit while opposing a motion in the House of Lords for the withdrawal of English forces in America.

Bulwer Lytton called Edward Geoffrey Stanley 'frank, haughty, rash, the Rupert of debate'. He was Prime Minister three times, though he held the office only briefly. He first entered Parliament in 1822. In 1834 he inherited the title Lord Stanley and in 1851 he succeeded to his father's title as Earl of Derby. A contemporary found his way of life in St James's Square, where he lived from 1837 to 1855, 'unwholesome': 'he never walks or rides, but sits all day in a back room without taking any exercise, until he goes to the House of Lords'.

W.E. Gladstone lived at the house in 1890. He received the

William Pitt, Edward Geoffrey Stanley, William Ewart Gladstone,
10 St James's Square

Pitt, William

freedom of Dundee during his residence and published some of his most important studies on the scriptures and Homeric literature.

Both 9 and 10 St James's Square were designed by Henry Flitcroft, who earned the name of 'Burlington Harry' after Lord Burlington became his principal patron. No.10 was built in 1734 and the first owner, Sir William Heathcote, paid £2970 for the house, excluding outbuildings, door furniture and the architect's fee.

Pitt [the Younger] , **William.**

120 Baker Street, W1
William Pitt (1759–1806) lived here 1803 to 1804 (LCC 1949).

William Pitt spent most of his official life in Downing Street (he became Tory Prime Minister at the age of 24) but in October 1802 he 'acquired a new residence in London...no 14, York Place, Portman Square', now 120 Baker Street. William Hunt described the statesman at this period: 'his hair became almost white and his face bore the marks of disease, anxiety and indulgence in port wine.... He lived for his country, was worn out by the toils, anxieties and vexations that he encountered, and died crushed in body, though not in spirit, by the disaster that wrecked his plans for the security of England and the salvation of Europe'. War with France exhausted Pitt and he died after the news of Napoleon's victory at Austerlitz.

Place, Francis.

21 Brompton Square, SW3
Francis Place (1771–1854) political reformer lived here 1833–1851 (LCC 1961).

Francis Place was trained as a leather breeches maker. He ran a successful tailor's shop in Charing Cross and the library he kept behind the shop was the regular resort of reformers inside and outside Parliament, including James Mill, Robert Owen and George Bentham. He never became an MP but he was able to steer a Bill through the House of Commons in 1824 which repealed the Combinations Act, which had made trade unions illegal. After Place's first wife died in 1827 he began visiting a middle-aged actress at 15 Brompton Square and married her in 1830. The couple moved to 21 Brompton Square in 1833 and five years later Place drafted the People's Charter for the Chartists in his Knightsbridge home.

21 Brompton Square is a four-storey terrace house, built in about 1825. Two other personalities lived there: Paolo Spagnoletti, the

214

Italian violinist (1826–33), and William Chippendale (1865–71), an actor famous for playing elderly men in classical comedy.

Playfair, Sir Nigel.

26 Pelham Crescent, SW7
   Sir Nigel Playfair (1874–1934) actor-manager lived here (GLC 1965).

The house in which Playfair lived in Pelham Crescent (1910–22) was built in the 1830s by George Basevi. Playfair made his professional début as an actor in London in 1902. He formed a syndicate with Arnold Bennett and Alistair Tayler to buy the derelict Lyric Theatre in Hammersmith which achieved fame in the 1920s: John Drinkwater's *Abraham Lincoln* ran for 466 performances in 1919. Playfair did much to popularise English classic drama by combining meticulous dedication to the original text with a sense of style that made the plays vital to contemporary audiences.

Pombal, Marquess of [Sebastian de Carvalho].

23/24 Golden Square, W1
   These two houses were the Portuguese Embassy (1724–1747) The Marquess of Pombal Portuguese statesman Ambassador 1739–1744 lived here (GLC 1980).

Sebastian de Carvalho, Marquess of Pombal, was head of the Portuguese legation in London from 1739 to 1744. He was particularly interested in the contrast between the expansion of English industry and trade and the commercial decay of his own country, and when he returned to Portugal many of his reforms were aimed at establishing a commercial system along English lines. Pombal was Joseph I's chief minister (1750–76) and proved ruthless and sometimes cruel, expelling the Jesuits and dealing harshly with any threat to the monarchy's absolute power. He was also a reformer and rebuilt Lisbon after the earthquake of 1775.

Pope, Alexander.

Plough Court, 32 Lombard Street, EC3
   In a house in this court Alexander Pope poet was born 1688 (City of London).

Alexander Pope's father was a Catholic merchant and linen draper. His business premises were in Lombard Street where Pope was born.

The young poet was a precocious child and called the 'little nightingale' for his melodious voice. He was considered the master of classical forms of poetry and his influence on 18th-century verse was not challenged until Wordsworth and Coleridge published the *Lyrical Ballads* in 1798. He is remembered today for *The Rape of the Lock*, a poem in mock heroic style, and for his verse satires including *The Dunciad* and the philosophical poem *The Essay on Man*.

Portuguese Embassy. *See* POMBAL, Marquess of.

Primrose, Archibald Philip. *See* ROSEBERY, 5th Earl.

Priory of St John the Baptist.

86–8 Curtain Road, EC2
The site of this building forms part of what was once the precinct of the Priory of St John the Baptist Holywell Within a few yards stood from 1577 to 1598 the first London Building especially devoted to the performance of plays and known as 'The Theatre' (LCC 1920).

The Priory of Holywell was founded shortly before 1128 for nuns of the Benedictine order. It was dissolved in 1539 and the site and all its property passed to the crown. In 1576 the actor-manager James Burbage built a theatre on part of the Holywell precinct. Its position was ideal: close to the city walls, and therefore easily accessible to Londoners, but outside the jurisdiction of the City Corporation who were consistently hostile to actors. Marlowe's *Dr Faustus* was performed at 'The Theatre' and from 1594 it appears that Shakespeare often acted there. Burbage's lease expired in 1597 and all the materials were taken across the Thames to be used in the construction of the Globe Theatre.

Pryde, James. *See* RICKETTS, CHARLES.

Pugin, Augustus Charles; Pugin, Augustus Welby Northmore.

106 Great Russell Street, WC1
Here lived the architects Aug. Charles Pugin Born 1762 Died 1832 Aug. Welby N. Pugin Born 1812 Died 1852 (Duke of Bedford).

Augustus Charles Pugin moved to 106 Great Russell Street when his son Augustus Welby Northmore was a boy. Pugin the elder established a school in the house for architects and architectural illustrators and the students were kept to a strict timetable by Mrs Pugin, who rose at

Augustus Charles and Augustus Welby Northmore Pugin,
106 Great Russell Street

4 a.m.; work began at 6 a.m.

A.W.N. Pugin learnt about Gothic architecture from his father and in 1827 he designed Gothic furniture for Windsor Castle. Two years later he designed scenery for a new ballet, *Kenilworth*, which was produced at Covent Garden; he converted the upper floor of his parents' house into a model theatre where 'he designed the most exquisite scenery, with fountains, tricks, traps, drop-scenes, wings. . .and every magic change of which stage mechanism is capable'. In 1832 his frail young wife Anne died a week after the birth of their only child, 'a fearful blow to a sensitive mind'. His parents died within the following year and Pugin moved to Salisbury. His most influential work, *Contrasts; or, A Parallel Between the Nobel Edifices of the Fourteenth and Fifteenth Centuries, and Similar Buildings of the Present Day; shewing the Present Decay of Taste*, was published in 1836.

Quaid i Azam. *See* JINNAH, MOHAMMED ALI.

Rackham, Arthur.

16 Chalcot Gardens, NW3
Arthur Rackham (1867–1939) illustrator lived here (GLC c1981).

Arthur Rackham bought 16 Chalcot Gardens soon after his marriage to Edyth Starkie in 1903, remaining there until 1920. The house was built in 1881 and enlarged to the design of C.F.A. Voysey in 1889; Michael Ayrton later added a studio for Rackham.

Rackham gave up his job with the Westminster Fire Office in 1892 to become a full-time illustrator. He was an enthusiast for German culture, usually spending part of each year in Germany or the Alps, and was inspired by German artists. While he lived in Hampstead he became established as the leading Edwardian illustrator with his *Rip Van Winkle* (1905), *Peter Pan* (1906), *Alice in Wonderland* (1907) and *A Midsummer Night's Dream* (1908).

Radcliffe, John. *See* BOW STREET.

Raffles, Sir Stamford.

Highwood House, Mill Hill, NW7
Sir Stamford Raffles, LLD, FRS, Founder of Singapore lived here June 1825 to July 1826 (Hendon Corporation).

Stamford Raffles spent most of his life in the East. He was forced

219

to return to England in 1824 because of ill-health and in May 1825 bought the 112-acre estate at Highwood. It adjoined the property of William Wilberforce whose anti-slavery campaign Raffles supported. Raffles was an enthusiastic collector of natural history and helped to found London Zoo, becoming its first president. He died only 13 months after moving to Highwood House. The local vicar refused to conduct his funeral or sanction a memorial to him because he was opposed to the ideals of both Raffles and Wilberforce (his private income came from a slave plantation). Raffles's coffin was only discovered in 1915 when St Mary's church was enlarged; an inscription was finally erected in his memory.

Most of Highwood House dates from the early 19th century but it incorporates part of an older house which had belonged to Lord William Russell in the 17th century.

Raglan, 1st Baron [Lord Fitzroy Somerset].

5 Stanhope Gate, W1
First Baron Raglan: Lord Fitzroy Somerset (1788-1855) commander during the Crimean War lived here (LCC 1911).

Lord Raglan lived at 5 Stanhope Gate from about 1835 until his departure to the Crimea. When he moved from Stable Yard, St James's, to Stanhope Gate he was acting as military secretary at the Horse Guards, a position in which, according to the *Morning Chronicle*, he revealed his talents 'for business, benevolence, justice, unwearied diligence, decision and clearness'. He was chosen to command the British forces when war was declared between England and Russia in 1854 but had not seen military action since the Peninsula War against Napoleon when he had attended the Duke of Wellington. He had an unfortunate habit of referring to the French (now allies) as the enemy. He was too old for such a demanding position and fell ill with the armies besieging Sebastopol, dying on 28 June 1855.

Ratcliff Cross. *See* WILLOUGHBY, Sir HUGH.

Reading, 1st Marquess of. *See* ISAACS, RUFUS.

Red House.

Red House Lane, Bexleyheath, Bexley
Red House built in 1859-60 by Philip Webb architect for William Morris poet and artist who lived here 1860-1865 (GLC 1969).

The Red House, Bexleyheath

William Morris bought an orchard and meadow in rural Bexleyheath in 1859 and employed Philip Webb to build his house. Webb kept as many of the original orchard trees as possible: some were so close that apples fell into the open windows on hot autumn nights. The house was built almost entirely of red brick with Gothic painted arches, high-pitched roofs, stained-glass windows and a well in the garden: Dante Gabriel Rossetti commented 'more a poem than a house'.

The Red House is now surrounded by suburban houses and it is hard to imagine how isolated it was in the 1860s. Morris would meet his visitors at the nearest station, Abbey Wood, and drive them home through three miles of Kent countryside, in a wagonette designed by Webb. Poets and artists of the Pre-Raphaelite movement were frequent visitors: D.G. Rossetti, Swinburne, Burne Jones and Ford Madox Brown. They played harmless jokes on one another and Morris, with his red hair and fiery temper, was a favourite figure of fun.

Morris left the Red House in 1865. It was exceptionally cold in winter and he had suffered a serious attack of rheumatic fever the previous year. He moved to 26 Queen Square, Bloomsbury, the new headquarters of his design firm Morris, Marshall, Faulkner & Co. (*See also* WILLIAM MORRIS.)

Relph, Harry.

93 Shirehall Park, NW4
   Harry Relph (1851–1928) 'Little Tich' Music hall comedian lived and died here (GLC 1969).

Harry Relph, who appeared under the name 'Little Tich', was an extraordinary figure. He was 4 feet 6 inches tall with an extra finger on each hand. He deliberately appeared with larger than average accomplices and was described as 'this grotesque homuncule, this foot-light Quasimodo'. His greatest success came from the 'Big Boot Dance' which he played all his life, even in the royal command performance of 1912. Paul Nash saw the act: 'his strangest and most compelling asset were his feet. These I think were normal in themselves, but were habitually inserted into the most monstrous boots, long, narrow and flat, so long that he could bow from the boots and lean over at almost an acute angle from his heels'.

Repton, Humphrey.

Lloyds Bank, 182 Main Road, Gidea Park, Romford, Essex
   On this site lived the landscape gardener Humphrey Repton 1752–1818 (private).

Humphrey Repton lived at Romford from 1783 until his death. He took up landscape gardening after losing money in a scheme to improve delivery of mail. His first adviser was Lancelot Brown but he soon developed his own, less formal, more natural approach to garden design. His first major project was at Cobham, Kent, in 1790. In London he designed the gardens of Russell Square and altered Kensington Gardens. He had a successful practice patronised by the nobility and became friends with William Wilberforce, William Pitt and Edmund Burke.

Reschid, Mustapha Pasha.

1 Bryanston Square, W1
   Mustapha Pasha Reschid (1800–1858) Turkish statesman and reformer lived here as an ambassador in 1839 (GLC 1972).

The handsome pavilion at 1 Bryanston Square was designed by Joseph Parkinson and built in 1811. The Turkish Embassy moved to the house from Regent's Park in March/April 1839 and Reschid lived there from early April to mid-August. Reschid was ambassador 1836–7 and again in 1838–9 and gained a knowledge of the West which informed his subsequent attempts to modernise the Ottoman Empire. His historical standing rests on his achievements as a political and social reformer in Turkey.

Reynolds, Sir Joshua.

5 Great Newport Street, WC2
Sir Joshua Reynolds Artist (1753–1761) lived here

Fanum House, (site of 47) Leicester Square, WC2
Sir Joshua Reynolds (1723–1792) portrait painter lived and died in a house on this site (LCC 1960).

After two years' travelling and studying in Italy Reynolds established a studio for portrait painting in St Martin's Lane in 1753 and within two years had 125 sitters. He moved to 5 Great Newport Street late in the 1750s. The street was not finished when he lived there and his house was pulled down in about 1766. Nos.10 and 11 were erected in its place so the present no.5 was not his residence.

In 1760 Reynolds moved to Leicester Fields (now Square) where he built a magnificent studio and reception rooms in which to entertain clients and visitors, including Fanny Burney, Dr Johnson, Edmund Burke, David Garrick and James Boswell. The 'painting room was of octagonal form, about 20 feet long and about 16 in breadth . . . the chair for his sitter was raised 18 inches from the floor'.

Reynolds was interested in all the arts. He was president of the Royal Academy from its foundation in 1768 and a founder-member of the Literary Club. He gave up painting in 1789 after losing the sight of his left eye and died three years later.

Reynolds, Saint Richard.

Stable Block, Syon House, Isleworth
St. Richard Reynolds a monk of Syon Abbey lived within these premises till martyred at Tyburn 4th May 1535 (private).

Syon House and its outbuildings are on the site of the Bridgettine Abbey established in 1422. The abbey was founded by Henry V soon after his victory at the Battle of Agincourt. All that remains of the monastic buildings are some rib-vaulting in the ground floor of Syon House and a few lengths of stone walling. Richard Reynolds was chaplain to the Bridgettine Abbey for many years before he was martyred at Tyburn in 1535. He was among 40 English martyrs to be canonised in 1970.

Richmond, George.

20 York Street, W1
   George Richmond (1809-1896) painter lived here 1843-1896 (LCC 1961).

Richmond studied at the Royal Academy where he was influenced by William Blake and Fuseli. He had to take up portrait painting to earn a living after eloping to Gretna Green with an architect's daughter. He became extremely successful, aiming to paint 'the truth lovingly told'. His son recalled some of the visitors to 20 York Street: 'Mrs Fry (Elizabeth Gurney), John Ruskin, Mr Gladstone and Mrs Gladstone . . . Archdeacon Henry Edward Manning, afterwards Cardinal Archbishop of Westminster . . . Few houses in London can have been visited by a greater variety of interesting people, ranging from the Duke of Wellington to Mrs Manning, the murderess, who came as lady's maid to the Duchess of Sutherland'.

Ricketts, Charles.

Lansdowne House, Lansdowne Road, W11
   In these studios lived and worked the artists Charles Ricketts (1866-1931) Charles Shannon (1863-1937) Glyn Philpot (1884-1937) Vivian Forbes (1891-1937) James Pryde (1866-1941) and F. Cayley Robinson (1862-1927) (GLC 1979).

Lansdowne House was designed by William Flockhart and built in 1904. The first artists to work at the studios were Ricketts and Shannon (1904-23) who had jointly edited the influential magazine *The Dial* and who collaborated on the design and illustration of books for Ricketts's Vale Press. Ricketts was also a stage designer, his work anticipating the designs of Bakst.
   Philpot was at Lansdowne House from 1925 to 1935 making a close study of the old masters' techniques to produce experimental sculpture and painting using under-painting and glaze in the manner of Titian and Goya. Vivian Forbes studied under him (1923-7). Pryde died at Lansdowne House in 1941. With Sir William Nicholson he invented the famous Beggarstaff Brothers, producing posters using a new technique with paper cut-outs to produce striking silhouettes.

Ripon, Marquess of [George Frederick Robinson].

9 Chelsea Embankment, SW3
   George Frederick Robinson Marquess of Ripon (1827–1909) states-
man and Viceroy of India lived here (LCC 1959).

G.F. Robinson lived at 9 Chelsea Embankment from 1890 until his death. He first entered Parliament in 1852 as an advanced Liberal MP for Hull. When Lord Lytton resigned in 1880 he became Viceroy of India and tried to involve Indians in the government and administration of their country; the Conservatives called it a 'policy of sentiment'. He served as Colonial Secretary (1892–5) and held the Privy Seal in Campbell-Bannerman's government (1905–8). He resigned in 1908.

Rizal, José.

37 Chalcot Crescent, NW1
   Dr Jose Rizal (1861–1896) Philippine patriot and hero lived here
(Embassy of the Philippines and Philippine Society of London 1955).

Jose Protasio Rizal y Mercado Alonso was born in Calambo in the Philippine Islands and died at Manila. He studied medicine in Spain and travelled widely, working part of the time as a journalist; he also wrote two long novels. He stayed briefly at 37 Chalcot Crescent (1888–9). Rizal is remembered for the leading part he played in the Philippine independence movement against Spain and his execution was the signal for renewed revolt.

Roberts, Frederick Sleigh, Earl.

47 Portland Place, W1
   Earl Roberts (1832–1914) Field-Marshal lived here (LCC 1922).

Earl Roberts took 47 Portland Place from January 1902 until 1906 shortly after he returned to England as commander-in-chief of the British army. He had served in India (1852–1900) and in South Africa (1900–02). Roberts became involved in army reform and the reorganisation of the military system at the War Office; in *The Defence of the Empire* (1905–6) he wrote of the necessity of realizing the country's unpreparedness for war.

Robinson, F. Cayley. *See* RICKETTS, CHARLES.

Robinson, George Frederick. *See* RIPON, Marquess of.

Rokesley, Gregory de.

72 Lombard Street, EC3
In a house on this site lived Gregory de Rokesley, eight times Mayor of London 1274–1281 and 1285 (City of London).

Gregory de Rokesley was one of the most successful wool merchants and the richest goldsmith of his time. Eight times Mayor of London, he was also king's chamberlain (1276) and Master of the Exchange (1278). He owned property in London, Canterbury and Rochester, eight manors in Kent, two in Surrey and one in Sussex.

Romilly, Sir Samuel.

6 Gray's Inn Square, WC1
Sir Samuel Romilly Solicitor General 1806 occupied chambers here 1778–1791 (Benchers of Gray's Inn).

21 Russell Square, WC1
Here lived Sir Samuel Romilly law reformer Born 1757 Died 1818 (Duke of Bedford 1919).

Samuel Romilly was admitted a member of Gray's Inn in 1778 and called to the Bar in 1783. He was descended from a Huguenot family and grew up an ardent disciple of Rousseau. He became acquainted with some of the English and French radical thinkers of the day, including Jeremy Bentham, Diderot and Mirabeau, and stayed in Paris during the French Revolution. As a law reformer he attempted to reduce the number of offences punishable by death. He supported the emancipation of Catholics and, with his friend William Wilberforce, worked for the freedom of slaves. Romilly's wife died in 1818 and he committed suicide only a few days afterwards in his house in Russell Square (where he had moved in 1805).

Romney, George.

Holly Bush Hill, NW3
George Romney (1734–1802) painter lived here (LCC 1908).

Romney bought a house in Hampstead in 1796 for £700, pulled down the stables, and erected an 'ambitious gallery for statuary and paintings, with a few living rooms attached'. Romney had moved from his former residence in Cavendish Square to his new gallery by 1798 but his physical and mental health were rapidly declining. His successful period as a portrait painter and rival of Joshua Reynolds was over: his friend Hayley reported in 1799 that 'his increasing weakness of body and mind afforded only a gloomy prospect for the residue of his life'. Romney left Hampstead the same year, returning to the wife he had deserted in Kendal many years before, and died insane.

Ronalds, Sir Francis.

Coach House, 26 Upper Mall, W6
The first electric telegraph 8 miles long was constructed here in 1816 by Sir Francis Ronalds F.R.S. (private).

Francis Ronalds laid down eight miles of wire, insulated in glass tubes and surrounded by a wooden trough filled with pitch, in the garden of his house at 26 Upper Mall (later called Kelmscott House). He published an account of his invention in *Descriptions of an Electric Telegraph and of some other Electrical Apparatus* in 1823 but received no official recognition or encouragement until his electric telegraph was developed by Charles Wheatstone. Wheatstone had seen some of the Hammersmith experiments and produced his model in 1837, working with William Fothergill Cooke. Ronalds was finally knighted for his services in 1871. Part of the original telegraph was dug up from the garden of 26 Upper Mall in 1871 and is now in the Science Museum, South Kensington.

Rosebery, 5th Earl [Archibald Philip Primrose].

20 Charles Street, W1
5th Earl Rosebery (1847-1929) Prime Minister and first Chairman of the London County Council was born here (LCC 1962).

The 5th Earl Rosebery was the first to suggest that the LCC 'should found an historical department which would commemorate the houses of famous men' (*see* INTRODUCTION). He took his seat in the Lords as a Liberal after being sent down from Oxford in 1869 for refusing to give up his stud. Throughout his political career he tried to reform the Lords by making it more representative; he favoured the election of peers by local authorities and the curtailment of hereditary rights to a seat. In 1889 Rosebery was elected to the LCC for the City and became the first chairman. The first street improvement to be completed by the council was named after him: Rosebery Avenue. He was Prime Minister for a year (1894-5) after the resignation of Gladstone.

Ross, Sir **James Clark.**

2 Eliot Place, SE13
  Sir James Clark Ross (1800–1862) polar explorer lived here (LCC 1960).

James Clark Ross lived at Eliot Place, Blackheath, after he returned from his famous expedition to the Antarctic (1839–43). He crossed the Antarctic Circle on New Year's Day 1841 and sailed on to discover a long range of high land he called Victoria, a volcano over 12,000 feet high (named Mount Erebus after one of his ships), the Great Ice Barrier and Coulman Island (named after his fiancée). On earlier voyages Ross had discovered the position of the north magnetic pole (1831) and found Ross Island and Ross Sea in the Antarctic.

Rossetti, Christina Georgina.

30 Torrington Square, WC1
  Christina Georgina Rossetti (1830–1894) poetess lived and died here (Duke of Bedford 1913; GLC 1975).

Christina Rossetti moved to 30 Torrington Square, 'a comfortable residence', in 1876. Her brother was the Pre-Raphaelite artist Dante Gabriel Rossetti and she contributed some of her earlier verse to the Pre-Raphaelite magazine *The Germ* under the pseudonym 'Ellen Alleyne'. She was profoundly religious and refused to marry John Collinson and Charles Cayley because they did not share her High Anglican beliefs: her poetry dwells on the agonies of hopeless love. Her finest collection, *Goblin Market and other Poems*, was published in 1862. She spent her last years producing works of religious edification which achieved a wide circulation and showed her concern for contemporary social problems, prostitution, unemployment and poverty.

Rossetti, Dante Gabriel.

110 Hallam Street, W1
  Dante Gabriel Rossetti (1828–1882) poet and painter born here (LCC 1906; premises rebuilt and plaque refixed 1928).

17 Red Lion Square, WC1
  In this house lived in 1851 Dante Gabriel Rossetti (1828–1882) poet and painter and from 1856–1859 William Morris (1834–1896) poet and artist and Sir Edward Burne-Jones (1833–1898) painter (LCC 1911).

Dante Gabriel Rossetti, 16 Cheyne Walk

16 Cheyne Walk, SW3
Dante Gabriel Rossetti (1828–1882) and Algernon Charles Swinburne (1837–1909) lived here (LCC 1949).

Dante Gabriel Rossetti was born to an Italian father and half Italian mother at 38 Charlotte Street (now 110 Hallam Street). The family remained there until 1836 and received some distinguished foreign visitors, including Mazzini and Louis Napoleon.

By the time Rossetti took lodgings in Red Lion Square in 1851, sharing a studio with a fellow artist Walter Deverell, he had fallen in love with Elizabeth Siddal. 'Guggums', as he called her, was the model for many Pre-Raphaelite paintings, including his own 'Beata Beatrix' and Millais's 'Ophelia'. Rossetti and Guggums lived together in Blackfriars; although he married her in 1860 he continued to see other women and she committed suicide in 1862.

William Morris and Edward Burne-Jones took over Rossetti's studio on the first floor of 17 Red Lion Square in 1856. Morris's work as a designer began with the furnishing of their rooms: 'Topsy has had some furniture made after his own design; they are as beautiful as medieval work, and when we have painted designs of knights and ladies upon them they will be perfect marvels'. Morris, Marshall, Faulkner & Company was established at 8 Red Lion Square in April 1861: Morris meanwhile had moved to the Red House and Burne-Jones to Kensington.

Rossetti lived at 16 Cheyne Walk from 1862 to 1882. At first he shared it with his brother William, the poet Swinburne and novelist George Meredith. William and Meredith only stayed a short time. Meredith is supposed to have been put off by the sight of Rossetti's 'uneaten breakfast of five eggs which had bled slowly to death on slabs of coagulate bacon'. Swinburne wrote *Atalanta in Corydon* and his most impressive and notorious volume of poetry *Poems and Ballads* (1866) in the house. Rossetti's own poems were published in 1870 after he had recovered his only manuscript copy from inside Guggums's coffin in Highgate cemetery.

16 Cheyne Walk, with its magnificent iron gates and railings, was built in 1717 but the central bay window is a later addition. Rossetti surrounded himself with his collection of blue and white Nankin china and exotic animals, a wallaby, kangaroo, two wombats, an armadillo, peacocks and a Brahmin bull — this last because its eyes were like Morris's wife Janey. Rossetti fell hopelessly in love with her and the house deteriorated into disorder as he took increasing doses of chloral and whisky to combat his melancholia and insomnia.

Rossi, Charles. *See* HAYDON, BENJAMIN.

Rowlandson, Thomas.

16 John Adam Street, Adelphi, WC2
*Thomas Rowlandson (1757–1827) artist and caricaturist lived in a
house on this site* (LCC 1950).

Rowlandson lived in the basement of 2 Robert Street, Adelphi, from
1793 to 1795, 'a dismal uninhabited place and likely to remain so'. In
1800 he moved to the attic of 16 John Adam Street. Rowlandson was
born in Old Jewry and studied painting at the Royal Academy Schools
and then in Europe, returning to contribute regularly to the Academy
(1777–81). The publisher Rudolph Ackermann stimulated most of his
later work, including *The Microcosm of London* (1808–10), in which
Augustus Charles Pugin assisted with the drawings, *The Three Tours of
Doctor Syntax* (1812–21) and *The English Dance of Death* (1815–16).

Roy, William.

10 Argyll Street, W1
*Major General William Roy (1726–1790) founder of the Ordnance
Survey lived here* (GLC 1979).

Major General William Roy moved into Argyll Street in 1779 and
lived there until his death. The house had a plain brick frontage and
simple Georgian windows at that time but has since been camouflaged
with stucco. It is one of the only two surviving buildings of the Duke
of Argyll's estate.

Roy's cartographic talent was revealed during the Duke of Cumber-
land's campaign against the supporters of Bonnie Prince Charlie in the
Highlands of Scotland. Roy spent nine years mapping the entire
Scottish mainland to open the wild landscape to the English troops. He
joined the army and produced maps for the Duke of Brunswick during
the Seven Years' War. His greatest achievement was laying the foundations for the national survey of Britain. The Ordnance Survey was
created a year after his death as a result of his last scientific undertaking,
the triangulation of south-east England to discover the relative positions
of the Paris and Greenwich observatories.

Ruskin, John.

26 Herne Hill, SE4
John Ruskin (1819–1900) lived in a house on this site (LCC 1926).

231

Ruskin moved from his birthplace in Bloomsbury to 'rural' Herne Hill at the age of four. He recalled the house 'embowered in leafy seclusion and commanding from its garret windows a notable view, on one side, of the Norwood Hills, and, on the other, of the valley of the Thames'. He first learnt the difference between fact and fiction in its grounds: 'the differences of primal importance which I observed between the nature of this garden, and that of Eden, as I had imagined it, were that, in this one, *all* the fruit was forbidden; and there were no companionable beasts'.

After graduating from Oxford University Ruskin began *Modern Painters* at Herne Hill. The first volume was published in 1843, the year he moved to Denmark Hill. After a brief, disastrous and unconsummated marriage (his wife Effie left him for Millais) Ruskin spent much of his last 30 years in the Lake District, writing on art, architecture and social problems.

Russell, Edward.

43 King Street, WC2

Here lived and died Admiral Edward Russell Earl of Orford Born 1653 Died 1727 (Duke of Bedford).

Admiral Edward Russell moved to King Street in 1689/90 to a house that was part of the open arcade around the Piazza. The house was rebuilt for him in 1716/17 and probably designed by the architect Thomas Archer. It made the first breach in the architectural uniformity of the north and east sides of the Piazza and was heavily criticised: 'certainly one of the most expensive and worst buildings about London'.

Russell played a leading part in bringing William of Orange to England and as treasurer of the navy and Commander of the Fleet he was a dominant figure in the French War of 1689–97. He was made Earl of Orford in 1697 and was First Lord of the Admiralty for three periods between 1694 and 1717. He used the wood from his ship *Britannia* for the staircase of his Covent Garden home.

After Russell's death, the house and furniture were bought by the nephew of Thomas Archer. The house ceased to be a private residence in 1773. As 'Evans's Grand Hotel, Music and Supper Rooms' it was visited by Thackeray. The fruiterers who occupied it from 1929 until the closure of the market removed the columned entrance. The building has now been 'restored'.

232

Edward Russell, 43 King Street

Russell, Lord **John.**

37 Chesham Place, SW1
Lord John Russell, 1st Earl Russell (1792–1878) twice Prime Minister lived here (LCC 1911).

Lord John Russell moved to 37 Chesham Place in 1841. He had built the house for himself and it remained his town residence until 1870. When he became First Lord of the Treasury in 1846 his wife described the 'amount of mental toil which strained his naturally feeble frame'. However, he managed to fulfil 'his mighty daily task without the neglect of air and exercise, and without giving up the evening leisure with his children and me which he valued so much'. Russell was a writer as well as a reformist politician; he edited the letters of the 4th Duke of Bedford and of Charles Fox, of whom he wrote a biography.

Sackville, Charles [Earl of Dorset]. *See* BOW STREET.

Saint Thomas à Becket.

86 Cheapside, EC2
  St Thomas à Becket was born in a house near this site (City of London).

Thomas à Becket's father, Gilbert, was a merchant in the City of London and the descendant of a Normandy family of knightly rank. Thomas became Chancellor of England in 1155 and the intimate friend and counsellor of Henry II. Their friendship ended when Thomas was made Archbishop of Canterbury in 1162 and pursued ecclesiastical rather than secular interests. After his murder in Canterbury Cathedral in 1170, the cathedral became a place of pilgrimage: the abject king underwent penance in public.

Salisbury, 3rd Marquess of. *See* CECIL, ROBERT GASCOYNE.

Sambourne, Edward Linley.

18 Stafford Terrace, W8
  Edward Linley Sambourne (1844–1910) artist lived here (private).

Sambourne first began illustrating for *Punch* in 1876. Four years later he was made a full-time member of the staff and in 1900 he succeeded Tenniel as cartoonist-in-chief. He entertained many artists, politicians and actors in Stafford Terrace where he lived from 1876 until his death. Some of his finest work appeared in his illustrations to *The Water Babies*.

San Martin, José de.

23 Park Road, NW8
Jose de San Martin (1778–1850) Argentine soldier and statesman stayed here (LCC 1953).

San Martin was known as 'El libertador' in Argentina and acclaimed as a national hero after defeating the Spanish forces at San Lorenzo in 1813. Four years later he led an army across the Andes and defeated the Spanish at Chacabuco, earning the title 'Saint of the Sword', and in 1820 he entered Peru. While he was liberating the southern portion of the South American continent Simon Bolivar was acting similarly in the north and the two came into conflict in 1823. San Martin went into self-imposed exile in Europe, living in England, Brussels, Paris and finally Boulogne, where he died in 1850. His stay at Park Road was brief: from 12 June to 7 September 1824.

Santley, Sir Charles.

13 Blenheim Road, NW8
Sir Charles Santley (1834–1922) singer lived and died here (LCC 1935).

Charles Santley lived at 13 Blenheim Road from 1912 until his death. He had a long and distinguished career: he made his début as an opera singer in Italy in 1857 and gave one of his last recitals at the Mansion House in 1915, in aid of the Belgian refugees. He sang Valentine in the first performance of *Faust* in England (1863) and Vanderdecken in the *Flying Dutchman* (1870), the first Wagner opera given in an English-speaking country.

Sargent, John Singer.

31 Tite Street, SW3
John S. Sargent RA who was born in Florence Jan 12 1856 lived and worked 24 years in this house and died here April 15 1925 (private).

John Singer Sargent moved to a former studio of Whistler's in Tite Street in the 1880s. He studied painting in Florence and Paris and his first public success in England was 'Carnation, Lily, Lily, Rose', his depiction of childhood which was exhibited at the Royal Academy in 1887. Sargent became a Royal Academician ten years later, having gained an international reputation as a portrait painter. He was particularly appreciated in America (he was an American citizen) and carried out extensive decorations to the Public Library and Museum of Fine Arts in Boston.

Sartorius, John F.

155 Old Church Street, SW3
John F. Sartorius (c.1775–c.1830) sporting painter lived here 1807–1812 (LCC 1963).

Sartorius was the last of four generations of artists who all found popularity as painters of racehorses, hunters and other sporting subjects. He exhibited at the Royal Academy for the first time in 1802 and three years later married Zara Adamson of Chelsea. They lived in the Regency-type house at 155 Old Church Street until 1812. A large collection of Sartorius's work is at Elsenham Hall, Essex.

Savage, James. *See* ESSEX STREET.

Scawen-Blunt, Wilfred.

15 Buckingham Gate, SW1
Wilfred Scawen-Blunt (1840–1922) diplomat poet and traveller founder of Crabbett Park Arabian Stud lived here (GLC 1979).

Wilfred Scawen-Blunt was born at Petworth House, Sussex, and entered the diplomatic service, travelling extensively throughout Europe and the Near East. He fell in love with 'Skittles' (Catherine Walters) at the British Embassy in Paris, but his eventual wife was to be Byron's granddaughter. After inheriting Petworth, the Scawen-Blunts settled in England: Wilfred wrote poetry and founded the Crabbett Park Arabian Stud. He made frequent visits to Egypt and campaigned in Parliament for Egypt's freedom from Turkish domination.

Schreiner, Olive.

16 Portsea Place, W2
Olive Schreiner (1855–1920) author lived here (LCC 1959).

Olive Schreiner was born on a remote mission in South Africa. Her best-known work, *The Story of an African Farm* (1881), was based on her experiences as a governess in various Afrikaaner households.

237

Schreiner lived at the small Regency-type house at 16 Portsea Place for only a few months (August 1885 to January 1886).

Scotland Yard.

Whitehall Place, SW1
  Site of Scotland Yard first headquarters of the Metropolitan Police 1829–1890 (GLC *c*1981).

Scotland Yard lay on the north part of the precincts of the former Royal Palace of White Hall. The yards and buildings were used by servants of the royal household until the fire of 1698, when they were converted into private dwellings. The official residence of the Surveyor of Works to the Crown was in part of Scotland Yard; Inigo Jones, Christopher Wren and Sir John Denham lived there. Other famous residents included Milton, Sir John Vanbrugh, whose 'Goosepie House' was between Little Scotland Yard and Whitehall Court, and Thomas Campbell. The War Office, built in 1898, has replaced the first headquarters of the Metropolitan Police.

Scott, Sir George Gilbert.

21 Hampstead Grove, NW3
  Sir George Gilbert Scott (1811–1878) architect lived here (LCC 1910).

Gilbert Scott lived at 21 Hampstead Grove, a fine late 18th-century house, from 1856 to 1864. He had set up his own office off Trafalgar Square (G.E. Street was one of his most talented pupils) in 1838 and he began to practise during the boom in building of Poor Law Institutions. Scott and his partner W.B. Moffat built 53 of the 323 erected between 1836 and 1839. In 1855 Scott won the design competition for St Pancras Station and Hotel which were completed in 1874. He worked on the Albert Memorial while he lived in Hampstead, but Scott found it too cold in the winter and moved his family to Ham in 1864. He was knighted at Osborne for his work.

Scott, John. *See* ELDON, Lord.

Scott, Robert Falcon.

56 Oakley Street, SW3
  Robert Falcon Scott Antarctic explorer (1868–1912) lived here (LCC 1935).

Captain Scott lived at Oakley Street from about 1905 to early in 1908 but he was in active service with the Royal Navy for much of the time. He had returned to England in 1904 on *HMS Discovery* and moved to Oakley Street the following year, writing part of his *Voyage of the Discovery* there. His expedition to Antarctica had discovered King Edward VII Land, made a survey of the coast of South Victoria Land and survived two years icebound in McMurdo Sound. In 1908 Scott was posted to the *Essex*. He was already planning his next — and last — Antarctic expedition. The *Terra nova* sailed in 1910; Scott and four others reached the South Pole on 18 January 1912 but all perished on the return journey. Two of Scott's companions, Edward Wilson and Captain Oates, have plaques commemorating their London residences.

Seferis, George.

7 Sloane Avenue, SW1
George Seferis (1900-1971) poet Nobel prizewinner Greek Ambassador lived here (Greek Embassy 1975).

George Seferis first went to London in 1924 to spend a year learning English. He returned, serving as consul at the Greek Consulate General (1931-4) and later as Greek ambassador (1957-62). Seferis's first volume of poetry, *Turning Point*, was published in 1931 but was not translated into English until 1938. By the time Seferis was Greek ambassador in London he was recognised as one of the leading 20th-century European poets and in 1963 he was awarded the Nobel Prize for Literature in recognition of his art and his struggle for human rights.

Shackleton, Sir Ernest.

12 Westwood Hill, SE26
Sir Ernest Shackleton (1874-1922) Antarctic explorer lived here (LCC 1928).

Shackleton lived at 12 Westwood Hill from 1884 until his apprenticeship on the White Star shipping line in 1890. He returned at intervals to the family home until his marriage in 1904; his sister recalled 'he used to bring back all sorts of trophies from abroad . . . the grandest thrill of all was when Ernest turned up with three baby alligators in a cardboard box'.

Shackleton made his first voyage to Antarctica with Captain Robert Scott on the *Discovery* in 1901. He led his own expedition, in 1907-9, discovering Beardmore Glacier and sending parties to the south magnetic pole and to the summit of Mount Erebus. His 1914-16 expedition to cross the Antarctic continent almost ended in tragedy when the *Endurance* was crushed by ice 1000 miles from habitation, but Shackleton led a dramatic rescue which he later recounted in *South* (1919).

Shannon, Charles. *See* RICKETTS, CHARLES.

Shaw, George Bernard.

29 Fitzroy Square, WC1
George Bernard Shaw lived in this house from 1887–1898 'From the coffers of his genius he enriched the world' (St Pancras Borough Council 1951; GLC 1975).

George Bernard Shaw lived off his mother, a music teacher, until he was 30. 'I did not throw myself into the struggle for life', he confessed, 'I threw my mother into it.' He wrote numerous novels, none of which was published, and his career as a writer only took off when he began to work as a critic in 1886. His first plays, *Plays Unpleasant*, were written in the 1890s and brought him instant notoriety, shocking their audiences and readers by examining prostitution, male chauvinism and slum landlords in their middle-class context.

Shaw continued to live in squalor in Fitzroy Square even when he was relatively well-off. His room was cluttered with books and the cold congealed remains of meals the servants no longer bothered to remove. Shaw described his reading habits: 'Whilst I am dressing and undressing I do all my reading. The book lies open on the table. I never shut it, but put the next book on top of it long before it's finished. After some months there is a mountain of buried books, all wide open, so that all my library is distinguished by a page with the stain of a quarter's dust or soot on it'.

Shaw was removed from the squalor by Charlotte Payne-Townshend, 'a green-eyed Irish millionairess', whom he married in 1898. Both were over 40 and settled down to a long, contented and almost business-like marriage, first living in Charlotte's flat in Adelphi Terrace — 'delightful rooms overlooking the river'. From 1905 their permanent country home was at Ayot St Lawrence, Hertfordshire.

Shaw, Richard Norman.

Grimsdyke, Great Redding, Harrow Weald, Harrow
This house designed by R. Norman Shaw architect for Frederick Goodall painter was later the home of W.S. Gilbert writer and librettist (GLC 1976).

Richard Norman Shaw, Frederick Goodall and Sir William Gilbert, Grimsdyke, Harrow Weald

Richard Norman Shaw established his own architectural practice at 30 Argyll Street early in the 1860s. 'Tall, thin and distinguished-looking . . . quick of mind, easily amused, suave and persuasive with his clients', he was also 'generous to his clerks.' He made a study of Wealden houses with his partner William Eden Nesfield. Grimsdyke was designed in 1870 for the painter Frederick Goodall in the 'Old English style', with half-timbered gables, tile-hanging and tall, irregularly placed chimney-stacks. Goodall (1822–1904) surrounded the house with exotic shrubs and Egyptian sheep. He made two trips to Egypt, specialising in Egyptian scenes and biblical genre paintings; he was elected RA in 1863.

William S. Gilbert moved to Grimsdyke in 1890. While living there he wrote *Utopia Limited*, his satire of the Victorian world. At the time he was himself surrounded by the material benefits of the age: 110 acres of farmland, tennis courts, greenhouses filled with peaches and melons, and 40 servants. Gilbert drowned in 1911 attempting to save a female guest bathing in the lake.

Shelley, Mary.

24 Chester Square, SW1
  Mary Shelley author and wife of the poet lived and died here (Keats–Shelley Memorial Association 1977).

The GLC agreed to erect a plaque to Mary Shelley including a reference to her most famous work, *Frankenstein* (1818). The house at 24 Chester Square had become a vicarage and neither the vicar nor the London Diocesan Fund were willing to allow the work to be mentioned, so the GLC withdrew and the Keats–Shelley Memorial Association erected their own plaque.

Mary Shelley's parents were the radical philosopher William Godwin and Mary Wollstonecraft, the campaigner for female emancipation. Godwin described his daughter when she was 15 as 'singularly bold, somewhat impervious, and active of mind. Her desire of knowledge is great, and her perseverance in everything she undertakes almost invincible'. *Frankenstein* was written in 1816 when the Shelleys were staying with Byron at the Villa Diodati near Geneva. The company agreed one evening each to write a tale of mystery. During the night Mary Shelley saw a man's form 'stretched out, and then, on the working of some powerful engine, showing signs of life'.

Shelley, Percy Bysshe.

15 Poland Street, W1
  Percy Bysshe Shelley (1792–1822) poet lived here (GLC 1979).

Percy Bysshe Shelley, 15 Poland Street

Percy Bysshe Shelley was sent down from Oxford in March 1811 after his submission of *The Necessity of Atheism* to the bishops and heads of the colleges. He arrived in London with a fellow rebel, Thomas Jefferson Hogg, and found lodgings in 15 Poland Street. Hogg said the name of the street reminded Shelley 'of Thaddeus of Warsaw, and of freedom'. Shelley occupied himself attending anatomical lectures at St Bartholomew's Hospital and circulating broadsides exposing the corpulence of the prince regent, whose 'pantaloons are like half-moons/ Upon each brawny haunch'. In August Shelley eloped to Edinburgh with Harriet Westbrook, a schoolfriend of his sister. The marriage was not successful and Shelley left England in July 1814 with Mary Godwin (Harriet was found drowned in the Serpentine in December 1816). Mary and Shelley had an artistically rewarding life in Switzerland and Italy in the company of Byron and his mistress, the Leigh Hunts, Trelawnay and T.L. Peacock. *Ode to the West Wind* was written in Florence in 1819 and *Adonais* in Pisa in 1821. Shelley drowned in July 1822 sailing between Leghorn and Spezzia. His body was found in August and cremated on the sands by Trelawnay, Leigh Hunt and Byron.

Shepherd, Thomas Hosmer.

26 Batchelor Street, N1
   Thomas Hosmer Shepherd (1793–1864) artist who portrayed London lived here (GLC 1976).

T.H. Shepherd and his wife moved to 26 Batchelor Street, a modest three-storey terrace house to the west of the Liverpool Road, in 1818, remaining there until 1841. The house was then on the edge of the built-up area of Islington with the unspoilt fields of Barnsbury to the north. Shepherd became the best-known topographical artist of his day through specialising in contemporary London. He produced the aquatints for *A Picturesque Tour on the Regent's Canal* in 1825, and a year later began *Metropolitan Improvements*. He made 159 steel engravings for the work, published in 41 parts, and it was a great success, appealing to a wide readership. Shepherd's last major commission was *Mighty London*, in the 1850s, by which time he had moved to Colebrooke Row, close to where Charles Lamb had lived 20 years earlier.

Sheraton, Thomas.

163 Wardour Street, W1
   Thomas Sheraton (1751–1806) furniture designer lived here (LCC 1954).

Sheraton described himself as a 'mechanic, one who never received the advantage of a collegial or academical education'. He carried on the trade of a journeyman cabinet maker when he first went to London in 1790 but soon devoted himself to writing technical treatises. His first book of decorative designs, *The Cabinet Maker and Upholsterer's Drawing-Book*, was published between 1791 and 1794, when he was living in Wardour Street; although he received many orders he remained poor all his life. His surroundings in Golden Square, Soho, where he had moved in 1795, were humble, dirty and ill-kept and his obituary recorded that he 'left his family, it is feared, in distressed circumstances'.

Sheridan, Richard Brinsley.

10 Hertford Street, W1
   Richard Brinsley Sheridan (1751–1816) dramatist and statesman lived here 1795–1802 (LCC 1955).

14 Savile Row, W1
   Richard Brinsley Sheridan dramatist lived here b.1751 d.1816 (RSA 1881).

Sheridan's best-known plays were produced early in his life, *The Rivals* in 1775 and *The School for Scandal* in 1777. He bought David Garrick's share in Drury Lane in 1776 and became manager, but the theatre suffered after he entered Parliament four years later. Sheridan was a supporter of Charles James Fox. He was a notable orator, and his most celebrated speech (1787), supporting the impeachment of Warren Hastings, lasted over five hours. Sheridan's last years were marred by insomnia, varicose veins and serious financial worries. Drury Lane had to be rebuilt twice during his management. Friends helped him to move to 14 Savile Row but when he died he was £5000 in debt. Only the physician in attendance prevented Sheridan from being carried to the sponging-house in his blankets as he lay dying.

Short, Sir **Frank.**

56 Brook Green, W6
Sir Frank Short (1857–1945) engraver and painter lived here (LCC 1951).

Frank Short lived at Brook Green from 1893 to 1944. During this period he was president of the Royal Society of Painter Etchers (1910–38) and treasurer of the Royal Academy (1919–32). He was also director of the etching and engraving school at the Royal College of Art. Sir Henry Badeley wrote: 'his own etchings will live for their clearness of expression and delicacy of execution: in mezzotint and aquatint he could give free scope to his sense of poetry'.

Sickert, Walter.

6 Mornington Crescent, NW1
Walter Sickert (1860–1942) painter and etcher lived and worked here (GLC 1977).

1 Highbury Place, N1
W.R. Sickert (1860–1942) had his school of painting and engraving here 1927–34 (London Borough of Islington).

Sickert took many studios and apartments in London (Islington and Camden were his favourite areas) as well as living in France, Italy and on the south coast of England. He lived at 6 Mornington Crescent in 1907 and painted some of his most immediately attractive pictures there, domestic interiors with 'Little Rachel', 'a little Jewish girl of 13 or so with red hair', for his model. In 1911 with Gore and Gilman he founded the Camden Town Group which introduced post-impressionism into British art.

Sickert opened the last of his private ateliers at 1 Highbury Place in 1927, keeping the studio until he left London in 1934. Robert Emmons described the school: 'most of the time we sat in a semi-circle round the fire and listened to the professor talk. . . . Little by little he came less often. The students drifted away. The school came to an end by a process of evaporation!'

Silver Studio.

84 Brook Green, W6
The Silver Studio established here in 1880 Arthur Silver (1852–1896) Rex Silver (1879–1965) Harry Silver (1881–1971) designers lived here (GLC 1981).

The Silver Studio closed in 1963 and four years later its contents were left to Hornsey College of Art, now part of Middlesex Polytechnic. The Polytechnic proposed the erection of a plaque to the studio and made its own to council standards, the first time this has been done.

Arthur Silver, a successful designer, established the studio when he had too many orders to be able to cope with them alone. Nearly 30,000 designs were produced by the studio, mostly for furnishing textiles and wallpapers. Between 1895 and the early 1900s it was given over entirely to Art Nouveau designs, in particular the wallpapers of John Illingworth Kay and Harry Napper. In the 1920s and 1930s the studio produced chintzes and needlework designs. After World War II it supplied its oldest customers, Liberty and Sanderson, with mainly period designs.

Simon, Sir John.

40 Kensington Square, W8
Sir John Simon (1816–1904) pioneer of public health lived here (LCC 1959).

John Simon was elected to the Royal Society when he was only 29 after writing a paper on the thyroid gland. He qualified as a surgeon at St Thomas's Hospital and in 1848 was appointed medical officer of health to the City of London. He became chief medical officer to the Board of Health, to the Privy Council and to the Local Government Board. His reports on the health of London were published in 1858 and 1859 and his *English Sanitary Institutions* has remained a classic study. Whenever Simon found any spare time he studied oriental languages and prints at the British Museum and read metaphysical works. He lived in Kensington Square from 1868 to 1904.

Sloane, Sir Hans.

4 Bloomsbury Place, WC1
Sir Hans Sloane (1660–1753) physician and benefactor of the British Museum lived here 1695–1742 (GLC 1965).

King's Mead, King's Road, SW3
The ground to the west of this building was given to the Parish of Chelsea in 1733 by Sir Hans Sloane President of the Royal Society Born 1660 Died 1753 (LCC 1953 stolen; GLC 1977).

Hans Sloane began his plant collection while studying medicine in France and he became a Fellow of the Royal Society in 1685 when he was only 25. Two years later he travelled to Jamaica as physician to the

Duke of Albemarle, returning with some 800 specimens of plants and animals, which formed the basis of his famous collection and of his *Catalogus plantarum quae in Insula Jamaica sponte proveniunt aut vulgo coluntur* (1696). Sloane set up a private practice at 4 Blooms-bury Place but the size of his museum forced him to expand into no.5 next door in 1708. The late 17th-century houses still survive though the street façade was refaced in the Italianate style in about 1850.

In 1712 Sloane bought the Manor House and its lands in Chelsea but he did not live there permanently until 1742. His property included the Physic Garden, which he permanently leased to the Society of Apothe-caries, laying the foundations of a new greenhouse, library and gar-deners' quarters. When he moved his collection to the Manor House it filled the ground floor. His library contained some 40,000 volumes. On his death Sloane's collection was sold to the nation and formed a sub-stantial part of the British Museum.

Sloane left a burial ground and the site for a workhouse to Chelsea — commemorated by the plaque at King's Mead. The bronze plaque was stolen so the GLC replaced it with one of enamelled steel: 'of low scrap value and moderately resistant to vandalism'.

Smiles, Samuel.

11 Granville Park, SE13
  Samuel Smiles (1812-1904) author of 'Self Help' lived here (LCC 1959).

After studying medicine in Edinburgh and editing the *Leeds Times* Samuel Smiles joined the Leeds and Thirsk Railway. He went to London in 1854 as secretary to the South Eastern Railway and worked on the extension of the line from Charing Cross to Cannon Street. Smiles's best-known work is *Self Help* (1859). He worked for social and political reform, championing state education, supporting workmen's benefit societies and helping in the foundation of public libraries.

Smirke, Sir Robert.

81 Charlotte Street, W1
  Sir Robert Smirke (1781-1867) architect lived here (GLC 1979).

Robert Smirke designed the British Museum. The original museum, which opened in 1759, was in Montagu House. After various additions to the collection, including (in 1823) the magnificent library of George III, a new building was required. Smirke was devoted to the neo-classical style and his Grecian design was immediately accepted. The

King's Library was begun in 1823 but Smirke was still at work on the southern colonnade in the 1840s. His brother Sydney erected the 'domed rotunda entirely fabricated of metal' over the Reading Room (1854–7).

Sydney and Robert worked together on the Oxford and Cambridge Club House (1835–7). Robert's original Carlton Club building of the 1820s was remodelled by Sydney in the 1840s after it had become overshadowed by Sir Charles Barry's new Reform Club next door.

Smith, Frederick Edwin [Earl of Birkenhead].

32 Grosvenor Gardens, SW1
   F.E. Smith Earl of Birkenhead (1872–1930) lawyer and statesman lived here (LCC 1959).

F.E. Smith was the favourite subject of caricaturists: over six feet tall, he invariably wore his hat on the back of his head, sported a red flower in his buttonhole and smoked a very long cigar. He was called to the Bar in 1899 and within five years had a large and lucrative practice. His best-known case was the defence of Ethel le Neve, mistress of Crippen. He wrote widely on international law, famous trials, histories and biographies and was renowned for his biting wit. When Smith moved to Grosvenor Gardens in 1915 (his home until his death) he was an MP and Attorney General. In 1919 he became Lord Chancellor, in 1922 the Earl of Birkenhead, and from 1922 to 1926 Secretary for India.

Smith, John Christopher.

6 Carlisle Street, W1
   John Christopher Smith Handel's friend and secretary (1712–1763) lived and died here (Handelian Society 1958).

J.C. Smith was a pupil and friend of Handel and acted as his amanuensis after Handel's sight failed. Smith wrote several operas, and his adaptation of *A Midsummer Night's Dream* (called *The Fairies*) was successfully produced by Garrick in 1754 at Drury Lane.

Smith, Sydney.

14 Doughty Street, WC1
   Sydney Smith (1771–1845) author and wit lived here (LCC 1906).

Sydney Smith moved to 14 Doughty Street from Edinburgh in 1803 and remained there for three years. Shortly after moving, his infant son died, and sorrow was added to the family's poverty. However, 'there was much quiet happiness . . . and though there was strict economy visible in all its arrangements, fine taste and loving care were equally conspicuous; and if the rooms were small and modestly furnished, they were none the less bright and pleasant places'. Smith continued to contribute to the *Edinburgh Review* which he had helped to found with Francis Jeffrey and Henry Peter Brougham. He tried to make a living from preaching, but the turning-point came when he lectured at the Royal Institution in 1804 and received £50 for the series. The Smith family were then able to move to a larger and more comfortable house. Smith's best-known work is *The Letters of Peter Plymley* (1807), a good-humoured tract in support of Catholic emancipation.

Smith, William.

16 Queen Anne's Gate, SW7
William Smith MP (1756–1835) pioneer of religious liberty lived here (GLC 1975).

16 Queen Anne's Gate was built between about 1775 and 1778 and William Smith lived there from 1794 until about 1819. He was active in the anti-slavery movement and the campaign for giving non-Anglicans freedom of worship and basic rights of citizenship. A member of a prosperous dissenting family in Clapham, he became chairman of the Committee of the Dissenting Deputies and entertained fellow reformers in Queen Anne's Gate, including Zachary Macaulay and Charles James Fox. He had ten children, one of whom was to be the mother of Florence Nightingale.

Smith, W.H.

12 Hyde Park Street, W2
W.H. Smith (1825–1891) bookseller and statesman lived here (GLC 1966).

12 Hyde Park Street was W.H. Smith's first home after his marriage in 1858. The large mid-Victorian house was once one of a row but now it is the only one standing and contrasts with the low modern terrace houses next to it.

Smith joined his father's newsagent business and in 1851 obtained the monopoly of station bookstalls on the London and North Western Railway, earning the title of 'North-Western Missionary' for selling only respectable literature. In 1868 Smith was elected Conservative MP for Westminster, joining Disraeli's cabinet as First Lord of the Admiralty nine years later. *Punch* nicknamed him 'Old Morality' for his term as

Leader of the Commons (1886–91). He was made Lord Warden of the Cinque Ports in 1891, and died that year at Walmer Castle, the warden's official residence.

Smollett, Tobias. *See* CHELSEA CHINA.

Spencer, Herbert.

37–8 Queen's Gardens, W2
  Herbert Spencer philosopher lived here 1866–1887 (Tepal Residential Hotels Ltd).

Herbert Spencer first went to London when he was appointed sub-editor of *The Economist* in 1848. He remained on the paper until 1853 and became acquainted with George Eliot and G.H. Lewes, T.H. Huxley and Tindall. He was an ardent follower of Darwin and adapted his theory of evolution to philosophy, sociology and aesthetics. He took lodgings in a boarding-house in Queen's Gardens in 1866, remaining there for 21 years.

As philosopher, sociologist and educationist, Spencer profoundly influenced European and American thought in the latter half of the 19th century through such works as *The Principles of Biology* (1864), *The Principles of Psychology* (1855, 1870–72), *The Principles of Ethics* (1892–3) and *The Principles of Sociology* (1876–96). He defended the sciences rather than the arts as the sound basis of education in *Education, Intellectual, Moral and Physical* (1861).

Spurgeon, Charles Haddon.

99 Nightingale Lane, SW12
  Charles Haddon Spurgeon (1834–1892) preacher lived here (GLC 1971).

Charles Spurgeon became a Baptist in 1850. Three years later he went to London and preached at the new Park Street Chapel. His sermons were a great success and after the chapel could be extended no further, Spurgeon transferred his Sunday services to Exeter Hall in the Strand. In June 1855 12,000–14,000 people listened to one of his sermons in a Hackney field. He lived in Nightingale Lane from 1857 to 1880, rebuilding the house in 1869. The Metropolitan Tabernacle was built in Newington Butts in 1861 to accommodate his vast congregations, and in 1867 he founded an orphanage in Stockwell.

Staël, Madame **de.**

Rear of Dickins & Jones, Argyll Street, W1
1813–1814 Germaine Necker Baronne de Staël-Holstein lived in a house on this site during the last ten years of exile (La Société d'Etudes Staëliennes).

Madame de Staël was the daughter of Jaques Necker, a Swiss banker and minister to Louis XVI. She married the Swedish ambassador to Paris, Baron de Staël-Holstein, and established a salon in Paris which attracted some of the great liberal intellectuals of the day, many of whom were disillusioned with Napoleon. She separated from her husband in 1798 but had already begun a new relationship with the French novelist Benjamin Constant and they shared exile together. She travelled throughout Europe while in exile and her experiences were post-humously published in *Dix années d'exil* (1821). She re-established her salon in Paris after the restoration of the monarchy and helped intro-duce German literature to the French.

Stanfield, Clarkson.

Stanfield House, Hampstead High Street, NW3
Clarkson Stanfield (1793–1867) Theatrical scenic-artist, Marine and Landscape painter, Royal Academician lived here 1847–1865 (Hamp-stead Plaque Fund).

Clarkson Stanfield was the son of the anti-slavery writer James Field Stanfield. After training as a heraldic painter and spending ten years at sea he went to London to earn a living as a scene painter and lived in William Etty's rooms in Essex Street from 1826 to 1831 (*see* SAMUEL PEPYS). His seascapes were exhibited at the Royal Academy and Ruskin called him 'the leader of the English realists'.

Stanford, Sir **Charles.**

56 Hornton Street, W8
Sir Charles Stanford (1852–1924) musician lived here 1894–1916 (LCC 1961).

Charles Stanford went to Queen's College, Cambridge, as a choral scholar in 1870. Three years later he was organist at Trinity College and in 1876 his music to Tennyson's *Queen Mary* was produced at the Lyceum. When he was living in Hornton Street his opera *Shamus O'Brien* had a long successful run in London though it has since been forgotten. Stanford's church music is still played but he also composed symphonies, operas and many choral works.

Stanhope, Charles, 3rd Earl.

20 Mansfield Street, W1
Charles 3rd Earl Stanhope (1753–1816) reformer and inventor lived here (LCC 1951).

Charles Stanhope was an ardent reformer, supporting the abolition of the slave trade and religious liberty. He was absent from Parliament from 1780 to 1786 because of his sympathy with revolutionary France even when his country was at war with Napoleon. Not only his colleagues in Parliament disapproved of his radical views, treating him like a 'political Ishmael'; in 1794 a mob attacked his home in Mansfield Street (where he lived 1787-95) demonstrating against 'Citizen Stanhope's' revolutionary sentiments. As an inventor, Stanhope proved the value of lightning conductors and perfected a microscopic lens which is named after him. To printing he contributed the iron hand-press and a process of stereotyping.

Stanley, Edward Geoffrey [Earl of Derby]. *See* PITT, WILLIAM [Earl of Chatham].

Stanley, Sir Henry Morton.

2 Richmond Terrace, SW1
Sir Henry Morton Stanley (1841–1904) explorer and writer lived and died here (GLC 1979).

Stanley's real name was John Rowlands. He was brought up in a Welsh workhouse and in 1859 sailed to New Orleans where he was adopted by a cotton-broker, whose name he took. He fought on both sides in the American Civil War and then took up journalism. In 1869 the *New York Herald* commissioned Stanley to find David Livingstone who was lost in the African interior and he found him in November 1871. He returned to equatorial Africa three years later and traced the course of the Congo. Stanley's final journey to Africa (1887) was an attempt to rescue the Emir Pasha but he failed and went to live in London soon afterwards. He married Dorothy Tennant in 1890 and they settled first in De Vere Gardens (where both Henry James and Robert Browning are commemorated by plaques) and then 2 Richmond Terrace.

Steer, Philip Wilson.

109 Cheyne Walk, SW3
Philip Wilson Steer (1860–1942) painter lived here (GLC 1967).

Wilson Steer lived at 109 Cheyne Walk from 1898 until his death. He was a founding member of the New English Art Club (1886) which helped introduce the work of the French impressionists to England. His house was built in the late 18th century but has been extensively altered. Steer was a bachelor with a housekeeper to look after him. He painted in the first-floor drawing-room studio, and his collections of pictures and antiques, coins, bronzes and Chelsea porcelain filled the house. William Rothenstein said: 'he was extremely matter of fact; in life, for him, there was little romance. Without a brush in his hands, he was indifferent to most things save dry feet and freedom from draughts . . . content to meet the same people every day. He liked too, to hear the same jokes; with a little gossip, a naughty story or two, the evenings passed pleasantly. Sickert and George Moore, Tonks and Harrison, MacColl, Frederick Brown, Sargent and myself formed his regular circle'.

Stephen, Sir Leslie.

22 Hyde Park Gate, SW7
Sir Leslie Stephen (1832–1904) scholar and writer lived here (LCC 1960).

Leslie Stephen's great work was editing the *Dictionary of National Biography*, which he began in 1882. He supervised the first 26 volumes and wrote many of the articles.

The Stephens added two storeys to the original five of 22 Hyde Park Gate to provide nurseries for the children. One of them (later Virginia Woolf), wrote the 'Hyde Park News' (1891–5) in which she recounted the activities of the family: eight children, seven servants, dogs, rats, bugs and visiting relations. After the death of Leslie Stephen's second wife Julia in 1895 the family began to disintegrate. Virginia suffered the first of several breakdowns which were finally to cause her suicide. Leslie Stephen was knighted in 1902 but died in 1904. That year the four Stephens children, Virginia, Vanessa, Thoby and Adrian, left the elegant surroundings of Kensington to live at 46 Gordon Square, Bloomsbury.

Vanessa married the painter Clive Bell in 1907 and they settled in Gordon Square, leaving Virginia and Adrian (Thoby had died in 1907) to find a new home. They moved across Tottenham Court Road to 29 Fitzroy Square *(see also* LEONARD and VIRGINIA WOOLF).

Stephenson, Robert.

35 Gloucester Square, W2
   Robert Stephenson (1803–1859) engineer died here (LCC 1905; premises rebuilt and plaque refixed 1937).

Stephenson moved to Gloucester Square in 1847. His first few years there were some of his most active as an engineer. He constructed a railway from Alexandria to Cairo, supervised a scheme for uniting two Norwegian lakes, constructed the Conway Bridge, the High Level Bridge at Newcastle, the Britannia Bridge, the York and North Midland Railway Bridge over the River Ayre and the Royal Border Viaduct over the Tweed. He also served on various parliamentary commissions and committees and was president of the Institution of Civil Engineers (1856–7). The drawing-rooms of his house in Gloucester Square were like museums, full of unusual clocks, electrical instruments, microscopes and toys.

Stevens, Alfred.

9 Eton Villas, NW3
   Alfred Stevens (1817–1875) artist lived here (LCC 1924).

Alfred Stevens worked with his father, a house painter and decorator, before going to Italy to study art. He became involved in political intrigues in Naples, walked to Rome and then to Florence where he copied paintings in the Uffizi, making a living by producing forgeries for dealers. He returned to England in 1842 and was employed by industrialists to construct exhibits for the 1851 Great Exhibition. Stevens's most notable work is the Wellington Memorial in St Paul's Cathedral, which he began in 1858. Long years of struggle with unsympathetic officials and the financial hardship the commission involved undermined his health, and when he moved to Eton Villas in 1865 Stevens had only another ten years to live. He intended to build a larger house on the adjoining plot of land but only completed a studio.

Stoker, Bram.

18 St Leonard's Terrace, SW3
   Bram Stoker (1847–1912) author of 'Dracula' lived here (GLC 1977).

Bram Stoker moved into 18 St Leonard's Terrace in 1896, the year before his most famous work *Dracula* was published. He began working as a civil servant in the Irish Civil Service (he was born in Dublin) and his first book was on the duties of clerks of Petty Sessions in Ireland (1878). He also wrote drama criticism for newspapers and in 1878 went to London to join Sir Henry Irving in the management of the Lyceum Theatre. Stoker left St Leonard's Terrace in 1906, the year he published his biography of Irving.

Stothard, Thomas.

28 Newman Street, W1
Thomas Stothard (1755–1834) painter and illustrator lived here (LCC 1911).

When Thomas Stothard's home in Henrietta Street became too small for his increasing family he bought the freehold to 28 Newman Street, which he acquired 'with a considerable quantity of handsome furniture, especially that of the drawing-room, for the very moderate sum of one thousand pounds'. Stothard's daughter-in-law described the studio: 'tolerably large, it possessed the very necessary advantage of an excellent light, and was so filled with pictures, drawings, portfolios, books, prints, and all the *et cetera* of a studio, that there was not, literally, a vacant chair for a visitor . . . in some drawers of the same apartment there was, beautifully preserved, a most gorgeous collection of butterflies, collected by Stothard himself in the fields near Norwood and Highgate . . . and he generally had his china jars filled with some most beautiful nosegays, that he was in the habit of choosing himself'.

Strachey, Lytton.

51 Gordon Square, WC1
Lytton Strachey (1880–1932) critic and biographer lived here (GLC 1971).

Lytton Strachey was at the centre of the Bloomsbury group both as a literary figure and geographically. When he bought 51 Gordon Square in 1919 he wrote to Virginia Woolf: 'very soon I foresee that the whole square will become a sort of college and rencontres in the garden I shudder to think of'. Strachey was a conscientious objector during World War I. *Eminent Victorians* was published in 1918, a new style of biography in which, according to David Cecil, 'fact and reflection are fused together into a work of art, individual and creative as a novel'.

Strang, William.

20 Hamilton Terrace, NW8
William Strang (1851–1921) painter and etcher lived here 1900–1921 (LCC 1962).

William Strang made 20 Hamilton Terrace his home 13 years after George Macfarren died there. Strang studied art at the Slade School and learnt etching from Alphonse Legros. He went on to produce over 700 plates and was often attracted by grim or fantastic objects. His illustrations of the *Ancient Mariner* were published in 1896, of Kipling's short stories in 1900, and of *Don Quixote* in 1902.

Street, George Edmund.

14 Cavendish Place, W1
George Edmund Street (1824–1881) architect lived here (GLC 1980).

G.E. Street was one of the most important architects of the high Victorian period, and his talented pupils included Philip Webb, William Morris and R. Norman Shaw. He himself worked in the office of Gilbert Scott (1844–8). His most famous work, the Law Courts in the Strand, was built between 1874 and 1882. The building took 35 million bricks, one million cubic feet of stone and 11 miles of pipes for heating; *The Builder* denounced it as 'a deformity and eyesore for all time'.

Strype Street.

10 Leyden Street, E1
Strype Street (formerly Strype's Yard) derives its name from the fact that the house of John Strype, silk merchant, was situated there. At that time was born, in 1643, his son John Strype, historian and biographer, who died in 1737 (LCC 1929).

John Strype the elder (*d* 1648) established his business as silk merchant in Strype's Yard, Petticoat Lane, and became a freeman of the City. His son based his literary works on his enormous collection of charters, letters and state papers of the Tudor period. He was nicknamed the 'appendix-monger' for his cumbrous and tiresome appendixes. His work includes *Memorials of Thomas Cranmer, Archbishop of Canterbury* (1694) and *Annals of the Reformation in England* (1709).

Stuart, Prince Charles Edward. *See* ESSEX STREET.

Stuart, John McDouall.

9 Campden Hill Square, W8
John McDouall Stuart (1815-1866) first explorer to cross Australia lived and died here (LCC 1962).

On 22 April 1862 John McDouall Stuart became the first explorer to reach the geographical centre of Australia. He had emigrated to Australia in 1838 and first worked as a surveyor, joining Charles Stuart's expedition to the interior in 1845. Stuart then became involved in the search for a route across Australia from north to south. This was of political importance; the overland telegraph had reached India so the discovery of a north-south route could be the basis for a continuing telegraph line. Stuart completed the first crossing in 1862 under government auspices and on his return was given a grant of £2000 and the gold medal of the Royal Geographical Society. With failing eyesight and declining health he returned to England in 1864. He lived with relatives in the four-storey late Georgian terrace house in Campden Hill Square from 1865 until his death. In 1942 the Stuart Highway was built along the route he had opened across Australia.

Suess, Edward.

4 Duncan Terrace, N1
In this house was born Edward Suess (1831-1914) geologist, economist, statesman (Geological Society of London).

Edward Suess lived in Duncan Terrace for the first three years of his life, moving with his family to Prague in 1834. He was professor of geology at the University of Vienna for most of his professional life. He served as municipal councillor of Vienna and was responsible for regularising the course of the Danube and providing the city with clean drinking water. In 1873 he became a deputy and was leader of the Liberals for many years.

Sun Yat-Sen.

4 Gray's Inn Place, WC1
Sun Yat-Sen (1866-1925) Father of the Chinese Republic lived in a house on this site while a political exile from his country (private).

After the failure of Sun Yat-Sen's attempt to overthrow the Canton government in 1895 he went into 16 years' exile. He was detained by the Chinese legation in London the following year but the British Foreign Office intervened; he spent eight months studying in the

British Museum Reading Room. On returning to the Far East he became an early leader of the Chinese Nationalist Party and played a leading role in the overthrow of the Ch'ing (Manchu) dynasty in 1911. He was the first provisional president of the republic of China and the Nationalists called him the 'Father of China'.

Swinburne, Algernon Charles.

The Pines, 11 Putney Hill, SW15

Algernon Charles Swinburne (1837-1909) poet and his friend Theodore Watts-Dunton (1832-1914) poet novelist critic lived and died here (LCC 1926).

Seriously ill from years leading a dissipated life, and suffering from a form of epilepsy, Swinburne was taken in hand by Theodore Watts-Dunton and lived in his Putney House from 1879 until his death. Swinburne had lived for a time with Dante Gabriel Rosetti in Cheyne Walk. Watts-Dunton was also a friend of some of the Pre-Raphaelites and had given up his career as a solicitor to become critic, novelist and poet. His fantasy *Aylwin* (1898) was wildly popular when published but Ford Madox Ford called it 'bilge'.

Watts-Dunton succeeded in stifling Swinburne's creative talent and he produced little work equalling his first series of *Poems and Ballads* (1866). He could satisfy some of his more unusual desires, however, at The Pines, including sliding down the wooden bannisters, an act followed by the exquisite pleasure of Watts-Dunton removing the splinters. Ford Madox Ford was a frequent visitor to the house, which presented a depressing aspect: 'the most lugubrious London semi-detached villa that it was ever my fate to enter. It was spacious enough, but, built at the time of the 1850-60 craze for Portland cement its outer surfaces had collected enough soot to give it the aspect of the dwelling of a workhouse-master or chief gaoler'.

Symons, George James.

62 Camden Square, NW1

George James Symons F.R.S. pioneer of the scientific study of rainfall, founder of the British Rainfall Association, twice President of the Royal Meteorological Society lived here 1868-1900 (1957).

Symons kept an unbroken record of the weather at his house in Camden Square for 42 years, as meteorological reporter to the registrar-general. He organised a system for observing rainfall which expanded from 168 stations in 1860 to 3404 in 1898, manned by over 3000 volunteer observers. He was elected FRS in 1878 and in 1883 was chairman of the committee on the eruption of Krakatoa. His last paper, completed just before his death, was on *The Wiltshire Whirlwind of October 1, 1889.*

Szabo, Violette.

18 Burnley Road, SW9
  Violette Szabo G.C. (1921–1945) Secret Agent lived here She gave her life for the French Resistance (GLC c1981).

Violette Bushell moved with her parents to Burnley Road in 1935. She joined the Land Army at the outbreak of World War II and in 1940 married Etienne Szabo, an officer in the French Foreign Legion. After he was killed at El Alamein Violette was recruited to the French section of the Special Operations Executive as a secret agent. In June 1944 she was used as a courier to take vital plans to mobilise groups of the Maquis in the Limoges district but she was captured by the Germans. After imprisonment and torture in France she was moved to Ravensbruck. On the journey the train was attacked by the Allies and when the guards left their prisoners for a moment Violette was able to supply water to the tightly packed carriages of men. She was executed at Ravensbruck with two other British girls. The War Office wrote to her parents: 'it was with her dignified courage that she impressed and moved even those responsible for her death'. She was posthumously awarded the George Cross in 1946 and the Croix de Guerre in 1947.

Taglioni, Marie.

14 Connaught Square, W2
Marie Taglioni (1809–1884) ballet dancer lived here in 1875–1876 (LCC 1960).

Marie Taglioni was the first notable exponent of dancing 'sur les points' and helped to free dance from the stiff formalism of the early 19th century. She had established an international reputation by the time she went to London in 1829 and danced in *Les sylphides* at Covent Garden. Thackeray referred to the grace of her dancing in his novel *The Newcomes*. She retired in 1847 because singing, particularly with the advent of Jenny Lind, was becoming more popular than dancing. She continued to teach deportment and dancing and her pupils included the youngest members of the royal family.

Tagore, Rabindranath.

3 Villas on the Heath, Vale of Health, NW3
Rabindranath Tagore (1861–1941) Indian poet stayed here in 1912 (LCC 1961).

Tagore made several visits to England. His ambition was to establish an international university for the study of different cultures and religions to create 'that mutual sympathy, understanding and tolerance on which alone can the unity of mankind rest'. His visit to London in 1912 began inauspiciously: 'I reached London and stayed in a hotel. Here I suffered great disappointment. Everyone seemed like phantoms. The hotel used to empty after breakfast and I watched the crowded streets. I was in despair. It was not possible to know this humanity or enter into the heart of another place'. However, William Rothenstein found him lodgings near his own residence in Hampstead. Rothenstein was impressed by *The Songs of Gitanjali* and they were published by Macmillan, becoming an instant success. When Tagore won the Nobel Prize for Literature he donated the £8000 to the Santinekatan Centre of Learning which he founded in 1921.

Talleyrand, Prince.

21 Hanover Square, W1
Prince Talleyrand (1754–1838) French statesman and diplomat lived here (GLC 1978).

Talleyrand lived in Hanover Square from 1830 to 1834. Though an elderly man, his diplomatic skills were unrivalled and as French ambassador he worked with Lord Palmerston to secure the independence of the Belgian nation. A renegade priest and married bishop, he had talents that kept him alive and nearly always in a position of power throughout the French Revolution and the reigns of Napoleon, Louis XVIII and Louis Philippe. Lord Sefton visited Talleyrand in Hanover Square and described him 'in a loose flannel gown: his long locks (for it is no wig), which are rather scanty, as may be supposed, were twisted with the curling iron, saturated with powder and pomatum, and then with great care arranged into those snowy ringlets which have been so much known and remarked upon all over Europe. His under attire was a flannel pantaloon, loose and undulating in those parts which were restrained by the bandages of the iron bar which supports the lame leg of this celebrated cul-de-jatte'.

Tallis, John.

233 New Cross Road, SE14
John Tallis (1818–1876) publisher of 'London Street Views' lived here (GLC 1978).

John Tallis lived at the semi-detached mid-19th-century house at 233 New Cross Road from 1870 until his death. He joined his father's bookselling business and because of his initiative the firm expanded into publishing. *London Street Views* appeared in 1838–40 and by 1853 the turnover of the business had more than doubled. Tallis then set up the London Printing and Publishing Company and launched his *Illustrated News of the World* as a rival to the *Illustrated London News*. The magazine had high production costs and in 1861 Tallis went bankrupt.

Tawney, Richard H.

21 Mecklenburgh Square, WC1
  R.H. Tawney (1880–1962) historian teacher and political writer lived here (GLC 1980).

When Lady Jeger unveiled the plaque to Tawney she commented 'his friends would be pleased. But I'm sure he would be furious and declare that it was utter rubbish'. The notion of any honour was anathema to the author of *Religion and the Rise of Capitalism* (1926) and *The Acquisitive Society* (1921) and he refused a peerage. Tawney lived at 21 Mecklenburgh Square from 1852 to 1862. He was professor of economic history at the London School of Economics from 1931, president of the Workers' Educational Association (1928–44) and a leading thinker in the labour movement.

Tempest, Dame Maria.

24 Park Crescent, W1
  Dame Maria Tempest (1864–1942) actress lived here 1899–1902 (GLC 1972).

Maria Tempest's real name was Mary Susan Etherington. She made her stage début in 1885 as a singer at the Comedy Theatre but after her first straight role in 1901 as Becky Sharp she made her reputation in drawing-room comedies. She introduced new plays of Noel Coward and Somerset Maugham to the London stage and Coward wrote *Hay Fever* for her.

Temple, Henry John. *See* PALMERSTON, Lord.

Terry, Ellen.

22 Barkston Gardens, SW5
  Ellen Terry (1847–1928) actress lived here (LCC 1951).

215 King's Road, SW3
  Ellen Terry the Great Actress lived here from 1904 to 1920 (private 1951).

Richard H. Tawney, 21 Mecklenburgh Square

Ellen Terry made her début when she was only five, in Charles Kean's production of *A Winter's Tale*. In 1864 she married the middle-aged artist G.F. Watts, but the marriage lasted only a year. From 1868 to 1875 she lived with E.W. Godwin by whom she had two children, Edith and Edward Gordon Craig. Her most triumphant period as an actress was after she had left Godwin. She was Henry Irving's leading lady at the Lyceum from 1878 to 1902 and her performances of Shakespeare's heroines were legendary.

When she settled in Barkston Gardens in 1888, Ellen Terry had divorced her second husband, the actor Charles Wardell, and began her long love-affair by letter with George Bernard Shaw. In 1902 she took up managing, putting on performances of Ibsen's *The Vikings* and *Much Ado About Nothing* with sets designed by her son. The performances were acclaimed but had little financial success and she returned to the stage and to the new playwrights, Shaw and Barrie. Her third marriage, to a young American, lasted three years, but by 1910 she was single again, still acting but suffering from failing eyesight and memory.

Thackeray, William Makepeace.

16 Young Street, W8
 William Makepeace Thackeray (1811–1863) novelist lived here (LCC 1905).

36 Onslow Square, SW7
 William Makepeace Thackeray (1811–1863) novelist lived here 1854–1862 (LCC 1912).

2 Palace Green, W8
 William Makepeace Thackeray novelist lived here Born 1811 Died 1863 (RSA 1887).

Thackeray moved to Kensington in 1846 and settled with his two daughters in the double-fronted Georgian house in Young Street. His wife had been insane for some years and the girls had spent their early years in Paris with their grandparents. Anne later recalled how Thackeray would 'write in his study at the back of the house in Young Street. The vine shaded his two windows, which looked out upon the bit of garden, and the medlar tree, and the Spanish jessamine of which the yellow flowers scented our old brick walls ... the evening bells used to ring into it across the garden, and seemed to come in dancing and clanging with the sunset'. Thackeray wrote *Vanity Fair, Pendennis* and *Henry Esmond* in the Young Street house and much of the action of *Henry Esmond* was set in nearby Kensington Square.

William Makepeace Thackeray, 16 Young Street

In 1855 Thackeray's daughters were 15 and 18 and he moved to the new, more fashionable district of South Kensington on the advice of friends. They lived at 36 Onslow Square for the next eight years. *The Virginians* was completed in 1859 and, in 1860, Thackeray became the first editor of the *Cornhill* magazine.

By 1862 Thackeray's health was failing and he decided to return to the higher ground of Kensington. He bought an old house in Palace Green with the intention of altering and restoring it but, as Anne recalled, 'the old house which my father had intended to alter and live in was found to be tumbling to pieces and not safe to knock about. After some demur it was pulled down and the Queen Anne building was erected'. Thackeray was pleased with the new house but worried about its cost. He died after living there a year.

Thomas, Edward.

61 Shelgate Road, SW11
Edward Thomas (1878-1917) essayist and poet lived here (LCC 1949).

Edward Thomas was born in Lambeth and spent his youth in Wandsworth, Clapham and Shelgate Road, Balham, attending St Paul's School and Oxford University. His first book, *The Woodland Life*, was published in 1897. He was encouraged by the critic James Ashcroft Noble and married his daughter Helen in 1899. The couple lived in cottages in Kent and Hampshire while Thomas earned a precarious living as a Grub Street hack. He only began to write poetry shortly before the outbreak of World War I and produced almost 150 poems before he was killed at the Battle of Arras. Quintessentially English, he was inspired by love and an intimate knowledge of the countryside; his poetry has earned him a permanent place in English literature alongside two of his favourite poets, Thomas Hardy and John Keats.

Thornycroft, Sir Hamo.

2a Melbury Road, W14
Sir Hamo Thornycroft (1850-1925) sculptor lived here (LCC 1957).

Hamo Thornycroft studied sculpture with his father Thomas before attending the Royal Academy Schools and travelling to Italy. When he returned to England his sculpture 'Teucer' (1881) was bought by the Chantry bequest for the Tate Gallery. His works in London include Oliver Cromwell in Old Palace Yard, the Gladstone memorial in the

267

Strand and General Gordon in Trafalgar Square. Thornycroft helped his father with the Poet's Fountain in Park Lane and modelled the figures of Shakespeare, Fame and Clio. He lived at Moreton House, Melbury Road, from 1878 to his death.

Thorpe, John.

High Street House, Bexley High Street, Bexley
   John Thorpe Kent antiquary lived in this house 1750-1789 (London Borough of Bexley 1976).

John Thorpe bought High Street House in 1750, rebuilding it in 1761. His father was a physician in Rochester who studied the history of the diocese of Rochester in his leisure. John Thorpe edited and published much of his father's research which constituted his major works, *Registrum Roffense* (1769) and *Customale Roffense* (1783), which his daughter illustrated.

Thurloe, John.

Wall of Lincoln's Inn, Chancery Lane, WC2
   John Thurloe Secretary of State 1652 Bencher of Lincoln's Inn 1654 lived at Old Square at various times until his death Born 1616 Died 1668 (Cromwell Association).

Thurloe was admitted to Lincoln's Inn in 1647 and five years later was made Secretary of State. When Cromwell became protector, Thurloe took charge of the intelligence department, whereby 'Cromwell carried the secrets of all the princes of Europe at his girdle'. After the Restoration Thurloe was accused of high treason but survived to live on in Great Milton, Oxfordshire, and his chambers in Lincoln's Inn. His correspondence remains a major source for the history of the protectorate. It was discovered 'in a false ceiling in the garret belonging to Secretary Thurloe's chamber, no.xiii near the chapel of Lincolns Inn', during the reign of William III.

Tree, Sir Herbert Beerbohm.

31 Rosary Gardens, SW7
   Sir Herbert Beerbohm Tree (1853-1917) actor-manager lived here (LCC 1950).

76 Sloane Street, SW1
   On this site lived Sir Herbert Tree 1853-1917 Actor Manager.

Herbert Beerbohm Tree was the half-brother of Max Beerbohm. He lived in Rosary Gardens from 1886 to 1888 and during that period he took over the management of the Comedy Theatre and the Haymarket. From the profits of *Trilby*, George Du Maurier's play (performed at the Haymarket in 1896) in which Tree gave one of his most successful performances as Svengali, he was able to build the palatial Her Majesty's Theatre across the street. At the new theatre he produced sumptuous performances of Shakespeare's plays, never hesitating to cut the original lines in order to add his own ideas. (*See also* Sir CHARLES WENTWORTH DILKE.)

Trevithick, Richard.

University College London, Gower Street, WC1
   Close to this place Richard Trevithick Born 1771 Died 1833 Pioneer of High Pressure Steam ran in the year 1808 the first steam locomotive to draw passengers (Trevithick Memorial Committee).

Richard Trevithick conveyed the first passengers to be moved by the force of steam in one of his earliest steam locomotives, 'Captain Dick's Puffer', near his home in Redruth in 1801. By 1808 he had built a more advanced locomotive, the 'Catch-me-who-can'. It was erected on the site now occupied by Euston Square and Trevithick offered rides at a shilling a head. A rail broke and the engine overturned: the perfection of the locomotive was left to the Stephensons.

Trollope, Anthony.

39 Montague Square, W1
   Anthony Trollope (1815–1882) novelist lived here (LCC 1914).

Anthony Trollope began writing to supplement his income working for the General Post Office and his first successful novel was *The Warden* (1855), the first of the Barsetshire series. He moved to 39 Montague Square 'early in 1873 . . . a house in which I hope to live and hope to die'. He had resigned from the Post Office in 1867 and spent 1871–2 travelling round Australia.

Trollope's first act in his new home was to organise his library of 5000 books, 'they are dearer to me even than the horses which are going, or than the wine in the cellar, which is very apt to go, and upon which I also pride myself. When this was done . . . I began a novel, to the writing of which I was instigated by what I conceived to be the commercial profligacy of the age'. The result was *The Way we Live Now* (1875), his keenest satire, which explored the inroads of the

Anthony Trollope, 39 Montague Square

speculative financier in English political and social life. Trollope was himself to make a very adequate income from his writing.

Turner, Charles.

56 Warren Street, W1
Charles Turner (1774-1857) engraver lived here (LCC 1924).

Charles Turner lived at 56 Warren Street from December 1799 to March 1803, spending his first year of married life there. His first child was born in the house, which was soon too small for Turner's engraving business. In April 1803 the family moved a short distance, to no.50, where Turner died. He worked chiefly in mezzotint but also produced etchings, aquatints and stipple engraving, completing over 900 plates.

Turner, Joseph Mallord William.

23 Queen Anne Street, W1
J.M.W. Turner RA 1775-1851 lived here (Portman Estate Trustees *c*1883).

40 Sandycombe Road, Twickenham
J.M.W. Turner (1775-1851) painter designed and lived in this house (GLC 1977).

119 Cheyne Walk, SW3
J.M.W. Turner landscape painter Born 1775 and died 1851 lived and worked in this house (Turner House Committee 1900/1950).

North Side, Campden Hill Square Garden, W8
J.M.W. Turner RA landscape painter Born 1775 Died 1851 often painted sunsets near this tree (private).

Turner was born above his father's barber's shop in Maiden Lane, Covent Garden. The powder tax of 1795 forced many people to give up wearing wigs so Turner's father gave up his business and joined his son in lodgings in a mews between Harley Street and Queen Anne Street. During subsequent moves to Hammersmith (1807), Twickenham (1813) and Cheyne Walk (1839) Turner extended his property in Queen Anne Street, opening a gallery there in 1812.

Turner bought the plot of land on which he built Solus Lodge, later changed to Sandycombe Lodge, for £400. The son of the local vicar visited the artist and described the house and garden: 'it was an unpretending little place, and the rooms were small. There were several

J.M.W. Turner, 40 Sandycombe Road

models of ships in glass cases, to which Turner had painted a sea and background. They much resembled the larger vessels in his sea pieces'.

Visitors to Turner's cottage in Cheyne Walk found it a squalid place, but the view of the Thames was all that concerned the artist. 'The house had three windows in front, but possessed a magnificent prospect both up and down the river with this exception, the abode was miserable in every respect . . . Mr Turner pointed out, with seeming pride, to the splendid view from the single window, saying, "there you see my study — sky and water. Are they not glorious. Here I have my lessons night and day".' His final years were marred by sickness. Although he was well off he was regarded as 'grubby, miserly, jealous and squalid in his tastes'.

Twain, Mark.

23 Tedworth Square, SW3
   Mark Twain (1835-1910) American writer lived here in 1896-1897 (LCC 1960).

Before Samuel Longhorn Clemens took up writing and adopted the name of Twain he worked as a journalist, printer, a river pilot on the Mississippi and, during the Civil War, tried goldmining in Carson City. *The Adventures of Tom Sawyer* were published in 1873 and his masterpiece *The Adventures of Huckleberry Finn* in 1885. Twain made a fortune as a literary businessman; he lived extravagantly, speculating in inventions which eventually made him bankrupt. He came to Europe in 1891 to earn money to pay his debts. After the death of his daughter Susy, in August 1896, Twain led a secluded life in Tedworth Square, seeing only a few friends. The *New York Herald* started a public benefit fund to repay his debts and Twain returned to America in 1897.

Tyburn Tree.

Traffic island at junction of Edgware Road and Bayswater Road, W1
   The site of Tyburn Tree (LCC 1965).

The infamous Tyburn Tree gallows were moved to Newgate in 1783; for the previous 500 years they had been near Marble Arch. In medieval times Tyburn stream, which rises in Hampstead and flows down to the Thames, watered this lonely rural district. The western branch of the stream flowed along what is now Westbourne Terrace and the elms that grew along its banks were used as gallows and called 'Tyburn Trees'. By 1720 plans were being made to move the permanent site which had been established for hangings. The residents of the newly built Hanover

Square and neighbouring streets were offended by the frequent sight of the death-cart and noisy sightseers passing along Oxford Street to the gallows. 'Executions are frequent in London; they take place every six weeks, and five, ten or fifteen criminals are hanged on these occasions.' The complaints were effective and Tyburn Tree was removed to Newgate Prison. Tyburn Lane became Park Lane.

Underhill, Evelyn.

50 Campden Hill Square, W8
Evelyn Underhill (1875-1941) Christian philosopher and teacher lived here 1907-1939 (GLC 1975).

Evelyn Underhill moved to 50 Campden Hill Square when she married Hubert Stuart Moore in 1907. She was brought up in an atmosphere of tolerant agnosticism and this stimulated her search for spiritual reality: by 1921 she was a practising Anglican. She studied botany, philosophy and social science at King's College London. *Mysticism*, her first important book, was published in 1911; it brought her into contact with the Catholic theologian Baron Von Hugel, with whom she remained close friends.

United States Embassy. *See* ADAMS, HENRY BROOK.

Unwin, Sir Raymond.

Old Wyldes, North End, Hampstead Way, NW11
The original designer of the Hampstead Garden Suburb Sir Raymond Unwin architect and town planner lived here 1906-1940 (private).

Raymond Unwin went to live in Old Wyldes after Hampstead Garden Suburb Trust acquired 243 acres of land extending northwards from the house in 1906. Unwin was responsible for the layout of the suburb with his partner Barry Parker. They had already worked together on the plan of the most famous garden city, Letchworth. Both developments sought a way of uniting the finest qualities from rural and urban styles of living and followed the ideas of Ebenezer Howard. The farmhouse of Old Wyldes was probably built in the early 17th century though it has been added to substantially and weather-boarding has replaced the original plastering of the exterior.

There is a GLC plaque on the house to John Linnell and William Blake.

Vanbrugh, Sir John.

Vanbrugh Castle, Maze Hill, SE10
Sir John Vanbrugh architect and dramatist designed this house and lived here c.1719–26 (private).

Vanbrugh called the brick fort with round towers and pointed roofs which he built for himself at Greenwich his 'Bastille', no doubt remembering the period he spent in the original Bastille as a suspected spy. He was the son of a rich sugar-baker and entered the Earl of Huntingdon's regiment in 1686. After reaching the rank of captain of marines, Vanbrugh turned dramatist; *The Provok'd Wife* was produced in 1697. Two years later 'without thought or lecture' (Swift), he became an architect and built Castle Howard and Blenheim Palace, with the assistance of Nicholas Hawksmoor. In 1716 he succeeded Sir Christopher Wren as surveyor at Greenwich and built his castle the following year.

Van Buren, Martin.

7 Stratford Place, W1
Martin Van Buren (1782–1862) eighth US President lived here (GLC 1977).

Stratford Place was laid out in 1773 by Richard Edwin for the Hon. Edward Stratford: nos.1–7 were completed in 1776. Martin Van Buren came to England as American ambassador in 1831 but he returned to

277

Sir John Vanbrugh, Vanbrugh Castle, Maze Hill

America in April 1832. The senate had refused his appointment because of old political rivalries. Instead Van Buren accepted the vice-presidential nomination under Jackson and became the eighth president (1837-41). When Van Buren first came to England Washington Irving was secretary and chargé d'affaires at the American legation; he was a constant visitor to Stratford Place and wrote most of *The Alhambra* in the house.

Vane, Sir Harry.

Gatepost of Vane House, Rosslyn Hill, NW3
Sir Harry Vane statesman lived here Born 1612 beheaded 1662 (RSA 1897).

All that remains of the 17th-century Vane House (with an 'entry' by Sir John Soane) is a gatepost to which the RSA plaque is attached.

Henry Vane became a Puritan as a young man and went to New England rather than conform to Church of England restrictions. He was governor of Massachusetts (1636-7) and on returning to England became joint treasurer of the navy and an MP. Though Vane took no part in the trial and execution of Charles I he was an ardent member of the Commonwealth government and on intimate terms with Cromwell. He was beheaded for high treason on the Restoration of Charles II.

Van Gogh, Vincent.

87 Hackford Road, SW9
Vincent Van Gogh (1853-1890) painter lived here 1873-1874 (GLC 1973).

160 Twickenham Road, Twickenham
Vincent Van Gogh the famous painter lived here in 1876 (private).

Van Gogh was transferred from The Hague to the London branch of the art dealers Goupil & Co. in June 1873. He worked at their gallery in Southampton Street as an apprentice art dealer. In August he moved into the house of Mrs Loyer, a curate's widow from the south of France, at 87 Hackford Road. Van Gogh longed for Holland and his homesickness was exacerbated by unrequited love for his landlady's daughter Ursula, who was already engaged to someone else; he left Hackford Road in July 1874.

Van Gogh worked for Goupil & Co. in Paris but returned to England in 1876, working as a curate in a London school and passing his spare time visiting Hampton Court. He recalled his first attempts to paint while living in London: 'how often I stood drawing on the Thames Embankment, on my way home from Southampton Street in the evening and it came to nothing. If there had been somebody then to tell me what perspective was, how much misery I should have been spared'.

Vardon, Harry.

35 Totteridge Lane, N20
Harry Vardon professional golfer Born May 9th 1870 lived in this house from 1903 until he died in 1937 (London Borough of Barnet).

Harry Vardon was born in Jersey. He was in his prime as a professional golfer at the turn of the century, winning the British Open Championship six times, the US Open in 1900 and the German Open in 1911. He won 62 major competitions and broke many records, raising the standard of the game in Britain and abroad. When he lived in Totteridge Lane he was professional to the South Herts Golf Club and wrote several books on golf, including his autobiography *My Golfing Life* (1933).

Vaughan Williams, Ralph.

10 Hanover Terrace, NW1
Ralph Vaughan Williams (1872-1958) composer lived here from 1953 until his death (GLC 1972).

Ralph Vaughan Williams moved to 10 Hanover Terrace after his second marriage and his widow wrote that it: 'was exactly what we wanted, quite central and beautiful . . . before long we felt we had lived in the house for years!' John Nash designed the terrace in 1822-3 and it was built by John Mackell Aitkens: no.10 is now the official residence for the Provost of University College London.

After studying at the Royal College of Music and Cambridge, Vaughan Williams went to study with Bruch in Berlin and Ravel in Paris. In 1904 he joined the Folk Song Society with Cecil Sharp; folksong was to be an abiding interest and influence. He became a pioneer of English nationalism in music and *The Times* obituary wrote that he 'spoke with the authentic voice of England so that its accent was unmistakeable'. His Ninth Symphony was completed in Hanover Terrace shortly before his death.

Voltaire.

10 Maiden Lane, WC2
1694–1778 Voltaire French poet, historian, satirist and humanitarian lodged near this spot 1727–1728 (private).

Voltaire was the pseudonym of François-Marie Arouet, dramatist, novelist, moralist, philosopher, satirist, historian and genius of 18th-century European culture. He was exiled to London in 1726 after a quarrel with the powerful aristocrat Chevalier de Rohan. *Lettres philosophiques* (1734) revealed the profound impression the comparative freedom and justice of English society made on him and he was forced into exile once more, this time in Champagne, for his outspoken criticism of France. *Candide* (1759) remains his most famous novel. His plays include *Mahomet* (1741) and *Zaire* (1732).

Von Hugel, Baron Friedrich.

4 Holford Road, NW3
Baron Friedrich Von Hugel (1852–1925) theologian lived here 1882–1903 (GLC 1968).

Von Hugel was born in Florence and educated in Brussels by a Protestant tutor under Catholic supervision. He was particularly interested in biblical scholarship and mysticism, 'the mature man's approach to religion and the foundation of true humanism'. It was a dangerous area for a Catholic to investigate and Von Hugel's friends Father Tyrrell and Abbé Loisy were both excommunicated. Von Hugel's first important work was *The Mystical Element of Religion as studied in St Catherine of Genoa and her Friends* (1908).

Wainwright, Lincoln Stanhope.

Clergy House, Wapping Lane, E1
Lincoln Stanhope Wainwright (1847–1929) Vicar of St. Peter's London Docks lived here 1884–1929 (LCC 1961).

Lincoln Wainwright worked for over 50 years for the poor of St Peter's parish, London Docks, where he bcame vicar in 1884. In his overcrowded parish he helped to provide the poor with schools and clubs (he founded the Church of England Working Men's Society), with medical and nursing facilities, clothing and holidays.

Wakefield, Charles Cheers, Viscount.

41 Trinity Square, EC3
Viscount Wakefield of Hythe who with his wife led Tower Hill Restoration and gave this house for good to church and people MCMXXXVII (private 1937).

Charles Wakefield moved to London in 1891 after working for an oil broker in Liverpool and in 1899 founded his own firm dealing in lubricating oils and appliances. He became extremely wealthy, devoting his business to locomotive lubricants at a time when the motor industry was rapidly expanding: 'Castrol' was the trade name he adopted. He gave much of his fortune to causes in the City of London, including the

Guildhall Library and Art Gallery, the League of Mercy, the Tower Hill Improvement Fund and the Bethlem Royal Hospital.

Wakley, Thomas.

35 Bedford Square, WC1
   Thomas Wakley (1795–1862) reformer and founder of 'The Lancet' lived here (LCC 1962).

Thomas Wakley went to London in 1815, married the daughter of a wealthy merchant and set up a medical practice in Argyll Street and then the Strand, from where he launched *The Lancet* on 5 October 1823. Wakley's paper attacked the nepotism and malpractices in London hospitals and he was involved in many libel actions. As independent radical MP for Finsbury (1835–52) he helped to secure the free pardon of the Tolpuddle martyrs; he also obtained Sunday opening of museums and art galleries and constantly advocated higher wages and improvements in housing for working people. When he was coroner for West Middlesex he stopped the flogging of soldiers and provided Charles Dickens, who often attended his inquests, with material for his novels. He lived at 35 Bedford Square from 1828 to 1848.

Walker, Sir Emery.

7 Hammersmith Terrace, W8
   Sir Emery Walker (1851–1933) typographer and antiquary lived here 1903–1933 (LCC 1959).

When Emery Walker moved to 7 Hammersmith Terrace in 1903, Edward Johnston took over his first home at no.3 in the terrace. Walker began work at the age of 14 for Alfred Dawson, who started the Typographic Etching Company. By 1886 he had founded his own firm in Clifford's Inn and was acquainted with William Morris, Walter Crane and other artists with whom he founded the Arts and Crafts Exhibition Society. Like Morris and Sidney Webb, he was involved in the beginnings of the labour movement and was secretary of the Hammersmith branch. He founded the Doves Press in 1900 with Cobden-Sanderson and they produced fine books printed in a clear type cut from drawings made in Walker's establishment and based on Nicholas Jensen's type.

Wallace, Alfred Russell.

44 St Peter's Road, Croydon
   Alfred Russell Wallace (1823–1913) naturalist lived here (GLC 1979).

44 St Peter's Road was built in 1880 shortly before Wallace moved in. Wallace stayed for about a year and his important work *The Geographical Distribution of Animals* was published during his residence (1880). He made his first visit to the Amazon Basin with the naturalist Henry Walter Bates in 1848-52. In Malaysia he discovered the line dividing Indo-Malaysian from Australasian fauna, since called the Wallace Line. He developed a theory similar to Darwin's theory of evolution and he and Darwin presented a paper to the Linnean Society in 1858 *On the Tendency of Species to form Varieties; and on the Perpetuation of Varieties and Species by Natural Means of Selection*. Darwin went on to publish his *Origin of Species* the following year, achieving fame and some fortune. Wallace was less fortunate and became associated with a number of unpopular and even eccentric causes.

Wallace, Edgar.

6 Tressillian Crescent, SE4
   Edgar Wallace (1875–1932) writer lived here (GLC 1960).

Junction of Fleet Street and Ludgate Circus, EC4
   Edgar Wallace reporter Born London 1875 Died Hollywood 1932 Founder member of the Company of Newspaper Makers 'He knew wealth and poverty yet had walked with kings and kept his bearing Of his talents he gave lavishly to authorship but to Fleet Street he gave his heart' (private).

Edgar Wallace, the illegitimate son of an actress, was raised by a Billingsgate fish porter and left school at the age of 12. He joined the army in 1893 and his dispatches during the Boer War brought him to the notice of Fleet Street. He returned to England and worked for the *Daily Mail*. His first novel *Four Just Men* was published in 1905. *Sanders of the River* and *Bones* were dictated in the upstairs back bedroom of his home in Tressillian Crescent, a sedate mid-Victorian house where he lived from 1908 to 1915. He was always poor because he continually bet on racehorses; the back gate to no.6 became a necessary exit to avoid his creditors. He died in Hollywood after moving there to write stories for films.

Walpole, Sir Robert; Walpole, Horace.

5 Arlington Street, SW1

Sir Robert Walpole (1676–1745) Prime Minister and his son Horace Walpole (1717–1797) connoisseur and man of letters lived here (GLC 1976).

Robert Walpole resigned as Prime Minister and left Downing Street for Arlington Street in 1742, dying there three years later. He had dominated English politics from early in the 18th century; A.J.P. Taylor characterised him as 'a coarse, pleasure-loving Norfolk squire, but the best financier and parliamentarian of his time'. His great ambition was to maintain peace in Europe through an alliance with France. He laid the foundations of free trade and of modern colonial policy and was responsible for transferring the centre of power in Parliament from the Lords to the Commons.

Horace was born at 17 Arlington Street, the fourth son of Robert Walpole. After attending Eton and Cambridge and spending a period in Europe on the Grand Tour, he moved into his father's last home at 5 Arlington Street which he inherited in 1742. Five years later Horace bought Strawberry Hill in Twickenham. He spent many years transforming the 'country box' into a Gothic castle, where he established a private press. The *Odes* of his old friend Thomas Gray were the first book to be published in 1757; his own Gothic romance *The Castle of Otranto* appeared in 1764. Walpole kept his London house in Arlington Street until 1779, when he moved to Berkeley Square.

Walter, John.

Gilmore House, 113 Clapham Common North Side, SW4

John Walter (1739–1812) founder of 'The Times' lived here (GLC 1977).

John Walter moved to Gilmore House in 1774 when he was head of a prosperous firm of coal merchants and underwriter at Lloyds. The handsome three-storey house was built in about 1763; busts of Shakespeare and Milton are set in roundels in the bay at the front. With the decline in the coal trade Walter went bankrupt and in 1784 was forced to leave Gilmore House on which he had spent so much. He set up as a printer in Printing House Square and in January 1785 issued the first number of *The Daily Universal Register*. The name was changed to *The Times* in 1788.

Walters, Catherine.

15 South Street, W1
   *Catherine Walters 'Skittles' (1839-1920) the last Victorian courtesan
lived here 1872-1920.*

Catherine Walters was born in the slums of Liverpool to a drunken
father who worked as a 'tide waiter' on the Mersey. Her good looks
attracted the attentions of a businessman who took her to London and
established her in Fulham. It was a common practice in the 1860s for
the most attractive prostitutes who were also skilled horsewomen to
advertise livery stables in Mayfair (as well as their own attributes) by
riding among the fashionable gentlemen in Hyde Park. Skittles joined
the 'pretty horse breakers' and in 1862 managed to catch Lord Harting-
ton, heir to the Duke of Devonshire. He settled an annuity on her and
she was able to live in style off the Devonshire estates for the rest of
her life. Her Sunday afternoon tea parties in South Street attracted
some of the most eminent politicians and aristocrats in the country,
including Gladstone, Kitchener and the Prince of Wales. She lived in
South Street until her death (aged 81).

Waltham, Abbots of.

4 Lovat Lane, EC3
   *Here stood the Inn of the Abbots of Waltham 1218-1540. Later the
residence of Sir Thomas Blanke Lord Mayor 1582-3* (City of London).

Watts-Dunton, Theodore. *See* SWINBURNE, ALGERNON.

Webb, Philip. *See* RED HOUSE.

Webb, Sidney; Webb, Beatrice.

10 Netherhall Gardens, NW3
   *Sidney Webb (1859-1947) and Beatrice Webb (1858-1943) social
scientists and political reformers lived here* (GLC *c*1981).

Sidney and Beatrice Webb lived at 10 Netherhall Gardens for some
months after their marriage while looking for a permanent home. As a
member of the LCC Sidney was particularly influential in developing
higher education in London, founding the London School of Economics.
Beatrice was a member of the Royal Commission on the Poor Laws
(1905-9) and they both drafted the important minority report of the
commission. They were leading members of the Fabian Society and

founded the *New Statesman* in 1913. Sidney Webb became President of the Board of Trade and Colonial Secretary, and was made Lord Passfield in 1929 and awarded the OM in 1944.

Weizmann, Chaim.

67 Addison Road, W14
 Chaim Weizmann (1874–1952) Scientist and Statesman First President of the State of Israel lived here (GLC 1980).

Chaim Weizmann first became a prominent figure in the Zionist Organization in 1914 when he was working as a reader in biochemistry at Manchester University. He discovered an improved method of producing acetone, the substance vital for the production of naval explosives. In 1915 he became Admiralty adviser on acetone supplies and he moved to London, where he began enlisting support for Zionist aims. He lobbied Balfour and Lloyd George and the Balfour declaration in favour of an independent Jewish state in Palestine was made in 1917, the year Weizmann moved to Addison Road.

The mid-Victorian villa in Addison Road was a centre of Zionist activity. Weizmann left the house in 1920 to become president of the World Zionist Organization and he played an important part in the negotiations over the partition of Palestine before the British withdrawal in 1948, becoming president of the new state of Israel.

Wells, Herbert George.

Alders, Bromley High Street, Bromley
 Site of birthplace of H.G. Wells born 21st September 1866 (Bromley Borough Council 1981).

13 Hanover Terrace, NW1
 H.G. Wells (1866–1946) writer lived and died here (GLC 1966).

H.G. Wells's early life was spent in poverty, and after an unhappy marriage he earned a precarious living as a journalist and teacher. Success came, however, with the publication of *The Time Machine* in 1894, followed by other scientific romances (like *The Invisible Man*) and more conventional novels (*Kipps* and *The History of Mr Polly*). Wells wrote his own obituary after he moved to Hanover Terrace in 1936, to 'an old, tumble-down house on the border of Regent's Park'. His 'bent, shabby, slovenly and latterly somewhat obese figure was frequently to be seen in the adjacent gardens, sitting and looking idly at the boats on the lake, or the flowers in the beds, or hobbling pain-

287

fully about with the aid of a stick'. The number of the house delighted him and he insisted on remaining there throughout World War II, placing a huge figure 13 by the front door.

Wesley, Charles.

13 Little Britain, EC1
Adjoining this site stood the house of John Bray scene of Charles Wesley's evangelical conversion May 21st 1738 (City of London).

24 West Street, WC2
West Street Chapel 1700 WMHS John and Charles Wesley preached here frequently leased by Methodists 1743-1798

1 Wheatley Street, W1
Charles Wesley (1707-1788) divine and hymn writer lived and died in a house on this site and his sons Charles (1757-1834) and Samuel (1766-1837) musicians also lived here

Charles Wesley claimed Whit Sunday 1738 as the date of his conversion to evangelicalism; his elder brother John was converted the following Wednesday. Charles lived at Great Chesterfield Street, now 1 Wheatley Street, from 1771 until his death. He preached at the City Road Chapel and was a regular visitor of condemned prisoners.

His sons pursued music as a profession rather than evangelicalism. Charles became a fine organist. Samuel was called 'an English Mozart' by William Boyce and he championed the works of J.S. Bach. The two brothers gave subscription concerts in their Great Chesterfield Street house until Samuel left the family circle in 1784 to become a Roman Catholic.

Wesley, John.

47 City Road, EC1
John Wesley (1703-1791) lived here (LCC 1926).

John Wesley, evangelist and the founder of Methodism, obtained a lease from the City of London in 1776 to build 'five substantial brick dwelling houses . . . and to erect a substantial brick building to be used as a house of worship' on a piece of land adjoining City Road. They were designed by George Dance the younger. Wesley's own house, which was opened as a museum and home for Christian workers in 1898, was the first to be built. His apartments were on the first floor and his bedroom was at the back. His brother Charles was a constant visitor: 'not infrequently . . . having left the pony in the garden in the

288

John Wesley, 47 City Road

front, he would enter, crying out, "Pen and ink! Pen and ink!" These being supplied, he wrote the hymn he had been composing'.

Westmacott, Sir Richard.

14 South Audley Street, W1
   Sir Richard Westmacott (1775–1856) sculptor lived and died here (LCC 1955).

Richard Westmacott's father was a monumental sculptor and Richard was sent to Rome as a pupil of Canova. On his return to London in 1797 he set up a studio and within six years had commissions amounting to £16,000. He succeeded Flaxman as professor of sculpture at the Royal Academy and his last important work was the group of sculpture in the pediment of the British Museum.

Wheatstone, Sir Charles.

19 Park Crescent, W1
   Sir Charles Wheatstone (1802–1875) scientist and inventor lived here (GLC c1981).

When Charles Wheatstone first went to London at the age of 21 he set up as a musical instrument maker and made scientific experiments with sound production. He invented the concertina and, through studying light and optics, established the principle of the stereoscope. His major achievement was the development of the electric telegraph on which he worked after being appointed professor of experimental physics at King's College in 1834. The device he invented to measure and compare resistances is known as 'Wheatstone's Bridge'. Wheatstone lived in Park Crescent from 1866 until his death.

Wheeler, Sir Charles.

Hereford Buildings, Old Church Street, SW3
   Sir Charles Wheeler PRA (1892–1975) lived here (private).

Charles Wheeler studied sculpture at Wolverhampton School of Art and the Royal College of Art and first exhibited at the Royal Academy in 1914. He became an RA in 1940 and was president of the Royal Academy (1956–66). His bronze and stone sculptures are in many public collections and cities throughout the world.

Whistler, James Abbott McNeil.

96 Cheyne Walk, SW3
James Abbott McNeil Whistler (1834–1903) painter and etcher lived here (LCC 1925).

The 12 years Whistler spent at 96 Cheyne Walk (1866–78) were some of his most creative: he painted the 'Nocturnes' and the portraits of his mother and Carlyle. He was continually harassed by creditors and had to pawn these paintings for cash. Visitors left his dinner parties still hungry, fed on little more than his extraordinary wit and conversation.

The orient influenced Whistler's house decorations. He slept on a large Chinese bed, ate off blue and white Chinese porcelain and covered the dining-room ceiling with Japanese fans. The drawing-room walls, pale yellow with a suggestion of pink, were still wet on the day of his first dinner party and his guests' clothes were tinted with the colours they brushed against. Comfort was not important to him.

Whistler left Cheyne Walk at the time of the libel case he brought against Ruskin in response to the art critic's humiliating judgment on his exhibition at the Grosvenor Gallery: 'I never expected to hear a coxcomb ask 200 guineas for flinging a pot of paint in the public's face'. Whistler was awarded a farthing damages and declared bankrupt in 1879.

White, William Hale.

19 Park Hill, Carshalton, Sutton
William Hale White (Mark Rutherford) (1831–1913) novelist lived here (GLC 1979).

William Hale White bought some land on Park Hill, Carshalton, in 1868 and built his own house to the design of Charles Vinall, a colleague of Philip Webb. White became friendly with both Ruskin and Webb through corresponding in the *Daily Telegraph* on the 'villainous' houses of the middle classes. His semi-autobiographical works were published under the name of Mark Rutherford. The first, *The Autobiography of Mark Rutherford*, was published in 1881. They trace the agonies of a man losing his faith. White was brought up in a dissenting family and trained for the ministry until he was expelled for questioning the inspiration of the Bible. He pursued a career in the civil service and journalism instead.

Whittington, Richard.

20 College Hill, EC4
The house of Richard Whittington Mayor of London stood on this site 1423 (City of London).

St Michael Royal, College Hill, EC4
Richard Whittington four times Mayor of London founded and was buried in this church 1422 (City of London).

The 15th-century chronicle of Gregory referred to Richard Whittington as 'that famous merchant and mercer Richard Whytyndone'. He served as Mayor of London on four occasions (1397, 1398-9, 1406-7, 1419-20) and was successful enough as a mercer to lend money to Richard II, Henry IV and Henry V. His legend developed early in the 17th century and a milestone at the foot of Highgate Hill marks the traditional spot where he heard Bow bells telling him to 'turn again'. The legend bears little resemblance to his life, but he did do much to enrich London, rebuilding Newgate Prison ('feble, over litel and so contagious of Eyre, yat his caused the deth of many men') and founding one of the principal almshouses and a hospital that still bears his name.

Wilberforce, William.

111 Broomwood Road, SW11
On the site behind this house stood until 1904 Broomwood House — formerly Broomfield — where William Wilberforce resided during the campaign against slavery which he successfully conducted in Parliament (LCC 1906).

Junction of Nan Clark's Lane and Highwood Hill (north side), Mill Hill, NW7
Site of Hendon Park Residence of William Wilberforce from 1826 to 1831 (Hendon Corporation).

44 Cadogan Place, SW1
William Wilberforce (1759-1833) opponent of slavery died here (LCC 1961).

Wilberforce lived at Broomwood House from 1797 to 1807. In 1807 Parliament made the slave trade illegal. Wilberforce then went on as MP for Hull to campaign for the abolition of slavery and for the complete emancipation of slaves. He had to retire from Parliament in 1825 because of ill-health. Thomas Buxton carried on his work and in 1833 slavery was abolished in all British territories, freeing some 800,000 slaves. On his retirement Wilberforce bought Hendon Park and 140 acres of land 'with convenient Offices, Pleasure Grounds, Park, Vegetable and Fruit Gardens'. He kept a large household, including two married sons and their families, and built a private chapel, later to become the Mill Hill church of St Paul's. He was forced to sell his estate in 1831 because of financial losses and he moved to the house of his cousin, Mrs Lucy Smith, in Cadogan Place.

Wilde, Oscar.

34 Tite Street, SW3
  Oscar Wilde (1854–1900) wit and dramatist lived here (LCC 1954).

When Oscar Wilde moved to 34 Tite Street in 1885 he was already a celebrity, known for his dandyism and aesthetic way of life. The house was decorated with white and yellow paint, with Japanese prints and etchings on the walls and elegant and simple furniture. Notoriety came with the publication in 1891 of *The Picture of Dorian Gray*, his infatuation with Lord Alfred Douglas, and predilection for boys from the Victorian underworld. While his brilliant witty plays (*Lady Windermere's Fan, An Ideal Husband* and *The Importance of Being Earnest*) were thrilling London audiences, Douglas's father, the Marquess of Queensberry, was campaigning for Wilde's exposure as a homosexual. Wilde left Tite Street in 1895 for prison, sentenced to two years' hard labour. Thereafter he lived in France, publishing *The Ballad of Reading Gaol* in 1898 and dying in poverty in Paris.

Willan, Robert.

10 Bloomsbury Square, WC1
  Dr Robert Willan (1757–1812) dermatologist lived here (LCC 1949).

The mid-Victorian stuccoed façades of 9–14 Bloomsbury Square cover houses built nearly 100 years earlier. Robert Willan lived at no. 10 from 1800 until shortly before his death in Madeira. He was appointed physician to the public dispensary in London and is chiefly known for his work as a dermatologist: he was the first physician in Britain to classify diseases of the skin in a clear and intelligible way. His major work *The Description and Treatment of Cutaneous Disease* was published between 1798 and 1808.

Willoughby, Sir **Hugh.**

King Edward Memorial Park, Shadwell, E1
This plaque is in memory of Sir Hugh Willoughby (d.1554) Stephen Borough (1525-1585) William Borough (1536-1599) Sir Martin Frobisher (1535?-1594) and other navigators who in the latter half of the sixteenth century set sail from this reach of the River Thames near Ratcliff Cross to explore the Northern Seas (LCC 1922).

India and China, with their wealth of precious silks and spices, held a particular fascination for English sailors in the 16th century and many lost their lives looking for routes to the orient by way of northern Europe and northern America. Three ships left the Thames in 1553 under Sir Hugh Willoughby's command, intending to sail to China by a north-east passage. The *Bona esperanza* and *Bona confidenza* sheltered in an inlet near the North Cape but were frozen in, and all (including Sir Hugh) died of cold and starvation. The *Edward Bonaventura* was more successful and with Richard Chancellor as pilot-general and Stephen Borough as master sailed into the White Sea and reached Archangel. For the first time the English discovered the wealth and power of the Russian emperor, and Chancellor set off to Moscow by horse-drawn sleigh to establish trading links between the emperor and Queen Elizabeth.

Stephen Borough's younger brother William served as ordinary seaman on the 1553 voyage to Russia. In 1587 he accompanied Sir Francis Drake on a military expedition to Cadiz in which over 100 Spanish ships were destroyed.

Martin Frobisher's aim was to find a north-west passage to the East and he made his first voyage in 1576. He crossed the Atlantic to Canada and discovered a deep inlet which he mistook for a passage to the East; it is now known as Frobisher Bay. He made two more voyages to the area but failed to find a passage or establish a colony.

Wilson, Edward Adrian.

Battersea Vicarage, 42 Vicarage Crescent, SW11
Edward Adrian Wilson (1872-1912) Antarctic explorer and naturalist lived here (LCC 1935).

Wilson went to London in 1895 to study medicine at St George's Hospital, Paddington. In 1896 he moved to Caius House (now Battersea Vicarage), then a mission house, where he worked in the evenings in addition to his day's study. Wilson joined Scott's Antarctic expedition (1901-4) as junior surgeon, zoologist and artist. When Scott planned a

Sir Hugh Willoughby, the Thames looking east

new expedition in 1910 Wilson was chief of the scientific staff and one of the five to reach the South Pole on 12 January 1912. Scott wrote of him: 'the life and soul of the party, the organizer of all amusement, the always good-tempered and cheerful one, the ingenious person who could get round all difficulties'. He died on the return journey with his four companions.

Winant, John Gilbert.

7 Aldford Street, SE1

John Gilbert Winant (1889–1947) United States Ambassador 1941–1946 lived here (GLC c1981).

John Winant succeeded the unpopular Joseph Kennedy as American ambassador to Great Britain in February 1941 and held the position until March 1946. After living at one of the flats above the embassy in Grosvenor Square, he moved to 7 Aldford Street, remaining there from 1942 until 1946. The house was lent to him by his close friend Winston Churchill. Perhaps because it was wartime, Winant made a great impact on the British press, intellectual community and general public. He was informed and compassionate, walking the 'streets of burning London at night in the midst of Luftwaffe bombings, instilling faith in the hearts of beleagured Britishers'. He was shattered by the death of his friend and benefactor Roosevelt in 1945 and two years later he committed suicide at his home in Concord.

Wolfe, James.

Macartney House, Greenwich Park, SE10

General James Wolfe (1727–1759) victor of Quebec lived here (LCC 1909).

Most of Macartney House was built about 1765 and therefore after Wolfe's residence (1751–9) but the part of it that faces Greenwich Park was probably built at the end of the 17th century. Wolfe's parents bought the house in 1751. Wolfe made only rare visits, as he was pursuing an active and successful career in the army on the Continent and in America. Early in 1759 he left England for the last time as brigadier-general in command of an expedition to the St Lawrence. He led the attack on Quebec, scaling the heights of Abraham in the dark; on 13 September he defeated the French, only to be killed in the action.

Wolseley, Garnet, 1st Viscount.

Rangers House, Chesterfield Walk, SE10
Garnet First Viscount Wolseley (1833–1913) Field Marshal lived in this house (LCC 1937).

Queen Victoria offered Wolseley Rangers House as a 'grace and favour' residence in 1888 after a distinguished military career. It had been bought by the crown as the official home of the Ranger of Greenwich Park and was empty, so Wolseley was able to live there until his departure for Ireland in 1891 as commander-in-chief. He was determined to modernise the army while working in the War Office but found his conservative commander-in-chief, the Duke of Cambridge, extremely unwilling to accept changes. Many of Wolseley's suggestions were not carried out until the Boer War, when their necessity was belatedly realised.

There is also a plaque on Rangers House to Philip, Earl of Chesterfield.

Wood, Sir **Henry.**

4 Elsworthy Road, NW8
Sir Henry Wood (1869–1944) musician live here (GLC 1969).

In 1894 Henry Wood was appointed music adviser for a series of Wagner concerts at the newly built Queen's Hall. The manager, Robert Newman, was planning a series of promenade concerts and realized that Wood, at only 25, would be the ideal musical director and conductor. The first promenade concert was given in the Queen's Hall in August 1895 and after Newman's death Wood negotiated for the BBC to sponsor the concerts. The BBC have broadcast them each year since the 1927 season and the Henry Wood Proms have more than fulfilled Wood's aim of 'truly democratizing the message of music and making its beneficial effects universal'. Wood lived in Elsworthy Road from 1905 to 1937.

Woolf, Leonard; Woolf, Virginia.

29 Fitzroy Square, W1
Virginia Stephen (Virginia Woolf) (1882–1941) novelist and critic lived here 1907–1911 (GLC 1974).

Hogarth House, Paradise Road, Richmond
Leonard and Virginia Woolf lived in this house 1915–1924 and founded the Hogarth Press 1917.

Virginia and her brother Adrian Stephen moved from Gordon Square to Fitzroy Square and occupied no.29, previously the home of George Bernard Shaw. Virginia held 'at-homes' on Thursday evenings and many of her brother's Cambridge friends, including Duncan Grant, Maynard Keynes, Lytton Strachey and E.M. Forster, were regular visitors. Virginia began her first novel, *The Voyage Out*, and was also reviewing for *The Guardian*, *The Times* and *Cornhill*.

On 10 August 1912 Virginia married Leonard Woolf, ex-member of the Ceylon Civil Service, political writer and critic. Just over a year later Virginia attempted suicide and Leonard began looking for somewhere quieter to live. When they moved into Hogarth House early in 1915 Virginia was still ill, but the favourable reception of *The Voyage Out*, published in March 1915, aided her recovery.

On 23 March 1917 the Woolfs went to the Faringdon Road and ordered their first printing press. It was delivered to Hogarth House in April and Virginia confessed to her sister Vanessa Bell 'I see that real printing will devour one's entire life'. The Hogarth Press was begun on a capital outlay of £41.15s.3d. and the first publication (150 copies of two stories, *The Mark on the Wall* by Virginia and *Three Jews* by Leonard) appeared in July 1917. The Woolfs moved back to Bloomsbury in 1924 taking the press with them. Throughout the 1920s and 1930s they published their own works and the poetry and prose of, among others, T.S. Eliot, John Middleton Murry and Katherine Mansfield.

Woolner, Thomas.

29 Welbeck Street, W1
Thomas Woolner RA sculptor and poet lived here 1860–92 (private).

Woolner met Dante Gabriel Rossetti in 1847 and became a member of the Pre-Raphaelite movement, contributing poetry to *The Germ*. His sculpture received little notice, and in 1852 he sailed to Melbourne, hoping to make his fortune in the Australian goldfields. Ford Madox Brown recorded his departure in the painting 'The Last of England'. Woolner returned two years later without a fortune, but his sculptures soon began to be more favourably received. He helped to restore the neglected art of medallion portraiture as well as executing many outdoor memorials including a statue to John Stuart Mill on the Thames Embankment. He produced busts of practically all the eminent men of his time, including Darwin, Tennyson, Cardinal Newman and F.D. Maurice.

Wren, Sir **Christopher.**

Cardinal's Wharf, 49 Bankside, SE1
Here lived Sir Christopher Wren during the building of St Paul's Cathedral Here also in 1502 Catherine Infanta of Castille and Aragon afterwards first Queen of Henry VIII took shelter on her first landing in London (private).

The Great Fire of London burnt from 2 to 3 September 1666 and on 12 September Wren presented his plan for the restoration of the city to Charles II. Though he was unable to complete his whole scheme, Wren, as surveyor-general and principal architect, rebuilt St Paul's, over 50 parish churches, 39 company halls, the custom house and several private houses. St Paul's was finished in all but a few details by 1716. Wren had also been employed to design the Ashmolean Museum in Oxford, Trinity College Library, Cambridge, the Temple and Chelsea Hospital, among other projects. His residency at Bankside has not been proven.

Catherine of Aragon (1485-1536) was betrothed to Prince Arthur, eldest son of Henry VII, and she arrived at Plymouth on 2 October 1501. The marriage was at St Paul's on 14 November. After Arthur's death, Catherine married his younger brother Henry on 11 June 1509.

Wyatt, Thomas Henry.

77 Great Russell Street, WC1
Thomas Henry Wyatt (1807-1880) architect lived and died here (GLC 1980).

Thomas Henry Wyatt and his brother Matthew Digby (1820-77) were the architect sons of a London police magistrate. Thomas Henry trained in the office of Philip Hardwick and set up his own practice in 1832. He built many churches, hospitals, barracks and country houses, many in Wales. He also designed the Assize Courts in Cambridge and, in 1845, three houses and the north gateway for Kensington Palace Gardens.

Wycherley, William. *See* BOW STREET.

Wyndham, Sir **Charles.**

43 York Terrace, NW1
Sir Charles Wyndham (1837-1919) actor manager lived and died here (LCC 1962).

299

Sir Christopher Wren, Cardinal's Wharf, 49 Bankside

York Terrace was designed by John Nash and built in 1822. Charles Wyndham lived at no.43 for about a year before his death. He made his London début in 1862 but that year went to America to work as a surgeon during the Civil War, appearing on the New York stage during the winter months. Wyndham made frequent visits to America throughout his life but his most famous acting part was created in London in 1886 — the title role in T.W. Robertson's *David Garrick*. Wyndham opened two new theatres in London, Wyndham's in the Charing Cross Road (1889) and the New Theatre in St Martin's Lane (1903).

Yeats, William Butler.

23 Fitzroy Road, NW1
  William Butler Yeats (1865–1939) Irish poet and dramatist lived here (LCC 1957).

5 Woburn Walk, WC1
  William Butler Yeats lodged here for 24 years (St Pancras Borough Council).

Yeats spent his childhood in Dublin, Sligo and London, staying in Fitzroy Road from 1867 to 1873. His father, John Butler Yeats, was a well-known artist and Yeats himself went to art school in Dublin though his central interest was already writing. When he returned to London he helped to found the Rhymers' Club with the 'decadent' poets Ernest Dowson and Lionel Johnson and became immersed in Far Eastern religion and magic. He took rooms in Woburn Walk at the end of 1895. Many contemporary writers attended his Monday evening 'at homes': George Moore, John Masefield, Rupert Brooke, Ezra Pound, Rabindranath Tagore and Lady Gregory. In 1940 John Masefield recalled Woburn Walk: 'forty years ago, that court of small houses was more romantic than it is today. At its western end in Upper Woburn Place, there were some late Georgian houses behind plane-trees, all long since destroyed and their site covered by the new hotel'.

As well as publishing many volumes of poetry Yeats was involved in the theatre, writing plays and helping to found the Irish Literary

William Butler Yeats, Woburn Walk

Theatre, later the Abbey Theatre Company. His interest in politics had been encouraged as a young man by his passion for the beautiful Irish nationalist Maud Gonne, and from 1922 to 1928 he served in the Irish Senate. In 1923 he was awarded the Nobel Prize for Literature.

Young, Thomas.

48 Welbeck Street, W1
Thomas Young (1773–1829) man of science lived here (LCC 1951).

Thomas Young had a prodigious intellect. By the age of 21 he had mastered half a dozen ancient tongues as well as French, Italian and Spanish and was elected to the Royal Society. After becoming a doctor of physics at Göttingen in 1796 he continued his studies at Cambridge, where he was known as 'Phenomena Young'. He practised as a physician in Welbeck Street (1800–25) and has been called 'the founder of physiological optics'. He was also a pioneer in the translation of hieroglyphics and was working on an Egyptian dictionary when he died.

Yovanovitch, Slobodan.

58–66 Cromwell Road, SW7
Professor Slobodan Yovanovitch (1869–1958) Serbian historian literary critic legal scholar Prime Minister of Yugoslavia lived here 1945–1958 (private).

Zangwill, Israel.

288 Old Ford Road, E2
Israel Zangwill (1864–1926) writer and philanthropist lived here (LCC 1965).

288 Old Ford Road was built in about 1870. Zangwill lived there between 1884 and 1887, perhaps longer. After graduating from London University with triple honours, he took up teaching and then journalism, and in 1892 *Children of the Ghetto* was published. This vivid account of cosmopolitan Jewish life in the East End was commissioned by the newly formed Jewish Publication Society of America and it brought Zangwill immediate fame. He became a leader of the Zionist movement working for the establishment of a Jewish Palestine and he founded the Jewish Territorial Organization.

Zoffany, Johann.

65 Strand-on-the-Green, W4
Johann Zoffany (1733–1910) painter lived here 1790–1810 (GLC 1973).

65 Strand-on-the-Green was built in about 1704 and has been known as Zoffany House since the 1850s. Zoffany went to London in the late 1760s after serving a long apprenticeship in Germany (he was born in Frankfurt) and Italy. He was introduced to George III and Queen Charlotte and received commissions to paint formal portraits and conversation pieces of the royal family. Between 1783 and 1790 he worked in India where he received so many lucrative commissions that he was able to buy the 'copyhold' of no.65. Zoffany managed to convey English social life in the late 18th century with remarkable vividness through developing the conversation piece into a sophisticated art form.

PEOPLE INDEX

STREET INDEX